ESSAYS ON THE CIVIL WAR
AND RECONSTRUCTION

ESSAYS ON THE CIVIL WAR AND RECONSTRUCTION

BY

WILLIAM ARCHIBALD DUNNING

Introduction by

DAVID DONALD

HARPER TORCHBOOKS ❧ The Academy Library
Harper & Row, Publishers
New York, Evanston and London

To My Wife

CHARLOTTE LOOMIS DUNNING

ESSAYS ON THE CIVIL WAR AND RECONSTRUCTION
Introduction to the Torchbook edition copyright ©
1965 by David Donald.

Printed in the United States of America.

This book was originally published in 1897 by The
Macmillan Company, with a second, revised edition in 1904.

First HARPER TORCHBOOK edition published 1965 by
Harper & Row, Publishers, Incorporated
49 East 33rd Street
New York, N.Y. 10016.

CONTENTS

INTRODUCTION TO THE TORCHBOOK EDITION

by David Donald

It is ironical that William Archibald Dunning's *Essays on the Civil War and Reconstruction* is being reprinted at a time when its author's reputation is at its lowest ebb. For nearly a generation historians of the Reconstruction era have been attacking Dunning and his students, and to brand a book as belonging to "the Dunning school" has come to imply that it is racist and partisan.

Yet only forty years ago W. A. Dunning was considered a model of historical excellence. By the time of his death in 1922 he was rich in honors and renown. Francis Lieber Professor of Political Philosophy at Columbia, he had trained a dynasty of historians and political scientists, and he had the rare honor of being President both of the American Historical Association and of the American Political Science Association.

Though political scientists still cite Dunning's multi-volumed history of political theories, he is best remembered today for his books on the Reconstruction era. Dunning came by his interest in this period naturally. Born in Plainfield, New Jersey, in 1857, he had boyhood memories of many of the events he described, and his father, a manufacturer who had intellectual interests and some artistic talent, encouraged his son to think about the problems of restoring the South to the Union. Dunning's studies at Columbia University, where he enrolled after Dartmouth College suspended him for a schoolboy prank, did even more to focus his attention on the post-Civil War period, for his principal professor, John W. Burgess, was at the time writing his several highly nationalistic volumes reinterpreting nineteenth-century United States history. The fact that James Ford Rhodes was beginning his massive history of the sectional conflict, which was to occupy the rest of his life, further convinced the young scholar that the Reconstruction years offered new sources, new problems, and an opportunity for new interpretations.

Dunning's first venture in this field was his doctoral dissertation at Columbia, published in 1885 as *The Constitution of the United States in Civil War and Reconstruction, 1860–1867,* a work written with the passion and the partisanship of a very young man, but one which already showed some of the technical mastery that was to characterize the mature scholar. Disgusted with the corruption of the dominant Republican party in his own day, Dunning looked back disapprovingly upon the events which had brought it to power. From his point of view, that of the "mugwump" Northern intellectual, it seemed obvious that

Thaddeus Stevens and the other architects of Congressional Reconstruction were "fanatics more extreme than the Southern fire-eaters who had precipitated the war."

The publication of Dunning's first book had three interrelated effects. First, it made the post-Civil War period a respectable field for academic historical investigation, for there could be no question that Dunning, unlike Rhodes, was no amateur but a true professional historian, whose qualifications included not merely advanced degrees from Columbia but postgraduate work at the University of Berlin under Heinrich von Treitschke. Second, it gave Dunning a permanent position on the influential Columbia faculty of political science, where he was to serve successively as fellow and lecturer, instructor, adjunct professor, and professor for the rest of his life. And third, it caused Dunning to be sought out by some of the very best graduate students entering the field of history.

Much of Dunning's fame—as well as much of the recent criticism of him—stemmed from the work of these students. Despite Dunning's own Northern origin and his interest in national problems, the best of his students came from the South and wanted to write on Southern topics. Forgotten now are such Dunning students as Homer A. Stebbins, who wrote on New York politics during Reconstruction, Harriette M. Dilla, who analyzed the politics of Michigan, and

Edith E. Ware, who discussed public opinion in Massachusetts. Instead, when one thinks of products of the Dunning seminar he remembers J. G. de Roulhac Hamilton's *Reconstruction in North Carolina* (1914), W. W. Davis's *The Civil War and Reconstruction in Florida* (1913), C. Mildred Thompson's *Reconstruction in Georgia* (1915), Walter L. Fleming's *The Civil War and Reconstruction in Alabama* (1905), J. W. Garner's *Reconstruction in Mississippi* (1901), Thomas S. Staples's *Reconstruction in Arkansas* (1923), and Charles W. Ramsdell's *Reconstruction in Texas* (1910).

Researched from the primary sources, factually accurate, and presented with an air of objectivity, these dissertations were acclaimed as triumphs of the application of the scientific method to historiography, and indeed they still provide our basic knowledge of the political history of the South during the postwar years. Yet, with every conscious desire to be fair, these students of Dunning shaped their monographs to accord with the white Southerners' view that the Negro was innately inferior. Since they thought it logical and inevitable that the white man should be superior to the Negro, they assumed that it was an obvious mistake to treat the Negro as a political, much less as a social, equal. Consequently, the Dunning students generally condemned Negro participation in the Southern Reconstruction governments, even while they condoned white terrorist organizations such as the Ku Klux Klan. Refusing to credit their own evidence that many white Southerners of high social and economic position collaborated with the Republican regimes in the South, they insisted that Southern white supporters of Radical Reconstruction were "carpetbaggers" or "scalawags." Naturally they welcomed the overthrow of the Republican governments and characterized the process by which the Negro was relegated to permanent second-class citizenship as "the restoration of home rule."

It was probably inevitable that present-day historians, who rightly regard such racist assumptions as intolerable, should link in condemnation Dunning's own writings with those of his students, but such a procedure is not entirely fair. In general, a historian cannot be justly praised, or blamed, for the work of graduate students who have studied under his direction. In Dunning's case caution is especially necessary, for he belonged to the "sink or swim" school of graduate instruction and had little to do with dissertations until they were submitted in virtually finished form for his criticism and approval. A broadly tolerant man, Dunning allowed his students to pursue their own paths, and it is hardly surprising that his young Southerners, themselves products of the dark days that followed Reconstruction, should have adopted sharply sectional views.

To be sure, Dunning himself, like most Northern whites of the period, shared many of their opinions. Like them, he saw "the ultimate root of the trouble in the South" not in the institution of slavery but in "the coexistence in one society of two races so distinct in characteristics as to render coalescence impossible." Slavery, he declared, had provided "a *modus vivendi* through which social life was possible," and any subsequent political arrangement in the South, to be enduring, must recognize "the same fact of racial inequality." Consequently, Dunning saw as a central theme of Reconstruction history "the struggle through which the southern whites, subjugated by adversaries of their own race, thwarted the scheme which threatened permanent subjection to another race." Disapproving of the "reckless enfranchisement of the freedmen and their enthronement in political power," Dunning condemned the "inefficiency, extravagance, and corruption" of the Southern governments supported by Negro ballots, and he concluded dryly: "To stand the social pyramid on its apex was not the surest way to restore the shattered equilibrium of the South."

This racial bias is unquestionably present in all of Dunning's own books on the Reconstruction era: his dissertation; the present collection of essays, originally published in 1898 and revised in 1904; his *Reconstruction, Political and Economic,* issued in *The American*

Nation Series in 1907 and recently republished as a Harper Torchbook. Belief in white supremacy, however, had very little functional relevance to Dunning's treatment of the period. A member of the Germanic "scientific" school of historians, he always tried to avoid generalizing, moralizing, and allocating praise and blame. "The many morals that may be drawn from the three decades of the [Reconstruction] process," he observed in the concluding essay in the present volume, "it is not my purpose to suggest." It is not too much to say that if a handful of quotations like those given in the previous paragraph—the same few quotations that have been endlessly repeated by Dunning's critics—were penciled out, his main theses and the logic of his argument would in no serious sense be affected. Even so hostile a critic as W. E. B. DuBois, who chided Dunning for the work of his students, was unable to produce much evidence that racism shaped the Columbia professor's own "often judicious" books.

Indeed, in a number of ways Dunning's views on Reconstruction are strikingly modern. Unlike most of his students, and unlike most later historians as well, he always tried to see the period in national perspective. The North, he declared, "claims our principal attention" during the whole era, for "the social, economic, and political forces that wrought positively for progress are to be found in the record, not of the vanquished, but of the victorious section." In all of his books, therefore, Dunning declined to take advantage of repeated opportunities to exploit either the pathos or the drama of conflicts within the South and kept his eye firmly on the national picture, especially on political and constitutional developments in Washington.

In tracing these developments, Dunning often anticipated the findings of later scholars. The incisive essay which opens this volume, for instance, might almost be a succinct prospectus for J. G. Randall's definitive *Constitutional Problems under Lincoln* (1926). Only a few years ago Dunning's condemnation of Andrew Johnson's "bad judgment and worse taste" in pursuing a Reconstruction policy which forced most Republicans into the Radical camp might have seemed unfairly hostile, but his verdict comes astonishingly close to that of Eric L. McKitrick in *Andrew Johnson and Reconstruction* (1960) and of LaWanda and John H. Cox in *Politics, Principle, and Prejudice* (1963). Then, too, Dunning's close analysis of the legislative history of the major Reconstruction acts and his attention to their constitutional implications foreshadow William R. Brock's careful study of these matters in *An American Crisis* (1963).

Even when dealing with events within the South, Dunning usually had perspicacious judgment. Unlike most historians who wrote of the period only to commiserate with the Southern whites upon their fate, he recognized the reconstruction of the Southern states as "one of the most remarkable achievements in the history of government" and as "a demonstration of political and administrative capacity . . . no less convincing than the subjugation of the Confederate armies as an evidence of military capacity." Nor, though his personal preference would have been for continued military rule in the conquered Confederacy, did he altogether undervalue the work of the so-called "carpetbag" government. As to corruption, he observed that the numerous undeniable instances of Southern graft were contemporaneous with the raids of the Tweed ring in New York, and he argued that the Southern governments had to make large expenditures in order to rebuild Southern roads, bridges, and levees and to extend basic social services to the freedmen. To these often maligned Reconstruction governments he gave full credit for creating the first real system of universal public education in the South.

In another sense, too, Dunning was prescient for, anticipating the later research of C. Vann Woodward, he denied that 1877 marked a sharp break in the continuity of Southern history. Unlike most of his students, who felt that the restoration of "home rule" meant the triumph of reason and justice in the South, Dunning recognized that the final undoing of Congressional Reconstruction did not come until the

Populist era, when the Negroes were disfranchised.

Dunning's *Essays on the Civil War and Reconstruction,* then, continues to have value, not merely to all students of American historiography but to all who wish to understand the postwar period of reorganization. To be sure, it has its limitations, but these are as obvious as they are indefensible; any undergraduate student can detect and correct them. They should not be allowed to obscure the fact that Dunning's book remains the best account of the constitutional and legislative history of the Reconstruction period.

The Johns Hopkins University
January, 1965

FOR FURTHER READING

There is no full-length biography of Dunning, but two brief, appreciative portraits are given by Charles Edward Merriam in *American Masters of Social Science*, edited by Howard W. Odum (New York, 1927), pp. 131–148, and by J. G. de Roulhac Hamilton in the *Dictionary of American Biography* (New York, 1930), V, pp. 523–524. See also Hamilton's introduction to Dunning's posthumously collected essays, *Truth in History* (New York, 1937), pp. xi–xxviii. Alan D. Harper's "William A. Dunning: The Historian as Nemesis," in *Civil War History*, X (March 1964), pp. 54–66, is sharply critical. More balanced are the discussions in Michael Kraus, *A History of American History* (New York, 1937), pp. 537–540, and in Harvey Wish, *The American Historian* (New York, 1960), pp. 231–235.

For more general appraisals of Reconstruction historiography, see the following essays, all of which are hostile to Dunning's point of view: W. E. B. DuBois, "The Propaganda of History," in *Black Reconstruction* (New York, 1935), pp. 711–729; A. A. Taylor, "Historians of Reconstruction," in *The Journal of Negro History*, XXIII (January, 1938), pp. 16–34; Howard K. Beale, "On Rewriting Reconstruction History," in *The American Historical Review*, XLV (July 1940), pp. 807–827; and Bernard A. Weisberger, "The Dark and Bloody Ground of Reconstruction Historiography," in *The Journal of Southern History*, XXV (November, 1959), pp. 427–447.

For a modern general history of the Reconstruction era see J. G. Randall and David Donald, *The Civil War and Reconstruction* (2nd ed.; Boston, 1961), which contains (pp. 776–788) an extensive bibliography.

D.D.

PREFATORY NOTE

Of the essays included in this volume all but one — that on "The Process of Reconstruction" — have been published before during the last eleven years: four in the *Political Science Quarterly*, one in the *Yale Review*, and one in the "Papers of the American Historical Association." For the purpose of their present appearance all have been subjected to revision, which has resulted in some cases in considerable modifications. The first five essays are devoted immediately to various phases of the Civil War and Reconstruction. The last two, while not concerned exclusively with those topics, have nevertheless such a relation to the legal and political questions treated as to justify their inclusion in the volume.

To the younger generation of reading men at the present day the military history of the Civil War is familiar or readily accessible; the constitutional and political history is neither. As to the Reconstruction, the term is to most people merely a synonym for bad government, and conveys no idea of the profound problems of statecraft that had to be solved between 1865 and 1870. The essays collected in the following pages have been written with reference to this situation. If in any degree they shall have contributed, either through statement, implication, or even omission, to throw light on the actual history of the time with which they deal, the end of the collection will have been attained.

LAKE SUNAPEE, N.H., Sept. 9, 1897.

NOTE TO THE REVISED EDITION

FOR the sake of greater homogeneity and with a view to completeness in the general survey of Reconstruction, the final essay in the first edition has been omitted, and for it has been substituted the essay on "The Undoing of Reconstruction," which appeared in the *Atlantic Monthly* in 1901.

April 14, 1904.

THE CONSTITUTION OF THE UNITED STATES IN CIVIL WAR

THE culmination of the differences between the sections in a definite political act occurred at a moment when the government was in the hands of that party whose principles were most susceptible of adaptation to the policy of the secessionists. Though the direct question of state or national supremacy was not met in the platform of either of the great parties in 1860, all the traditions of the Democracy were on the side of a strictly limited central government. For many years, now, the accepted narcotic for quieting any nervousness caused by threats against state rights had been the soothing formula: "Each government is sovereign within its sphere." The assertion in December of 1860 that South Carolina's "sphere" included the right to dissolve the Union, called for some decisive action in spherical delimitation.

President Buchanan had been with the extreme Democrats on the Territorial question. The rights and equality of all the states he had insisted on maintaining with the utmost care. But the demand that he should acknowledge what after all is only the logical conclusion of the state-rights doctrine, was more than he was prepared to accede to. His message, on the meeting of Congress in December, was a striking illustration of the difficulty with which all thoughtful Democrats were confronted by the action of South Carolina. Any such state right as that of secession, he claimed, was "wholly inconsistent with the history as well as the character of the federal constitution"; and his argument in support of this view contained practically all that had ever been said on the subject. Still he was far from excluding the idea of a "sphere" by which the central government was limited. "This government," the President stated, "is a great and powerful government, invested with all the attributes of sovereignty over the special subjects to which its authority extends." Not one man in the United States, probably, would have denied that. The whole constitutional development of the country had proceeded upon exactly that doctrine. But the President did not penetrate to the root of the difficulty by explaining definitely how the scope of those special subjects was to be determined. He did indeed refer to the wisdom of "the fathers" in adopting the rule of strict construction of the constitution; but all the world knew the unsatisfactory nature of that formula. No better illustration of its uselessness was needed than the results that were derived in the message itself from the application of the principle in the present crisis.

After reaching the conclusion that there was no constitutional right in a state to secede, he next examined the position of the executive under the circumstances. Following an opinion of Attorney-General Black,[1] he concluded that existing laws did not empower him to bring force to bear to suppress insurrection in a state " where no judicial authority exists to issue process, and where there is no marshal to execute it, and where, even if there were such an officer, the entire population would constitute one solid combination to resist him." His conclusion itself was reached by an exceedingly strict construction of the law of 1795, in reference to calling out the militia.[2] Having thus disclaimed any power in himself to resort to arms, he put the question: " Has the constitution delegated to Congress the power to coerce a state into submission which is attempting to withdraw, or has actually withdrawn from the confederacy?" Not being able to discover such a power among those delegated to Congress in the constitution, and not considering it " necessary and proper for carrying into execution" the enumerated powers, the President could not answer the question in the affirmative. " Without descending to particulars," he said, " it may be safely asserted that the power to make war against a state is at variance with the whole spirit and intent of the constitution."

[1] McPherson, History of the Rebellion, p. 51.
[2] 1 Statutes at Large, 424.

Such was the rather disheartening result of an examination of the situation from a strict-constructionist standpoint. A state had no right to secede, and the federal government had no right to prevent it from seceding. It was evident that if such were the true state of the case, a right must be evolved from somewhere to fill the vacuum. Much abuse has been heaped upon Mr. Buchanan as the originator of this constitutional paradox. Far from being responsible for it, however, he was only unfortunate in having officially to proclaim the disagreeable consequence of a long-established theory of governmental relations. The fixed form in which for years the doctrine of sovereignty had been enunciated by every department of the government was that referred to above. The relative force of federal and state action, when in conflict, was a question that had been sedulously avoided. Once only, in 1832, had the issue been fairly presented, but the result of the nullification controversy had given no conclusive answer. The Supreme Court had maintained an unbroken line of precedents on the double sovereignty basis.[1] It had asserted the supremacy of the federal laws, so far as they were within the powers granted or implied in the constitution, but it had admitted that many cases of dispute could arise in which the judiciary could not be called upon to give judgment. In such questions, of a political rather

[1] *Cf.* Brightly's Federal Digest, p. 142.

than a judicial character, the final authority as to the constitutionality of a given law was, by the doctrine of "spheres," undetermined. Though the ultra state-rights school of Calhoun had given a perfectly clear and definite solution to the problem, and Webster on the other hand had been equally explicit in his contradictory answer, it must be admitted that the general course of governmental action, and more important still, perhaps, the prevailing sentiment of the people as a whole, had followed the middle line of which the conservative Madison was a conspicuous adviser.

From this standpoint the only constitutional course in case of a conflict of the "sovereignties" was to deny that such a thing was possible, eulogize the constitution as the greatest extant production of the human intellect, point out the dreadful consequences that would follow the recognition of supremacy in either claimant, and end by compromising the difficulty in such a way as to furnish precedents for both sides in the future. It would be erroneous to maintain that this method of action was as unprofitable as it was illogical. On the contrary, it was probably the only course that could have brought the United States intact through to the year eighteen hundred and sixty. But more than one of the nation's true statesmen foresaw that it was only a question of time when "dodging the issue" would cease to give satisfaction as a principle of constitutional construction.

It was not understood by President Buchanan, or by the mass of the people, that the secession of South Carolina was the knell of the old principle. Mr. Buchanan promptly adopted the time-honored method of meeting the difficulty. His message in December, 1860, eulogized the constitution, and affirmed the supremacy of the general government in its sphere; he referred with emphasis to the reservation of rights to the states, and recoiled with horror from the idea of using force to preserve the Union, even if the power to do so were conferred. To Congress was left the devising of measures necessary to the circumstances, the President's only recommendation being an explanatory amendment to the constitution. The amendment, he thought, should deal not with the fundamental question, but with the status of slavery, so as forever to " terminate the existing dissensions, and restore peace and harmony among the states." [1]

The executive having thus failed to free itself from the shackles which precedent imposed, what did Congress effect in the way of meeting the emergency? In the House a special committee of one member from each state was appointed, to consider as much of the President's message as referred to the perilous state of the country. A special committee of thirteen was likewise appointed in the Senate. The most casual examination of the enormous mass of propositions submitted to

[1] McPherson, History of the Rebellion, p. 50.

these committees, as well as to the houses directly, will reveal the confidence that still remained in the "compromise" method of determining controversies, as well as the utter hopelessness of its successful application to the existing difficulty.[1]

The attention of Congress was directed chiefly to such measures as were embodied in the report of the House special committee, and in the resolutions proposed in the Senate by Crittenden of Kentucky. The Senate's special committee reported a failure to agree upon any general scheme of adjustment. The only proposition of the House committee's report to receive effective approval was that proposing an amendment to the constitution in these words: "No amendment shall be made to the constitution which will authorize or give to Congress the power to abolish or interfere, within any state, with the domestic institutions thereof, including that of persons held to labor or service by the laws of said state." This proposition secured the necessary two-thirds in both the House and the Senate, only the radical Republicans opposing it,[2] and it was ratified by the legislatures of Ohio and Maryland before its uselessness was appreciated.

It was upon the Crittenden resolutions, in the

---

[1] For digest of the propositions, see McPherson, Rebellion, p. 52 *et seq.* *Cf.* Bancroft, "The Final Efforts at Compromise," in *Political Science Quarterly*, VI, 401 (September, 1891).

[2] McPherson, Rebellion, p. 59.

Senate, that the friends of Union through con-
ciliation based their final hopes. The plan was
directed entirely to a settlement of the slavery
question. It provided for constitutional amendments dividing all United States territory by the
36° 30' line, and recognizing slavery south of the
line, while prohibiting it north. States formed
from this territory were to be admitted upon reaching a population requisite for a member of Congress, and were to make their own choice as to
slavery in their constitutions. The power to abolish slavery within its jurisdiction was denied to
Congress, if the places concerned should be within
the limits of states permitting slavery. The inter-
state slave trade was put beyond the interference
of Congress, and the United States was required
to compensate any owner for a fugitive slave violently rescued from him, at the same time having
action to recover the amount from the county in
which the rescue was effected. Such a scheme
did not seem to offer much consolation to the
Republicans, who had made it their cardinal principle that slavery was too horrible a thing to come
under the express recognition and protection of a
free government. The resolutions were opposed
by the united front of the Republican senators,
and finally, after the withdrawal of most of the
Southern delegation, they were rejected, on the
second of March, by a vote of 19 to 20.[1]

[1] McPherson, Rebellion, p. 64 *et seq.*

The Congress and the administration came to
an end on the fourth of March, 1861. How did
the constitutional question stand then? Had any
advance been made toward an answer to the vexed
question of sovereignty? The record sketched
above tells the gloomy tale. An emasculated
national sovereignty had been proclaimed by the
executive; a vigorous state sovereignty had been
actively asserted by seven of the commonwealths
of the Union; and no position whatever had been
assumed by the federal legislature.

I. *Principles of the Appeal to Arms*

It would be misleading to pass without notice
the idea of executive duty on which Mr. Buchanan
based his action in reference to the forts and other
property of the United States in the South. His
denial of the right of secession precluded, of course,
any recognition of the independence of the withdrawing states. Accordingly, a demand of the
commissioners from South Carolina for the removal of a hostile military force from her soil was
simply disregarded, and no admission was allowed
of her claim of eminent domain. Attorney-General Black had advised the President that "the
right of the general government to preserve itself
in its whole constitutional vigor by repelling a
direct and positive aggression upon its property

or its officers, cannot be denied." [1] The attitude of the administration was therefore manifested in its orders to the commander of Fort Sumter to stand strictly on the defensive, but to act vigorously if assailed.

In his personal defence, written after the war, Mr. Buchanan assigns as a reason for maintaining this position, that he was above all things desirous of avoiding bloodshed, and had high hopes of adjusting the difference by negotiation.[2] He had most convincing assurances that any aggressive action on his part would promptly lead to the withdrawal of several hesitating states; and, with the slender means at his disposition, he concluded that a preservation of the *status quo* was the most feasible as well as the most patriotic plan. It must be remembered, however, that Mr. Buchanan never abdicated the duty of administering justice and collecting the revenue in the seceded states. He declared his intention of performing these duties as soon as Congress should pass laws requisite to the novel circumstances. In case of action upon this line, armed collision with the state power would have resulted from the attempt to collect United States taxes. As a matter of fact, however, the opening of hostilities was precipitated on the issue of defending government property.

It will be profitable to determine as precisely as

[1] McPherson, Rebellion, p. 52.

[2] Mr. Buchanan's Administration on the Eve of Rebellion, ch. ix.

possible the theory of the constitution and of governmental relations upon which the exercise of force by the new administration proceeded. Mr. Lincoln's inaugural address was extremely moderate in tone. He did not announce any policy distinguishable from that of his predecessor. The constitutional perpetuity of the Union was his central proposition, and from this he deduced the nullity of all state ordinances of secession, and the necessity of enforcing the laws in all the states. But while, like Buchanan, Lincoln announced an intention to preserve the *status quo* till time should soothe excited passions, one feature of the former President's theory was conspicuously absent from the inaugural address: the "right to coerce a state" was not even alluded to. In view of the importance that had been ascribed to the search for such a right, the omission was significant. Under the impulse of actual hostilities, however, the contempt of the President for the state-sovereignty doctrine assumed a decidedly aggressive form. His message to Congress at the opening of the extra session on July 4 contained a severe denunciation of the dogma. The time had come for assuming a position that should at least be clear and intelligible; and the President planted himself unequivocally on the theory of national sovereignty. As his definition of a "sovereignty" he accepted this: "A political community without a political superior."

Tested by this [he said], no one of our states except Texas ever was a sovereignty. And even Texas gave up the character on coming into the Union. . . . The states have their *status* IN the Union, and they have no other legal *status*. . . . The Union is older than any of the states, and, in fact, it created them as states. Originally some dependent colonies made the Union, and in turn the Union threw off their old dependence for them, and made them states, such as they are. Not one of them ever had a state constitution independent of the Union.[1]

Such were the steps by which Lincoln reached his position of national supremacy. If a vote had been taken in 1861, in the Northern states alone, on the abstract constitutional question at issue, the President's view would in all probability have been defeated. But so skilfully were the theoretical assumptions blended with appeals to the Union sentiment of the people, that the whole doctrine enunciated in the message was accepted without discrimination. The same passion for territory which had made popular the extension of the boundaries to the Pacific, now clamored for the maintenance of the domain in its integrity. One theory of the constitution could not maintain it; the other could, and the other must be adopted.

The promptness of Congress in adopting measures for enabling the President to carry out his doctrine is sufficient evidence that the legislative department was one with the executive in his views of the constitution. The object of the war

[1] McPherson, Rebellion, p. 127.

was the subject of numerous resolutions proposed in both houses. But the majority showed no disposition to discuss abstractions when actions would more clearly proclaim their opinions. Hence, but one formal declaration of intention came to a vote. This was a resolution to the effect that the war forced upon the country by the disunionists of the South was

not waged in any spirit of oppression, or for any purpose of conquest or subjugation, or purpose of overthrowing or interfering with the rights or established institutions of those [the Southern] states, but to defend and maintain the supremacy of the constitution, and to preserve the Union with all the dignity, equality and rights of the several states unimpaired.[1]

It is beyond question that this declaration expressed the feelings of two-thirds of the Northern people at this time. The resolution, though not passed in joint form, was adopted by both House and Senate separately, with no substantial difference in the wording. In each case the vote was almost unanimous. On its face, the end of the war is proclaimed to be, not the overthrow of slavery, but the preservation of the Union. In respect to the dignity and rights of the states, the expression of intention is clearly inconclusive; for there were very widely varying views as to what was the extent of such dignity and rights under the supreme constitution. Were the rights to be preserved those that were claimed by the state-sover-

[1] McPherson, Rebellion, p. 286.

eignty politicians, or only such as were conceded by the centralizing school? All that appeared unmistakable was that some form of state organization was to be maintained when the rebellion was subdued.

But, even without any more definite declaration of Congress, it cannot be questioned that the doctrine of sovereignty enunciated by the President's message was the doctrine upon which the legislature planted itself for the struggle. Whatever may have been the defects of the theory, it certainly did not lack clearness and consistency. The nation is sovereign; the states are local organizations subordinate to the nation. The general government represents the nation, and is limited in no way by the local state governments, but only by the federal constitution. Of this constitution, however, the departments of the central government are the final interpreters; the limitations of the constitution, therefore, are practically guarded only by the mutual responsibility of the departments in action, and by the accountability to the people in the elections.

II. *The Presidential Dictatorship*

The circumstances in which the government found itself after the fall of Sumter were entirely unprecedented. The President was obliged to regard the uprising of the South as a simple insur-

rection; but the only parallel case, the Whiskey
Insurrection in Washington's administration, was
so insignificant in comparison, that from the very
beginning a system of original construction of the
constitution had to be employed to meet the varied
occasions for executive as well as legislative action.
Long before the end of the war, the principles
thus evolved had become so numerous and so far-
reaching in their application, as entirely to over-
shadow the most cherished doctrines of the old
system.

From the very outset the basis of the government's war power was held to be the necessity of
preserving the nation. The limit of its application
was not the clear expressions of the organic law,
but the forbearance of a distracted people. That
this forbearance extended so far as it did, is significant. The "necessity" thus sanctioned was not
the exigency of individual liberty that prompted
the Declaration of Independence, but the mortal
peril of a conscious nationality. For a third time
in a hundred years, the conviction of a fact beat
down the obstacles of established forms. The
revolution of 1776 secured liberty; that of 1789
secured federal union; and that of 1861–67 secured
national unity. In each case traditional principles were felt to be incompatible with existing
facts, and the old gave way to the new. The
question presented to the administration by the
commencement of hostilities was: Has this gov-

ernment the power to preserve its authority over all its territory? The answer of the old school of constitutional lawyers was: "Yes, so far as it is conferred by the constitution and the laws"; but the answer we derive from the actual conduct of the war is "Yes" without qualification.

Immediately upon the fall of Sumter, the assertion of the new doctrine began. Before the assembling of Congress, July 4, a series of proclamations by the President called into play forces deemed necessary to the preservation of the nation. The calling out of the militia was based upon the law of 1795. Buchanan had declined to consider this law as applicable to the present circumstances. His delicacy, however, was a phase of his scruples about coercing a state — scruples entirely foreign to his successor. It is enacted by the law in question that

whenever the laws of the United States shall be opposed, or the execution thereof obstructed in any state, by combinations too powerful to be suppressed by the ordinary course of judicial proceedings, or by the powers vested in the marshals by this act, it shall be lawful for the President of the United States to call forth the militia of such state, or of any other state or states, as may be necessary to suppress such combinations, and to cause the laws to be duly executed.[1]

Buchanan's interpretation of this was that the militia was to be employed only as a *posse comi-*

[1] 1 Statutes at Large, 424.

tatus to assist in executing a judge's writ.[1] While this may have been the immediate idea of the framer, there was not the remotest allusion to such an intent in the law itself, and it was no extraordinary stretch of construction for Lincoln to act in accordance with the plain terms of the statute. His proclamation avoided any reference to the state governments.

Four days after the call for militia, the President's purpose of ignoring the connection of the state governments with the rebellion was put to a severe test in his proclamation of a blockade of the ports of the Cotton States. He was obliged to speak of "the pretended authority" of those states, but only to declare that persons who, under such authority, molested United States vessels would be treated as pirates. This assumption by the executive of the right to establish a blockade was rather startling to conservative minds. It seemed like a usurpation of the legislative power to declare war. For blockade is an incident of actual warfare, and involves the recognition of belligerent rights. The constitutionality of the President's action, however, was affirmed by the Supreme Court in the Prize Cases,[2] and hence, Congress having acquiesced, it has the sanction of all three departments of the government. Accordingly, the President, as commander-in-chief, can determine,

---

[1] Attorney-General Black's opinion: McPherson, Rebellion, p. 51.
[2] 2 Black, 635.

without reference to Congress, the time when an insurrection has attained the proportions of a war, with all the consequences to person and property that such a decision entails.

Further action by the President previous to the meeting of Congress included a call for the enlistment of forty thousand three-year volunteers,[1] and the increase of the regular army by over twenty thousand men, and the navy by eighteen thousand. Mr. Lincoln himself doubted the constitutionality of these measures.

> Whether strictly legal or not [he says, they] were ventured upon under what appeared to be a popular demand and a public necessity, trusting then as now that Congress would readily ratify them.   It is believed that nothing has been done beyond the constitutional competency of Congress.[2]

This frank substitution of a " popular demand " for a legal mandate, as a basis for executive action, is characteristic of the times.   The President's course was approved and applauded.   Howe, of Wisconsin, proclaimed in the Senate that he approved it in exact proportion to the extent to which it was a violation of the existing law.[3]   The general concurrence in the avowed ignoring of the organic law emphasizes the completeness of the

[1] Under the law of 1795 the term of service of the militia, when called out by the President, was limited to one month after the next meeting of Congress.

[2] Message of July 4, 1861.   McPherson, Rebellion, pp. 125–6.

[3] Globe, 1st sess., 37th Cong., p. 393.

revolution which was in progress. The idea of a government limited by the written instructions of a past generation had already begun to grow dim in the smoke of battle.

The remaining subject dealt with in the President's proclamations was the suspension of the writ of *habeas corpus*. Southern sympathy in Maryland had taken so demonstrative a form that summary measures of repression were resorted to by the government. General Scott was authorized by the President to suspend the writ of *habeas corpus* at any point on the military line between Philadelphia and Washington. This assertion by the executive of an absolute control over the civil rights of the individual in regions not in insurrection excited rather more criticism than the measures which would unpleasantly affect only the rebellious states. A case was promptly brought before Chief Justice Taney for judicial interpretation.[1] Justice Taney's opinion took strong ground against the constitutionality of the President's act. The clause of the constitution touching the matter says: "The privilege of the writ of *habeas corpus* shall not be suspended, unless when in cases of rebellion or invasion the public safety may require it."[2] The implication is that in the cases mentioned the privilege may be suspended, but the clause is silent

---

[1] The case of John Merryman. For all the proceedings and the court's opinion, see McPherson, Rebellion, p. 155.

[2] Art. 1, sec. 9, clause 2.

as to who shall do it.   Precedent and authority were certainly with the chief justice in regarding the determination of the necessity as a function of the legislature.   But to have awaited the meeting and action of Congress in the present case might have been to sacrifice the government.   Lincoln therefore availed himself of the latitude of construction possible by the wording of the clause. Attorney-General Bates sustained the President in an elaborate opinion.   His ground was that in pursuance of the obligation to execute the laws, the President must be accorded the widest discretion as to means.   The use of military force to suppress insurrection was authorized by the constitution, and when such means had been determined upon by the executive, all the incidents of warlike action must necessarily be included.   Nor could the judicial department, being a co-ordinate and not a superior branch of the government, interfere.[1]

The position of the executive in this matter was entirely consistent with that assumed in the establishment of the blockade.   Granting the right in the President to decide when war has technically begun, both the powers in question spring naturally from the recognized authority of the commander-in-chief.   In the interval between April 12 and July 4, 1861, a new principle thus appeared in the constitutional system of the United States, namely,

[1] For the opinion, see McPherson, Rebellion, p. 158.

that of a temporary dictatorship. All the powers of government were virtually concentrated in a single department, and that the department whose energies were directed by the will of a single man.

The dictatorial position assumed by the President was effective in the accomplishment of two most important results, namely, the preservation of the capital and the maintenance of Union sentiment in the wavering border states. These ends achieved, the administration of the government fell back once more into the old lines of departmental co-ordination. Congress labored with the utmost energy to fill the gaps which the crisis had revealed in the laws. Small heed was given to the demands of the minority for discussion of the great constitutional questions that constantly appeared. The decisive majorities [1] by which the Republicans controlled both houses enabled work to be transacted with great vigor.

The first imperative duty of the legislature was to provide for defining the nature and extent of the insurrection which the President reported as existing. It has been shown how the executive had declined to recognize the state organizations as elements of the uprising against the general government. Congress necessarily adopted the same policy. Its measures were made to refer primarily to combinations of individuals against

[1] Practically 28 in a Senate of 50, and 92 in a House of 178. See Tribune Almanac for 1862, pp. 17 and 19.

the laws of the United States. But in the act of July 13, 1861, section five, the attitude of the state governments toward such combinations was taken into consideration as a means of determining the location and extent of the insurrection. In this section the obligation upon the state authorities to support the laws of the United States was distinctly assumed, and the refusal to fulfil this obligation was made a sufficient ground for proclaiming all the inhabitants of the delinquent community public enemies. The law in question, commonly called the "non-intercourse act,"[1] re-enacted the main features of the law by which President Jackson was empowered to collect the duties in nullification times; the fifth section provided further, that when the militia should have been called forth by the President to suppress the insurrection,

and the insurgents shall have failed to disperse by the time directed by the President, and when said insurgents claim to act under the authority of any state or states, and such claim is not disclaimed or repudiated by the persons exercising the functions of government in such state or states, or in the part or parts thereof in which said combination exists, nor such insurrection suppressed by said state or states, then and in such case it may and shall be lawful for the President, by proclamation, to declare that the inhabitants of such state, or any section or part thereof, where such insurrection exists, are in a state of insurrection against the United States; and thereupon all commercial intercourse by and between the

[1] Public Acts of the 37th Cong., 1st sess., ch. iii.

same and the citizens thereof and the citizens of the rest of
the United States shall cease and be unlawful so long as such
hostility shall continue.

A proclamation in pursuance of the authority
thus granted was issued by the President on
August 16. From that time the condition of territorial civil war legally and constitutionally existed
in the United States, with all the consequences of
such a condition which the law of nations recog-
nizes. Congress had exercised its power to declare
war, or, what has been admitted to be the same
thing, to recognize a state of war as existing.
From the time of such recognition, the acts of
the President involving technical war powers were
unquestionably in accordance with the constitution.

III. *The War Power in Relation to Civil Rights in the South*

Upon the passage of the " non-intercourse act,"
both political departments of the government had
given their recognition to the fact that all the
inhabitants of certain portions of United States
territory were at war with the government and its
loyal supporters. The duty of each department
thereupon was to use all constitutional means to
overcome in the shortest time possible the resistance to their authority. To what extent a strict
interpretation of the organic law would reveal

adequate powers, was a question; but the spirit of the people and general ideas of necessity were convenient sources of authority that never failed of application when the direct mandate of written law was lacking. A question that arose immediately was in reference to personal and property rights of dwellers in the insurrectionary districts. Such persons were still, on the theory of the government, citizens of the United States; but were they, as such, entitled, under the present circumstances, to the protection of their civil rights which is normally secured by our system?

War is the negation of civil rights. Granting the power in Congress to designate certain citizens as public enemies in the technical sense, the exercise of that power puts in the hands of the government a control over the life, liberty and property of all such citizens, limited only by the dictates of humanity and a respect for the practice of nations. The insurgents become, in short, belligerent enemies, with the rights and duties which international law ascribes to such. From the moment that they assume that character the constitutional guarantees of civil liberty lose their effect as against the executive. It becomes authorized to enforce submission to the laws by bullets, not by indictments. "Due process of law" ceases to be the necessary condition to a deprivation of civil rights. All the safeguards so carefully constructed by the constitution for the protection of citizens of the United States against oppression by their officers and legislators disappear when resistance by those citizens to law becomes so formidable as to be deemed war.

Such was the theory upon which the exercise of the war power was based by all three departments of the government. The Supreme Court, though divided, in the Prize Cases, upon the question of the exact time when the attitude of belligerency could be assumed, was unanimous in respect to the consequences after that time had arrived. Justice Nelson, dissenting, said:

There is no doubt the government may, by the competent power, recognize or declare the existence of a state of civil war, which will draw after it all the consequences and rights of war between the contending parties, as in the case of a public war. . . . The laws of war, whether the war be civil or *inter gentes*, convert every citizen of the hostile state into a public enemy.[1]

At the outbreak of the insurrection, then, two distinct courses lay open for the government to pursue. It could elect to repress the uprising by the civil power, through process of the courts, with the military arm as the marshal's *posse;* the insurgents then would be subject to the treatment of ordinary criminals. Or, on the other hand, the rebels could be recognized as belligerents and subdued by the exertion of military power alone. In the latter

---

[1] 2 Black, p. 693.

case, the insurgents would seem to be entitled to the treatment which public law secures to armed public enemies. But the question early arose, could not the government follow both courses at the same time, and be guided in its dealings with the rebels by international or by constitutional law, at its discretion? Could it not, for example, hang as traitors rebels taken in battle as prisoners of war? A practical application of some principle was early called for. In the fall of 1861 the crews of several Confederate privateers were brought as captives to New York, and were tried for piracy. The proceeding was in accordance with Mr. Lincoln's blockade proclamation, which ended with a declaration that rebels molesting United States vessels should be thus dealt with. But though a conviction was obtained in at least one case, the penalty was never enforced, for the reason that the Richmond government announced its intention to visit upon an equal number of prisoners in its hands exactly the same treatment that was accorded to the Confederates.[1]

The course of the administration in reference to the exchange of prisoners and other matters was dictated by the same considerations that were operative in the case of the privateersmen. It was desired to secure all the advantages which flowed from the exercise of the war power by the government, while not conceding belligerent rights to

[1] Annual Cyclopedia for 1861, pp. 585, 591.

those against whom that power was employed. In respect to life and liberty the practices of international war were followed, in order to avoid the barbarism of the *lex talionis;* though in theory the responsibility of the Southerners for their acts to the regular courts of law was always maintained. As to property, however, the course of the government was not so clearly defined. Measures looking to extensive if not general confiscation were broached early in the war. The basis for such a proceeding gave rise to animated controversy, and it was in connection with this discussion that the fullest light was thrown on the relation of the United States government to its citizens in the rebel states.

The first step taken by Congress toward confiscation was the act of August 6, 1861.[1] This made it the duty of the President to seize, confiscate and condemn all property used in aiding, abetting or promoting the present or any future insurrection against the government of the United States. Section four provided for the forfeiture of slaves employed in any military or naval service against the government and authority of the United States. This act was passed by virtue of the war powers of Congress. It was a legislative authorization for the exercise of an acknowledged belligerent right. For the purpose of freeing the slaves, the ultra anti-slavery men were perfectly willing to sacrifice

[1] Public Acts of the 37th Cong., 1st sess., ch. lx.

their old scruples about regarding men as property, and the provision on this subject was defended on the same ground as the rest of the bill.

This first act was somewhat crude and unsatisfactory in detail, but was in principle quite definite and distinct. War had been recognized as existing, and Congress had exercised the constitutional power of making "rules concerning captures on land and water." But during the next session of the Thirty-seventh Congress, the full development of the war gave rise to a more bitter spirit, which manifested itself in more radical and questionable measures. Many propositions looking to confiscation and emancipation were brought forward in both houses, and the debates upon these subjects were long and acrid. The dominant party became quite distinctly divided on the general policy of the war; and, behind all, the idea of finding in the existing crisis a definite settlement of the slavery question assumed a steadily increasing importance.

When it had been determined that the crimes of the secessionists called for vindictive punishment, serious constitutional difficulties were found to beset the path of the avengers. The House first passed a bill which surmounted all obstacles with gratifying ease. It simply provided that all property of whatever description, belonging to certain described classes of persons, was forfeited to the government of the United States, and declared lawful subject of seizure and of condemnation.

The judiciary committee of the Senate, to whom this and other bills were referred, recognized some of the objections that could be raised to the House proposition, and so reported a modification of it. By this it was enacted that the forfeiture should take effect only upon the property of persons "beyond the jurisdiction of the United States," or of persons in any state or district of the United States where, on account of insurrection or rebellion, the ordinary judicial process could not be served upon them; and the title to the property was to vest in the United States immediately upon the commission of the act, so that any subsequent alienation by the former owner would be void.

The objections raised against both these bills, on principles of both constitutional and international law, were very strong, and after long debates proved effective to prevent the passage of either. But a compromise bill, patched up from the many propositions that had been submitted during the discussion, became at last the law.[1] The first four sections fixed very severe penalties for the crimes of treason and rebellion, the latter being an addition to the catalogue of felonies. These provisions followed the suggestions of the more conservative Republicans, like Collamer, of Vermont, who expressed a strong desire to get at the property of the rebels, but insisted upon doing it by

[1] Public Acts of the 37th Cong., 2d sess., ch. cxcv.

regular judicial procedure.[1]   Sections five, six, seven and eight referred to confiscation proper. The President was directed to cause the seizure of all the property, of whatsoever kind, belonging to specified classes of persons, namely, officers of the rebel army or navy, officers of the civil administration of the so-called Confederate States, governors, judges or legislators of any of said states, ex-officials of the United States hereafter holding office under the Confederate States, and persons owning property in loyal states who should give aid and comfort to the rebellion.   Further, if any other persons, being engaged in the rebellion, or giving it aid and comfort, should not cease within sixty days of a proclamation to be issued by the President, such person's property should be liable to seizure in like manner.   The property so seized was to be proceeded against by action *in rem* in the United States courts, and condemned and sold as enemies' property, and the proceeds were to be used for the support of the army of the United States.

This act assumed the power in Congress to deprive several millions of persons of all their property, and this by simple legislative act.   By the theory of our constitution, such power must be granted by the organic law, or be inferable from some clearly granted power.   There was no claim of an express grant.   By implication,

[1] Globe, 2d sess., 37th Cong., p. 1812.

the power was held to be deducible from the clauses authorizing Congress "to declare war," "to make rules concerning captures on land and water," "to provide for calling forth the militia to . . . suppress insurrections," and finally, "to make all laws which shall be necessary and proper for carrying into execution the foregoing powers." On the other hand, the constitution contains the following prohibitions: "No bill of attainder . . . shall be passed;" "no person shall be . . . deprived of . . . property, without due process of law; nor shall private property be taken for public use without just compensation;" and finally, "no attainder of treason shall work . . . forfeiture except during the life of the person attainted." The exercise of authority under the grants above enumerated involved of necessity the violation of these prohibitions. Respect for both at the same time was inconceivable. The only escape from the dilemma was to assume that the constitution contemplated a state of affairs to which the prohibitions were inapplicable. And that indeed was the position taken by the advocates of confiscation. The existence of a state of war was held to bring into the sphere of legislative action any measures necessary to weaken the enemy that were recognized by the great system of international practice.

International law thus was set up as the source of Congress' power. But in the modern practice of civilized nations the general confiscation of

enemies' private property is unknown. It is as
obsolete as the poisoning of wells in an enemy's
country.   As a rule, real estate is left to its owners,
and movables are appropriated only so far as military necessity, as judged by the commander in the
field, seems to demand it.[1] Some vague idea of
such a justification seems to have suggested the
clause devoting the proceeds of the confiscations
to the support of the army. But it was rightly
argued that the determination of the army's necessities was a function of the President, and not of
Congress, and that legislation in such a case was
superfluous.[2] The justification of the Confiscation
Act by international law thus was no less difficult
than by constitutional law pure and simple. Only
as an abstract right of war, independent of all
convention and precedent, could the proceedings
contemplated by the act be consistently defended.

It appeared, however, from further developments, that the act was not based upon the war
power alone. After it had been sent to the President for approval, it became known that he proposed to veto it. His objections were ascertained,
and an explanatory resolution was hurriedly adopted
to meet his views.[3] Its most important provision
was that no punishment or proceedings under the
act should "be so construed as to work a forfeiture

---

[1] Halleck, International Law, pp. 456, 457, and authorities cited.
[2] *Cf.* Lincoln's message, McPherson, Rebellion, p. 198.
[3] Public Resolutions, 2d sess., 37th Cong., no. 63.

of the real estate of the offender beyond his natural life." This was an effort to reconcile the act with the prohibition in the constitution against forfeiture for treason; the futility of the effort appeared from the fact that the forfeiture contemplated by the act was in no sense the result of an attainder of treason. Attainder of treason does not result from a proceeding *in rem*, but from conviction in a criminal proceeding *in personam*.[1] The effect of the resolution, therefore, was simply to impair the utility of the act, while in no way affecting the constitutional question.[2]

Again, it was maintained that the action *in rem* provided for in the act was such "due process of law" as the constitution contemplates in the deprivation of property. This construction, however, is wholly contrary to the spirit of the bill of rights. The theory of the action *in rem* is that the "thing" is an instrument, a necessary participant, as it were, in the violation of some law. The provision of the constitution refers to criminal procedure against the person, and to apply it in other cases is mere distortion of the organic law. Any attempt to reconcile the act with the guarantee of civil rights leads to absurdities. Such was the con-

[1] Cooley, Constitutional Limitations, 4th ed., p. 317.

[2] As illustrating the struggles of the courts in construing the act, see decisions of District Judges Betts and Underwood, and others, collected in the Annual Cyclopedia for 1862–64, under the title "Confiscation."

sistent position taken by the radical advocates of confiscation, and such is the only position justified by the logic of facts.

But very important results are secured by pursuing further the line of argument adopted by the radicals. The benefits of the constitution must be denied to those who refuse to recognize its authority. Such denial, however, does not relieve the offenders of their responsibilities under the fundamental law. Circumstances may force the government to regard certain citizens of the United States as enemies engaged in war. In such a state of affairs, many provisions of the constitution become inoperative. In other words, since the government itself is the judge of the circumstances, the government may suspend certain parts of the organic law. But not only that. The suspension of the constitution is not absolute. While the right of jury trial, for example, may be denied under the authority of Congress, it may also be allowed. A man's property may be seized by virtue of the war power, but at the same time the man himself may be tried and hung for treason under the regular civil procedure. "We may treat them [the rebels] as traitors, and we may treat them as enemies," said Senator Trumbull, "and we have the right of both belligerent and sovereign, so far as they are concerned."[1] Such is undoubtedly the theory to be deduced from all

[1] Globe, 2d sess., 37th Cong., p. 943.

the circumstances of the government's action in reference to confiscation.

Sections nine to twelve of the Confiscation Act had reference to negroes. Slaves of persons engaged in rebellion against the government of the United States, coming into the lines of the army, or captured from their masters, or found in places once occupied by rebel forces, were declared free. Fugitive slaves were not to be given up except to such owners as would declare under oath that they had not borne arms against the United States in the present rebellion, or given aid and comfort thereto. The President was authorized to employ negroes in suppressing the rebellion, and also to make provision for the colonization of the freedmen in some foreign country.

The treatment of the negro question was freely admitted by all the friends of the confiscation bill to be a very important, and was asserted by some to be the most important, feature of the act. Vexatious complications had arisen in disposing of the fugitive slaves that could not be kept from coming within the lines of the army. The President's patience had been severely tried in his efforts to restrain the ardent abolition spirit of some of his generals.[1] While he looked forward to the possibility of a situation in which military necessity would justify emancipation, yet he considered the

---

[1] Especially Fremont and Hunter. See McPherson, Rebellion, pp. 247, 251.

political horizon, especially in the border states, too threatening to permit precipitate action. But the radicals in his party denounced his hesitation as pusillanimous, and were only too ready to attain their end through the legislative department. Confiscation seemed an easy and suitable path by which to penetrate the stronghold of slavery. By the act of August 6, 1861, slaves used for the purposes of the insurrection had been declared free. The principle was that, under such circumstances, slaves were contraband of war. But the basis of the later law was the right to free a man's slaves as a penalty for the master's participation in the rebellion. There was no essential distinction between the right of Congress to confiscate *choses in action* and its right to take from the rebel his claim to the services of a negro. The institution of slavery was not touched, and the peculiar significance of these provisions lay in the fact that they were dictated by a sentiment in the North that would not long be satisfied with such moderate measures.

By the Confiscation Act and the discussions incident to its consideration, the attitude and powers of the United States government in respect to such of its citizens as were proclaimed public enemies were more or less satisfactorily determined. In the struggle between those who upheld the restraints of the constitution and those who considered only the limits of international law, the government practically escaped all restrictions whatsoever. Side by side with the doctrine that all means looking to success in the war could be employed against insurgent citizens, developed the principle that a like absence of limitation characterized the relations of the government to citizens who were not public enemies. It was in connection with the civil rights of citizens in the loyal states that a far-reaching conception of the war power attained most distinct definition.

IV. *The War Power in Relation to Civil Rights in the North*

The question as to the extent of the government's authority over the life, liberty and property of the individual in states not in insurrection was complicated by the controversy over the proper department for exercising such authority. It has already been stated[1] that the action of the President in suspending the writ of *habeas corpus* of his own accord in 1861 had excited a discussion of his right to do it, and that Chief Justice Taney had given an opinion against the right. The impotence of the judiciary as against the executive, and the neglect of Congress to take any action on the matter, had left the administration in a position to realize its own ideas of its powers. Arrests of disaffected persons and Southern sympathizers under

[1] *Supra*, p. 19.

secret orders from Washington had gone on without ceasing, and in no case was the service of the great writ allowed.   Not only in Maryland, and the regions near the seat of war, but in the most distant parts of the land, from Maine to California, men were seized without any information as to the charges against them, and were confined in forts and prison camps.   It was not denied by the friends of the policy that frightful injustice was often done, but that fact was rightly held to have no bearing on the question of power involved.   If the constitution of the United States vested in the executive, in time of war, absolute discretion as to the means to be employed to carry on the war, whatever evils resulted from the exercise of this discretion must only be added to the aggregate of misery of which a resort to arms is the cause, and so must be regretted, but sternly endured.

For a year and a half after the beginning of the war the arrest and detention of citizens as "prisoners of state" went on without any formal announcement as to the principles of the proceedings.   Only when, in the autumn of 1862, a draft had become necessary to recruit the army, were the government's operations put upon a well-defined basis.   On September 24, a proclamation was issued by the President,[1] ordering, first, that as a necessary measure for suppressing the existing insurrection, all persons "discouraging volun-

[1] McPherson, Rebellion, p. 177.

teer enlistments, resisting military drafts, or guilty
of any disloyal practice affording aid and comfort
to the rebels," should be subject to martial law, and
liable to trial by courts-martial or military commissions; and second, that the writ of *habeas corpus*
should be suspended in respect to all persons arrested or held by military authority. In this paper
the President formally assumed the right to proclaim martial law and to suspend the writ of *habeas
corpus* at his own discretion throughout the United
States. On this assumption the power both to
arrest and to detain a citizen — and, indeed, to put
him to death — was complete.

The basis of this proclamation is to be found in
the apparently unimportant phrase with which the
orders are introduced. The whole proceeding is
"a necessary measure" of war. Granting that
the oath to "protect and defend the constitution,"
and the mandate to "take care that the laws be
faithfully executed," confer unlimited discretion
as to means, nothing can be said against the legality of the President's orders. But on any other
theory, it would be hard to justify them. The
fourth article of the amendments to the constitution guarantees the security of the people in their
persons against unreasonable seizures, and indicates that arrests are to be made through special
warrants. On the theory under which the President acted in ordering arrests by military authority,
this article of the constitution has no application

to times of civil war.[1]   It "speaks in reference to the normal condition of the country only."   When war exists, the President has the right to arrest and detain on his own motion; the Fifth Amendment, which forbids the holding of any one unless on action of a grand jury, loses its force under such circumstances.   As the policy of confiscation had been based on the nullity of constitutional restrictions as to the legislature, so the policy of military arrests was based on the nullity of those restrictions as to the executive.

The proclamation of September 24, 1862, constituted a perfect platform for a military despotism. The growing prominence of the emancipation policy during this year had dampened the enthusiasm of the Northern masses for the war, and in connection with the drafts the opposition to the government grew very demonstrative.   But this only tended to make military arrests more frequent.   As a result the widespread discontent with the administration's policy received additional stimulus, and the Congressional and state elections of 1862 were disastrous to the dominant party.   Some action by the legislature then became imperative.   Bills touching the subject were promptly taken up by Congress when it met in December, but the discussions were so violent that

[1] Binney, The Privilege of the Writ of Habeas Corpus (2d ed., Philadelphia, 1862), p. 55; Whiting, War Powers under the Constitution, p. 176.

no result was reached till just at the close of the session.

The interpretation of the clause of the constitution relating to the suspension of the writ of *habeas corpus*, was not, however, definitely decided even then. It was admitted on all sides that the general impression, from the foundation of the government, had been that the power of suspension was in Congress. The insertion of the clause in the article relating to Congress indicates that such was the idea of the committee on style and revision in the convention. As first presented to the convention and referred to the committee of detail, the clause contained the words " by the legislature." [1] Tucker's Blackstone and Story's *Commentaries* assume without discussion that Congress alone can suspend the writ. The Supreme Court indicated such an opinion in Bollman and Swartwout.[2] And especially significant of the early idea is the fact that when, in 1807, a bill was proposed suspending the writ in connection with Burr's conspiracy, a long and violent debate in the House disclosed not the slightest intimation that any one suspected that the power was in the President.[3] The action of Mr. Lincoln's administration, however, had been justified by opinions from eminent lawyers, and officially by that of the attorney-general. The grounds on which these

[1] Elliot's Debates, V. 445.   [2] 4 Cranch, 75.
[3] Annals of Congress, 2d sess., 9th Cong., p. 402 *et seq.*

views were based were generally technical rather than historical, and arguments were deduced from the circumstances and necessities of the present rather than from respect for the past.

Congress devoted itself to a course of procedure based upon a recognition of matters as they stood. The act of March 3, 1863,[1] first authorized the President, during the rebellion, to suspend the privilege of the great writ "in any case throughout the United States, or any part thereof." It then provided for the discharge of such persons as were in duress, upon failure of the grand jury to indict them, and for the judicial examination within twenty days of all persons hereafter arrested under orders of the administration. To check the torrent of prosecutions for malicious imprisonment that was threatening United States officers everywhere, it was enacted that the order of the President should be a sufficient defence in any such action. In other words, Congress declined to say whether or not the administration had acted illegally, but went so far as to protect it from any consequences if it had so acted. Provision was also made for the removal of all suits arising out of acts done under executive authority, from the state to the federal courts.

So far as concerned the past course of the administration, Congress undoubtedly took the wisest steps possible under the circumstances. Indem-

[1] Public Acts, 3d sess., 37th Cong., ch. lxxxi.

nifying the executive officers against suits for damages was a concession to the view that the President was correct in assuming the right to arrest and hold suspected persons; while the authorization to suspend the writ indicated that the power to suspend was in Congress. The only constitutional principle that can be deduced from the act as a whole is that the President may in an emergency exercise the right to arrest and detain individuals until Congress acts.

In pursuance of the authority of this act, Mr. Lincoln proclaimed a general suspension of the privilege of the writ of *habeas corpus* on September 15, 1863. The effect of the suspension was limited to persons held as "prisoners of war, spies, or aiders or abettors of the enemy," and such as were amenable to the Articles of War. How elastic these limits were may be judged by the interpretation put upon "aiders and abettors."

He is a public enemy who seeks falsely to exalt the motives, character and capacity of armed traitors, to magnify their resources, *etc.* He who overrates the success . . . of our adversaries, or underrates our own, and he who seeks false causes of complaint against the officers of our government, or inflames party spirit among ourselves, gives to the enemy that moral support which is more valuable to them than regiments of soldiers, or millions of dollars.[1]

With such perfect facilities afforded by law, it is scarcely to be wondered at that in many cases

[1] Whiting, War Powers, p. 197.

the practical construction of the proclamation was the arrest of anybody who expressed dissatisfaction with the administration. The boundary line between political opposition to the President and treason became extremely hazy in the eyes of the President's agents.

In addition to the free exercise of the right arbitrarily to arrest and hold citizens by military authority, the practice grew up, early in the war, of bringing arrested persons before military commissions and passing sentence upon them after summary proceedings of a *quasi*-judicial character. By the President's proclamation of September 24, 1862, all rebels and insurgents, and their aiders and abettors, and all disloyal persons generally, were declared subject to trial by court-martial or military commission. The latter organization had no legal existence in the United States when the President thus conferred jurisdiction upon it. Its actual power, however, became unmistakably manifest. It is to be noticed that with the recognition of the military commission a complete judicial system existed outside of the ordinary civil and criminal courts. The whole process of arresting, trying, convicting and executing a man could be carried through without any recourse to the constitutional judiciary, and with no security whatever against the arbitrary will of the military commander. Such a state of things was held to be the necessary consequence of a rebellion which called for the exercise of the war power.

The *Habeas Corpus* Act of 1863 provided for the trial of all political prisoners by the civil authority, and thus seemed to cut off from the military courts the jurisdiction over civilians. But in spite of this the application of martial law continued in all the Northern states. Efforts to secure a judgment of the civil judiciary upon the validity of the extraordinary tribunals all proved ineffectual till after the war had ended. Then, in 1866, in the case of *Ex parte* Milligan,[1] the Supreme Court determined their relation to the constitution.

According to United States army orders, the military commissions were to administer the "common law of war," or, in other words, to execute martial, as distinct from military, law.[2] In assuming the right to try citizens of loyal states by purely military procedure, Mr. Lincoln asserted the existence of martial law, in its most unlimited sense, throughout the whole United States. Martial law is well understood to be practically no law — merely the unregulated will of a military commander, sanctioned by physical force.[3] Under its sway the whole machinery of civil justice disappears. The exigencies of active warfare bring

---

[1] 4 Wall. 2.

[2] *Ex parte* Vallandigham, 1 Wall. 249; *Ex parte* Milligan, 4 Wall. 142.

[3] See Garfield's argument, 4 Wall. 47.

the theatre of actual army operations into this condition by the very nature of the case. But the question raised by the President's action was whether there could be a constructive exigency of this sort — whether martial law could supersede civil law, not by the actual presence of contending forces and the actual destruction of the civil administration, but by the opinion of either the President or Congress that the necessity existed which would justify the supersession. It cannot be denied that the war was carried through on the latter theory. The records of the War Department contain the reports of hundreds of trials by military commissions, with punishments varying from light fines to banishment and death.[1] Congress, moreover, asserted its control over the subject by indemnifying officers against prosecutions for acts done under the President's orders organizing the commissions.[2] It further gave legal sanction to the military tribunals in the Reconstruction Acts, though here there was a doubt as to whether the status of the region was that of peace or of war.[3]

But the judgment of the Supreme Court in Milligan's case was a clear and explicit denial of any power in either executive or legislative department to suspend the operation of the laws protecting

[1] Digest of Opinions of the Judge Advocate General, p. 334.

[2] Act of May 11, 1866.

[3] See opinion of Attorney-General Hoar: McPherson, Reconstruction, p. 477.

civil liberty.   In the first place it was held that the suspension of the privilege of the writ of *habeas corpus* did not establish martial law, as had been claimed by the executive.   That act merely shuts off for the time civil inquiry into the reasons for military arrests.   As to. the main question, the government claimed :

When war exists, foreign or domestic, and the country is subdivided into military departments for mere convenience, the commander of one of them can, if he chooses, within his limits, on the plea of necessity, with the approval of the executive, substitute military force for and to the exclusion of the laws, and punish all persons as he thinks right and proper, without fixed or certain rules.

The necessities of the service, it was argued, required the division of the loyal states into military districts ; this, in a military sense, constituted them the theatre of military operations and therefore brought them under the authority of the commander.   This conclusion the court flatly rejected, and sought some palpable objective fact that should alone justify the existence of arbitrary rule.   This was found in the condition of the courts of justice.

Martial law cannot arise from a threatened invasion.   The necessity must be actual and present ;   the invasion real, such as effectually closes the courts and deposes the civil administration. . . .   Martial rule can never exist where the courts are open, and in the proper and unobstructed exercise of their jurisdiction.

The safeguards thrown about the liberty of the individual by the constitution could be disturbed by
neither President, nor Congress, nor the judiciary,
except so far as concerned the writ of *habeas
corpus.* Physical force alone could override the
organic law.

The opinion of the court was dissented from by
four of the justices on a single point, namely, the
denial of the power in Congress to declare martial
law. That this power was in the legislature,
though not exercised during the war, was deduced
by the minority from the authorization to make
rules for the army and navy, in connection with the
exception in the Fifth Amendment, of "cases arising in the land and naval forces, or in the militia
in actual service in time of war or public danger." [1]

The action of the political departments is in
direct contradiction of the judiciary on this vital
question of the war power. The whole subject of
extraordinary authority is involved in the determination of such a case as that of Milligan. To
maintain that the framers of the constitution contemplated vesting in any man or body of men the
discretionary right to set aside any of its provisions, seems too much like judging the past in
the light of the present. To believe that the nation
could have been preserved without the exercise of
such a discretionary power, involves too severe a
strain upon the reasoning faculties of the careful

[1] 4 Wall. 137.

student of the times. Two methods may be suggested of reaching a satisfactory conclusion on the question: either to consider that the war wrought a great modification in the canons of interpretation applicable to the organic law; or to recognize the fact that in the throes of the rebellion a new and adequate constitution developed out of the ruins of the old.

V. *The War Power and the Slaves*

All the circumstances connected with the origin of the war conspired to render the attitude of the government toward slavery the most delicate problem with which the administration had to deal. From the first contact of the Northern armies with Southern soil, questions arose that increased daily in both number and perplexity. Many slaves came into the control of the army, either through flight or by capture, and the generals pursued various policies as to the disposition to be made of the blacks. The device of the astute Butler, to seize them as contraband of war and then to set them free, was readily adopted in many quarters; but for months the condition of affairs in the border states caused the President to discountenance any procedure which would strengthen the idea that the war was becoming an anti-slavery crusade. Generals Fremont and Hunter were repressed with considerable abruptness when they undertook to apply a policy of emancipation in their respective departments, and Mr. Lincoln announced that he reserved to himself, as commander-in-chief, the exercise of whatever power was necessary in connection with this subject.

Meanwhile the abolition sentiment was rapidly gaining strength in the North, and with the growing sense of the meaning of war power the idea of general emancipation by military authority became increasingly attractive. President Lincoln long withstood the pressure that was put upon him to adopt this idea. He had grave doubts both as to his power in the premises and as to the wisdom of the policy. Eventually he gave way, and the Emancipation Proclamation was the result. The significance of this famous paper is generally misunderstood. As indicating the definitive adoption by the executive of a radical policy on a vital issue, the proclamation was of the highest importance; but it did not strike the shackles from a single slave. The proclamation did indeed declare the slaves in certain districts free: but as these districts were carefully defined so as to include only such as were under control of the Confederates, there could be no claim that the slaves therein were free in fact; and the basis of the proclamation was so formulated as entirely to preclude the contention that they were free in law. Mr. Lincoln gave as his authority for the proclamation "the power in me vested as commander-in-chief of the army and navy of the United States, in time of actual armed rebellion against the authority and government of the United States"; and he described the act as "a fit and necessary war measure for suppressing said rebellion," and as "warranted by the constitution upon military necessity." These expressions give to the paper the character of a military decree, pure and simple. The calling up or setting free of the enemy's slaves was both in theory and by precedent an incident of a commander's authority,[1] though it had always been looked upon as a desperate expedient. As military chief, then, Mr. Lincoln was within his rights in declaring the slaves free and in ordering his subordinates to enforce his decree. So far as the blacks came within the control of the army, their status was changed to that of freedom. As to those beyond the lines of the army, no change was effected; for it is the function of the military arm to effect changes primarily in fact and only indirectly in law. Had hostilities terminated before the whole South was occupied by the armies of the United States, there would have been no legal basis for a claim to freedom on the part of the slaves in the unoccupied regions. Even in the technically occupied regions there would have been some ground, in very many cases, for contesting the claim of the blacks to freedom after the re-establishment of normal conditions. Only by the adoption of the

[1] *Cf.* Whiting, War Powers, p. 69 *et seq.*

Thirteenth Amendment was the legal status of the freedmen put upon a clear and indisputable foundation.

The efficacy that was widely attributed to the Emancipation Proclamation as definitely freeing all the slaves in the Confederacy was a deduction from the prevalent doctrine which permitted of no distinction between the civil and the military powers of the President. On a correct understanding of his war power, it can attach only to his office as commander-in-chief of the army, and can have no effect on the performance of his civil duties. As chief civil executive, his actions relate to the laws; as chief officer of the army and navy, he is concerned with situations where there is no law. But in 1862 it was urgently insisted that a state of hostilities effected the immediate absorption of civil executive in the commander-in-chief. Hence to deny the instant validity of the Emancipation Proclamation throughout the Southern states, was considered equivalent to recognizing the independence of those states. But the deduction was quite fallacious. As civil executive Mr. Lincoln was still President of the whole United States, South as well as North; but as civil executive he could never have issued the proclamation. Only as commander of the army did he issue it; and the fact that his civil functions embraced the whole territory of the Union could in no way extend his military authority to regions

where he had no army to command. The confused
thinking of the time on this point probably accounts for the curious fact that the proclamation
was countersigned, not by the secretary of war,
but by the secretary of state. There seems to
have been some idea that this military decree
would be endowed with extraordinary efficiency
by the endorsement of the civil branch of the
administration.

While the President had been working con-
servatively toward the policy which he finally proclaimed, Congress had been pushing with rather
more vigorous strides toward the goal. The growing sentiment that the situation demanded the final
removal of the slavery question from politics found
expression first in assaults on the institution on the
lines of constitutional interpretation that had been
marked out by the Free-soil and Republican parties.
First in the District of Columbia and then in the
territories the powers that had long been held in
abeyance by threats of secession were in 1862
finally asserted.[1] Much time and ingenuity were
expended on the project of compensated emancipation in the border states, to which the President was so earnestly committed,[2] but the radical
sentiment, stimulated by military reverses, was
heedless of such moderate methods and urged

[1] For summary of war legislation on slavery, see Whiting, War
Powers, p. 393 *et seq.*
[2] McPherson, Rebellion, p. 213 *et seq.*

unceasingly the application of the war powers of Congress to the desired end, both in seceded and in loyal states.

We have already seen how adaptable the principles of the Confiscation Acts were to the purposes of emancipation in the rebel districts. Mr. Lincoln was careful to point out in his message of July 17, 1862,[1] that the method of setting free slaves here employed did not involve the assumption by Congress of the power to regulate the status of slaves within a state. The slaves, he showed, were forfeited to, and became the property of, the national government in consequence of their masters' crimes, and the government elected to set them free rather than to hold or sell them. Another means employed by Congress to make inroads on slavery was the peremptory prohibition of the return of fugitive slaves by the military authorities. By various prescriptions in the Confiscation Acts and in the Articles of War the return of fugitives to masters in the rebel states was rendered practically impossible.

Still another device for effecting emancipation was developed in the employment of negroes in the army. There was here, however, no new principle but merely a change of application. It was first enacted that any slave of a rebel should, upon entering the military service of the government,

[1] McPherson, Rebellion, p. 197.

become free.[1] But such a one would, under the Confiscation Act, be assured of his freedom by the mere fact of coming into the military lines ; so in this particular the law involved no innovation. A very distinct advance was made, however, in the further provision that, if owned by rebels, the mother, wife and children of such slave should also be free. This was a direct and unqualified assertion of the power to terminate the legal relation of master and slave, regardless of *de facto* conditions, by act of Congress. The provision was justified by the growing doctrine of military necessity, which was held to warrant Congressional as well as Presidential action. It was a "necessary and proper" means for carrying into effect the undisputed power to raise and support armies. As encouraging enlistments, it fell clearly within the war powers of the legislature. This line of reasoning was developed with ever-widening scope as the war progressed and the difficulty of procuring troops increased. In the Enrolment Act of 1864, which prescribed the drafting of negroes,[2] the principle was fully applied to the states not in secession. Slaves, when drafted into the service, received their freedom, but loyal owners were entitled to compensation. Later the wives and children of all persons in the army and navy

[1] Act of July 17, 1862; McPherson, Rebellion, p. 274.
[2] 13 Statutes at Large, 11.

were declared free.[1] With this the efforts to maintain a connection with the constitution became farcical ; for the act was retrospective, and the acutest
intellect must fail to discern how future enlistments would be encouraged by freeing the rela-
tives of persons who were already in the army
through conscription. In reality, however, little
attention was paid to this latest act. Slavery was
obviously on its last legs, and the Thirteenth
Amendment had already been submitted to the
legislatures.

VI. *Principles and Tendencies in the Exercise of the War Power*

Leaving out of account the dogma of state sovereignty, it had been a matter of faith with most
of the people of the United States that the federal
constitution embodied a peculiarly effective solution of the problem of liberty *versus* authority.
Many rights of the citizen were guaranteed by
direct and unequivocal prohibitions upon the government. But in addition to these the eternal
tendency of government to encroach upon the
individual was held to be counteracted by three
principles : first, that no department of the government should exercise any power not delegated
to it in the constitution ; second, that through the
clear separation of the three departments — execu-

---

[1] Joint resolution of March 3, 1865; 13 Stats. at Large, p. 571.

tive, legislative and judicial — each should act as a restraint upon the others ; and third, that the two most aggressive departments, executive and legislative, should be subject to frequent judgment by the people in the elections.

From the beginning of the government's career the efficiency of the first of these principles — that of delegated powers — had been weakened by the development of liberal construction under the doctrine of implied powers. But a limit to the implication of powers had always been recognized in the positive prohibitions of the constitution. That is, in selecting a "necessary and proper" means for carrying out an expressly delegated power, none could be chosen which was directly prohibited by the constitution. Upon resort to the war power, however, as we have seen, the prohibitions of the constitution had to be entirely disregarded. And the very first to go by the board were those that concerned the immediate rights of life and liberty. With the barriers down which had been so carefully constructed for the protection of these rights, the invasion of other regions, protected not by express prohibition but only by absence of delegation, could not meet with much resistance. When arrest without warrant, detention without hearing and conviction without jury were daily incidents, though distinctly forbidden, it could only seem ridiculous to haggle over the right to make treasury notes legal tender, merely because nothing was said about it in the organic law.   The whole spirit of war-time legislation compels recognition of the fact that the principle of delegated powers ceased to have great importance as a restraint upon government.

Nor, when the war power was fully developed, was any great influence exerted by the principle of the separation and co-ordination of departments. The judiciary simply became an "unconsidered trifle" as a restraint upon the legislature and the executive.   As to the relations of the latter two, a curious and interesting situation was developed. On the plea of "necessity" each disregarded both the doctrine of delegated powers and the explicit prohibitions of the constitution.   So far as the President was concerned, the "necessity" under which he acted was that of the military commander—the subjective motive on which an officer acts in adopting measures for the safety of an organized force, or for the success of its operations in the field when civil law is overthrown.   The only "necessity" which could rationally be made the basis of legislative action was that deducible from the "necessary and proper" clause of the constitution.   Between this and military necessity there is no connection, save in the identity of words.   But in the thinking of the war-time, the two ideas were completely confused, and the commander's privilege of doing whatever he regarded as likely to weaken the enemy was freely employed as a warrant for Congressional action. Both legislature and executive were on this theory "above law." Hence while Congress was endowed with authority to legislate entirely at its discretion, the President was privileged at his discretion to disregard all this legislation. Where such a conclusion was possible, the principle of departmental check and balance was obviously of little significance. Good statesmanship in both executive and legislature preserved the harmony of the two branches till the strain of armed hostilities was relaxed, but no longer. In the work of destruction the President was the real government, and Congress kept in the background; in the work of reconstruction Congress asserted once more its controlling power, and violently put the President into the background.

In the practice of the war-time the only principle working efficiently in limitation of the government was that of frequent elections. Public opinion, in short, and not the elaborate devices of the constitution, played the decisive rôle in the United States just as it had played it in earlier centuries and presumably less favored lands. American chauvinists had boasted long and loudly of the superior stability of the written constitution; a great national crisis quickly revealed that it was no more secure against the forces of popular passion than the less artificial structures with which it had been so favorably compared.

Side by side with the assumption by the national government of unlimited control over the rights of the people, the process of gathering in powers that had hitherto been left to the states went steadily on during the war. The association of the doctrine of state rights with that of secession was too close to permit of much resistance to this process. Centralization was the order of the day. Conspicuous among the illustrations of this fact appear the substitution of a national for a state system of banking and currency ; the creation of a national militia system to occupy the field once held by the state systems ; and the sweeping jurisdiction conferred by the *Habeas Corpus* Act upon the national judiciary at the expense of the state courts. The legislation by which these results were achieved was opposed on constitutional grounds which in earlier times would have been universally recognized as unassailable. But under existing circumstances, the territorial unity of the nation was held to outweigh all other considerations, and nothing could stand that either positively obstructed or even failed most effectively to promote this end.

It has sometimes been said that January 1, 1863, marks the most distinct epoch in the history of the war. The Emancipation Proclamation is assumed as the dividing line between the old system and the new. This view is more appropriate to the state of affairs in the South than to that in the

North. It is unquestionably true that Mr. Lincoln's decree furnished the Southern leaders with a most effective instrument for the consolidation of sentiment in the Confederacy. From that time the struggle on the part of the South was a desperate battle for existence. But in the North, on the other hand, the triumph of the radicals in securing the adoption of their policy by the President awakened feelings of apprehension among the other political factions. Mr. Lincoln admits, in his message to Congress in December, that the issue of the proclamation "was followed by dark and doubtful days." Nor was the gloom confined to the political arena. The bloody reverse at Fredericksburg, the narrow escape from disaster at Murfreesboro, and later the disheartening defeat at Chancellorsville, involved the military situation in hopeless uncertainty. Meanwhile, the discussion of the *habeas corpus* bill and the conscription act in Congress and in the country at large aroused the bitterness which culminated in the draft riots. In all respects the first half of the year 1863 was the period of lowest ebb of the national fortunes. The turn of the tide came with the nation's birthday. In the field, Gettysburg and Vicksburg marked the change. The stern enforcement of the conscription act was successful finally in putting the government on a firm footing with respect to men, while the enormous loan of $900,000,000, authorized by the last Congress, satisfactorily settled the matter of supplies.

By the summer of 1863, the question of war powers in the general government for the suppression of insurrection had been definitely settled. The military result of the war became only a question of time, and the legal and political results gradually began to assume the greatest importance. Most obvious of these was the final disappearance of the assumed right of state secession, and with it the whole doctrine of state sovereignty in all its ramifications. For, while it is often said that a right cannot be destroyed by force, the maxim refers rather to the abstract moral conviction than to the concrete legal privilege. The effort to exercise the alleged right had failed; and whether the means employed to prevent the exercise were revolutionary or not, the constitutional law of the country can take cognizance only of the results. But if the right of a state as an organized community to sever its political relations with other communities does not exist, there can be no claim of sovereignty for the state. For if political sovereignty means anything, it includes the attribute of self-determination as to its status in respect to other sovereignties. Limitation in this attribute is fatal to the conception of sovereignty, and accordingly, the failure of secession removed one pregnant source of confusion at the very basis of our system.

THE CONSTITUTION OF THE UNITED STATES IN RECONSTRUCTION

THE doctrine of state sovereignty perished in the destruction of the Confederate armies. With that dogma our constitutional law ceased to have any concern. Its principle was antecedent to and above the constitution. State rights, on the other hand, were, under the theory of national sovereignty, determined by the constitution itself. Before the war the scope of the powers assigned to the states had been influenced much by the state-sovereignty theory. The pressure of the government's peril during the rebellion, however, had caused a natural reaction, and many of the most widely recognized attributes of state authority had been assumed by the general government. With the assured success of Northern arms, a distinct definition of the rights of a state under the new situation became a matter of the first importance. The working out of such a definition was from the legal standpoint the main problem of reconstruction.

Inextricably involved in this leading legal question, was an even more troublesome practical difficulty. What was, and what should be, the civil and political status of the Southern blacks?

I. *Status of the Rebel States and of the Negroes at the Close of Hostilities*

The definition of state rights first presented itself as a vital political issue when the national authority began to be firmly re-established in the rebellious communities. In the course of the year 1863 the military situation in Tennessee and Arkansas seemed to justify the President in taking the preliminary steps towards the rehabilitation of those states with civil authority. His message of the 8th of December may be taken as the beginning of the process which only terminated with the withdrawal of the troops from the capitals of Louisiana and South Carolina by President Hayes in 1877. Between the close of 1863 and the end of hostilities no important progress was made towards a solution of either of the great problems which were now plainly confronting the nation. All phases of the matters were freely discussed, but the President and the legislature were unable to agree upon either the fundamental principles of a theory or the details of a practical measure. The immediate end sought at this time was the restoration to political rights of the people of the regions fully in the possession of the national forces. To effect this purpose a clear conception of the exact status of the districts in question was requisite. As to this status there were wide differences of opinion. Without considering at this point the various theories proposed, it will be well to sketch the public acts of the three departments which had had a bearing on the question at issue. Succinctly put, the question was this: Had the rebellious communities any rights as states under the constitution?

A review of the acts indicative of the view of the executive department of the government upon this point presents the following result: In his inaugural, President Lincoln stated his conviction that the Union could not be broken by any pretended ordinance of secession. This view was reaffirmed in his first message; and his non-intercourse proclamation of August 16, 1861, declared not the states, but the inhabitants of the states mentioned, to be in insurrection against the United States. In all the executive ordinances the illegal proceedings were assumed to be the acts of assemblages of individuals, and not the acts of the corporate states. A most important deduction from this theory was that the loyal element of the Southern people would be exempt from the penalties of the insurrectionary transactions. It was this element, indeed, which Lincoln adopted as the basis of the measures of restoration which he proposed in 1863. On the day Congress met, December 8, he issued a proclamation, the preamble of which recited the subversion of the state governments by persons in rebellion and hence guilty of treason, and the desire of certain of these persons to reinaugurate loyal governments "within their respective states." An oath was prescribed, the taking of which was to be a satisfactory proof of loyalty, and the President pledged himself to recognize any state government formed under certain conditions by a number of loyal persons equal to one-tenth of the voting population in 1860. Mr. Lincoln was thus true to the position assumed at the outbreak of the war. Nor did he recede from this position up to the time of his death. The executive department, in short, was fully committed to the doctrine that the corporate existence of the seceding states was not interrupted by the war.[1]

If we review the course of the legislature in its bearing on this question, we find up to a certain point a similar result. The act which provided for the definite recognition of the existence of a state of war, that of July 13, 1861, empowered the President to declare intercourse suspended with the inhabitants of certain enumerated districts, and gave no intimation that the states, as

[1] See Lincoln's speech just before his death; McPherson, Rebellion, p. 609.

such, were concerned. In imposing the direct
tax of twenty millions in 1861, the seceding states
were assigned their proportionate shares,[1] and by
a later law [2] the amounts thus assigned were made
a charge upon the land in the respective states.
Further, the creation of West Virginia was valid
only on condition that the consent of Virginia
was obtained; and we find, in the law erecting
the new state, that the legislature of Virginia did
give its consent.[3] Many other instances might
be adduced to illustrate the attitude of Congress
toward the question of state existence in the early
days of the war. It certainly was one with the
President in according to the state a being incapable of destruction by any unconstitutional
organizations of its inhabitants.

But there came a time when symptoms were
manifested of a change of heart in the majority
in Congress. With the brightening prospects of
the military situation, the anxiety to secure firmly
the settlement of the slavery question led to a
closer examination of the consequences that might
flow from too strict an adherence to a theory
better adapted perhaps to a time of doubt than
to a time of certain success. The subject of state

[1] 12 Statutes at Large, 295.

[2] *Ibid.*, 422.

[3] *Ibid.*, 633. This consent was given by a revolutionary organization formed by the Unionists after the triumph of their adversaries
in the adoption of the ordinance of secession.

status became very prominent through the steps toward restoration announced by the President in his message in December of 1863 and the accompanying amnesty proclamation.   So pronounced a movement towards the realization of the old state-rights doctrine aroused all the radical elements.   It was feared that Mr. Lincoln would be lax in exacting satisfactory conditions from the reorganized communities.   Accordingly, under the leadership of Senator Wade and Representative Henry Winter Davis, a bill was brought in, and after long discussion passed, prescribing conditions of restoration that were much more stringent than those contained in the President's plan, and making Congress instead of the executive the ultimate authority on the question of recognition. But so far as the matter of state status was concerned, the principle of the Wade-Davis bill was not different from that adhered to by the President. The rebellious states were regarded as having lost their governments through insurrection within their limits, and it was assumed as the duty of the national government, under the clause of the constitution directing the guarantee of a republican form in each state, to declare when such a form existed.   The whole plan of the bill, however, fell through, by the President's withholding his signature till the adjournment of Congress. He thereupon issued a proclamation stating his objections to the bill and renewing his encouragement to the loyal people of the states in the reorganization of their governments.[1]

Later on, in consequence of the practical application of the President's plan in Louisiana and Arkansas, the question was presented to the Thirty-eighth Congress in another shape. An organization had been effected in each of those states in accordance with Lincoln's proclamation, and credentials were accordingly presented to each house of persons claiming to represent the restored states. It became necessary for the houses to pass on the rightfulness of the claims. The Senate judiciary committee reported adversely to the admission of the claimants from Arkansas on the grounds, first, that the President's proclamation declaring the inhabitants of Arkansas in a state of insurrection had not been revoked; and second, that the supremacy of the military power in the state precluded the possibility of a civil organization that should be republican within the meaning of the constitution. In the House, the committee on elections reported favorably on the Arkansas claimants, but no action was taken on the report. As to Louisiana the result was no more conclusive. Favorable reports were made by committees in both houses, but were not acted upon. Again, in connection with the electoral count in February, 1865, the opportunity for an explicit declaration was evaded. By joint resolution it was enacted

[1] McPherson, Rebellion, p. 318.

that, because "the inhabitants and local authorities" of the eleven enumerated states were in
armed rebellion on election day, "the states" were
not entitled to representation in the electoral col-
leges.[1] No conclusive expression of opinion, in
fact, was made by the Thirty-eighth Congress on
the vital point of state status.[2] Resolutions without number were offered, embodying all conceivable shades of belief on the issue, but, after eliciting
much discussion, they were invariably consigned
to a permanent resting-place on the table, or to a
quiet grave in some committee.

There was a reason for this persistent ignoring
of so important a question. The sentiment in
favor of an absolute settlement of the slavery question had resulted in the submission to the states
of the Thirteenth Amendment; and it was evident

[1] McPherson, Rebellion, pp. 577, 578.

[2] The debates in the last session of this Congress (1864–65)
afforded abundant evidence that the doctrine of the continuous
existence of the states that had seceded was losing ground. The
Wade-Davis reconstruction bill contained clauses emancipating the
slaves and declaring them and their posterity forever free — that is,
practically abolishing slavery — in the rebellious districts. It had
been a universally accepted principle that Congress had no power to
enact any such law in respect to states. The passage of the bill
through the two houses was due in part to the theory that no states
existed in the regions designated. Many supporters of the measure,
however, considered that the war power was a sufficient basis for the
provision, and that no consideration of state status was involved.
The wording of the emancipation clause itself was: "All persons
held to involuntary servitude or labor in the *states* aforesaid are
hereby emancipated and discharged therefrom."

that until its adoption had put the question of slavery beyond the reach of the states, no further and conclusive steps toward restoration could be taken. But the Congress expired before the fate of the amendment was known, and shortly afterwards the collapse of the Confederacy left the national authority in the South supreme, but without any clear legislative expression as to the extent of that authority. It appears, then, that although the legislative department of the government had not, like the executive, consistently affirmed the persistence of the state entities as political units in our system, it had not, up to this time, rejected the theory.

The view held by the judiciary with respect to the war was first enunciated in the Prize Cases, decided in 1862. While a difference of opinion was manifested on the question, *when* an actual state of war began to exist, the Supreme Court was unanimous in its judgment as to the nature of the conflict. It was recognized as a military assertion of the authority of the general government over the inhabitants of certain states and districts. "Congress," the opinion declares, "cannot declare war against a state or any number of states, by virtue of the constitution." [1] Nor has the President any power to initiate or declare a war of any sort. He is only authorized by law "to suppress insurrection against the government of a state, or of the United

[1] 2 Black, 668.

States." The individuals conducting the present insurrection have taken advantage of the peculiar constitution of our system, and have "*acted as states* claiming to be sovereign"; but nowhere in either majority or dissenting opinion is any recognition given to the idea that the states as known to the constitution are concerned in the war. Again, in the case of The Venice,[1] Chief Justice Chase describes the government's policy as embracing no views of subjugation by conquest, but as seeking only "the re-establishment of the national authority, and the ultimate restoration of states and citizens to their national relations." There appears to be no indication, then, that the judiciary ever doubted the constitutional existence of the states. Circumstances had disarranged their relations with the federal government, but with the correction of the disturbance the former conditions would be resumed.

From the foregoing review of the attitude of all the departments of the United States government, it seems unquestionable that, while the necessities of war had made sad havoc with the rights of the states as well as of individuals, yet upon the return of peace a resumption was contemplated of the *ante bellum* status of both, subject only to such modifications as the now undisputed sovereignty of the nation should impose.

As to the status of the negroes, the whole

[1] 2 Wallace, 278.

question was in hopeless confusion. Under the operation of Mr. Lincoln's Emancipation Proclamation, and of the various acts of Congress containing provisions in reference to the subject, the number of freedmen dependent upon the government had become enormous. The care of these dependents became early a subject of considerable importance. Commanders were seriously embarrassed by the great crowds of improvident blacks that attached themselves to the armies in their campaigns. It was not considered just to the Southern slaves to give them their freedom and then leave them to be re-enslaved as soon as the national forces had gone by. Such a course indeed would have been impossible, since the freedmen themselves instinctively refused to stay. The border states protested vigorously against the influx of paupers to burden their already oppressed taxpayers. Private philanthropy took in charge the work of civilizing on the spot, but always under the protection of the army, such of the unfortunates as could be assembled at various points along the borders of the Confederacy. By act of March 3, 1865, the whole matter was systematized by the establishment of a bureau in the War Department [1] to have control of all subjects relating to refugees and freedmen from the territory embraced in the military operations of the war. The act authorized the issue of provisions, clothing

[1] 13 Statutes at Large, 507.

and fuel to destitute refugees and freedmen, and provided for their settlement on the abandoned or confiscated land of rebels. The existence of the bureau was limited to the duration of the rebellion and for one year thereafter. It was evidently the belief that the supervision of the general government would accomplish its object within a year after the cessation of hostilities, and that then the freedmen could be relinquished to the normal operation of the laws. Such, at least, was the view of the conservative Republicans, who hesitated to convert the national government into a permanent dispenser of charity. The act was regarded as based entirely upon the war power of the government, and was accordingly limited in its duration to the state of affairs which justified the exercise of such power.

Little more than a month after the passage of the bill, the Confederacy fell. The whole South came under the domination of the armies of the United States, and by the operation of the President's orders all the slaves in those regions became *de facto* free. Whether or not they rose immediately to a position of legal equality with their former masters was an unsettled question, now to become of the first importance. But whatever their rights at this period, the authority to which they looked for a guarantee of those rights divided the negroes distinctly from the other race. As has been indicated above, a reorganized state jurisdiction was to regulate the affairs of the restored commonwealths; but for the freedmen a bureau of the United States War Department had the indefinite jurisdiction conferred by the words, "the control of all subjects relating to refugees and freedmen from rebel states." The status of the negroes thus seems to have been practically that of wards of the national government, with rights totally undetermined.

II. *Presidential Restoration of the States*

Upon the theory which has been shown to have been recognized in the conduct of the war, the problem of restoring the states to their normal position in the Union was apparently simple. The instant the state of insurrection ceased which had given rise to the attitude of belligerency towards the inhabitants of the rebellious regions, *ante bellum* relations would be resumed, in so far as not modified by legislation during the war. That no such special modification had been effected in the relations of the insurrectionary states, had been assumed by all the departments of the government. But as to the individuals in rebellion, certain important measures had been passed. Most prominent were the provisions of the Confiscation Act of 1862, which declared severe penalties upon such persons. By section thirteen of this act, however, the President was authorized to extend amnesty and pardon at his discretion "to persons who may have participated in the existing rebellion in any state or part thereof." It was therefore left to the executive to relieve individuals from the consequences of their crimes so far as he saw fit. In pursuance of this authority, Mr. Lincoln had issued his proclamation of amnesty in 1863, prescribing a form of oath, the taking of which would restore to his normal relations a person who had incurred the disabilities resulting from participation in the rebellion. The nucleus of loyal citizens thus secured in any state was competent to take the steps necessary to the organization of a government for the state. Nor did it matter that they were a minority of the political people of the state — even the one-tenth that the President fixed upon arbitrarily as a sufficient number. The guaranty clause of the constitution would warrant the protection of a loyal minority by the national authorities against an overwhelming majority of disloyal and rebellious citizens.

In approaching reconstruction Mr. Lincoln's great anxiety was to get something in the nature of a state organization to recognize, without being over-critical as to how it was secured. Consistency required that the impulse to commonwealth organization should come, nominally at least, from the people of the unsettled community. His proclamation accordingly contained no mandate of action, but merely declared the circumstances under which he would recognize a government in any state. These circumstances were, (1) the completion of an organization by persons (2) who had subscribed to the oath of allegiance to the United States, and (3) who had pledged themselves to support the acts and proclamations promulgated during the war in reference to slavery. It is true that these terms were practically conditions imposed upon citizens of states as prerequisite to the exercise of their rights. But the plan, as Lincoln stated in his message,[1] was merely presented as a rallying point, which might bring the people to act sooner than they otherwise would, and was not intended as a final solution of all the delicate questions involved. In no rebellious state, save Virginia, was there a government whose members possessed the most fundamental qualification for legitimacy — namely, that secured by having taken the oath prescribed by article six of the constitution.[2] To obtain such a government was Lincoln's main object. In Louisiana and Arkansas he was successful. Congress, as has already been stated, declined to commit itself to such recognition of these governments as would have been implied in the admission of members chosen under their auspices. But under

[1] McPherson, Rebellion, p. 147.

[2] "The members of the several state legislatures, and all executive and judicial officers, both of the United States and of the several states, shall be bound by oath or affirmation to support this constitution."

executive protection their organizations were maintained till Congressional reconstruction supplanted them. In Tennessee, where there was a very strong Union sentiment, Andrew Johnson, in the capacity of military governor, effected an organization which went into full operation early in the spring of 1865. The government thus established also continued through the period of restoration.

Upon the collapse of the Confederacy and the death of President Lincoln, Mr. Johnson devoted himself to the application of his predecessor's plan in the other states. In Virginia, where a loyal organization had been maintained at Alexandria, with Mr. Pierpoint as governor, ever since the separation of West Virginia, he simply proclaimed his purpose to carry out the guarantee of a republican form of state government by supporting the measures of this authority.[1] By the same order, the administration of all the departments of the general government was put in operation throughout the state. Three weeks later Johnson's amnesty proclamation was issued. It followed Lincoln's closely in tenor, but the oath prescribed as a condition of pardon involved a more unqualified recognition of the validity of emancipation, and the classes of persons excluded from the benefits of the amnesty were more numerous. Accompanying the amnesty manifesto was issued the order to put in operation the plan of restora-

[1] Proclamation of May 9, 1865.

tion in North Carolina, and at intervals up to the middle of July successive proclamations inaugurated the system in all the other rebellious states. Johnson evidently aimed at operating on exactly the same theory as his predecessor. In the preamble of his proclamations he marked out the constitutional basis of his action : The United States must guarantee a republican form of government, and protect each state against invasion and domestic violence ; the President is bound to see that the laws are executed ; rebellion, "now almost entirely overcome," has deprived the people of the state of all civil government ; it is therefore necessary and proper to carry out and enforce the obligations of the United States to the people of the state. In consequence of these principles and facts, the President and commander-in-chief of the army and navy appointed a provisional governor for each of the disturbed states, with the duty of securing the re-establishment of the constitutional order. In the appointment of this special officer, Mr. Johnson followed the action of Mr. Lincoln in designating "military governors" for several of the states in which a firm foothold was early obtained by the army. The duty of the provisional governors was laid down in much the same terms that had been employed in Lincoln's instructions to Johnson when the latter held the office of military governor of Tennessee.[1] They were directed

[1] McPherson, Rebellion, p. 436.

to prescribe rules for the calling of a convention of delegates chosen by the loyal people of the respective states, and "to exercise all powers necessary and proper to enable such people to restore the states to their constitutional relations to the federal government." The test of loyalty was subscription to the oath of amnesty as set forth in the President's proclamation, and a prerequisite of voting was the qualifications of an elector under the laws of the state in force immediately before the act of secession. Further, the President decreed that the convention, "or the legislature thereafter assembled, will prescribe the qualification of electors, and the eligibility of persons to hold office under the constitution and laws of the state, a power the people of the several states composing the Federal Union have rightfully exercised from the origin of the government to the present time." [1]

In these electoral conditions was embodied the principle which developed at once a centre of antagonism to the President. It had already become a cardinal doctrine of the radical Republicans that the necessary corollary of emancipation and abolition was enfranchisement of the freedmen. By assuming that secession had effected the extinction of the states, they had removed all constitutional obstacles to the realization of this doctrine

---

[1] For Mr. Johnson's proclamations, see McPherson, History of the Reconstruction, p. 8 *et seq.*

by the general government. But here was a declaration by the President that the whole matter was to be left to the Southern whites; and the fate of negro suffrage in such hands was not doubtful. Around this rallying point, then, were speedily grouped all the elements of opposition to the President's policy. The conviction that the emancipated race, made by circumstances the wards of the nation, ought to continue under the nation's care, was common to all. But opinions as to the means of effecting this were of all degrees of diversity. Conservatives considered that if the civil rights of the blacks could be guaranteed by the general government, the political privileges could be left to the states. To assume this guarantee by law involved grave questions of constitutionality; to fix it by constitutional amendment seemed to require a previous determination of the status of the rebel states. In view of the difficulties that beset every plan that was suggested, many were inclined to give the President's experiment a fair trial, that the data thus obtained might be utilized in future adjustment.

In the midst of all this conflict of judgment, however, restoration on the line of the proclamation was accomplished. By the general amnesty and by special pardon of many in the excepted classes, a loyal population was secured in all the Southern states. Conventions revised the various state constitutions under the direction of the provisional governors, and also under immediate telegraphic supervision from Washington. The acts which the President demanded as conditions of his recognition were: the nullification of the ordinances of secession, the repudiation of the war debt, and the ratification of the Thirteenth Amendment by the first legislature. These measures were adopted with more or less grace; several of the states repealed, instead of declaring null and void, the secession ordinances, and South Carolina evaded altogether the repudiation of her war debt. But in spite of occasional manifestations of ill-feeling, the alluring prospect of self-government and representation in the national legislature kept the actions of the new governments in substantial accord with the President's wishes. The work of reorganization was completed, and by the opening of the Thirty-ninth Congress in December, 1865, representatives and senators from most of the rebel states were ready to present their credentials for admission to that body. In his annual message, Mr. Johnson formally called upon Congress to complete the work of restoration, by receiving the Southerners, subject to the constitutional right of each house to judge of the elections, qualifications and returns of its own members. On December 18, the secretary of state issued his proclamation that the Thirteenth Amendment was in force, having been ratified by twenty-seven states, among which were eight that had recently been in rebellion. On the same day the President in a special message to Congress announced specifically that the rebellion had been suppressed; that in all the insurrectionary states, except Florida and Texas, the people had reorganized their governments; and that in those two satisfactory progress was making. Upon the completion of the organization in these two states, then, the constitutional relations between commonwealths and national government would be, in the opinion of the executive, exactly as they had been before the war.

But the state of war which had been proclaimed in 1861 and 1862 by President Lincoln had not yet formally ceased to exist. By successive orders for particular localities, the blockade, the prohibition of commercial intercourse, and the suspension of the *habeas corpus* were revoked by Mr. Johnson; but it was not till August 20, 1866, that the final proclamation went forth that the insurrection was ended, "and that peace, order, tranquillity and civil authority now exist in and through the whole of the United States of America." Prior to that date, in all the states not declared at peace by special proclamations, the presumptive status of the inhabitants, under the unrevoked orders of Mr. Lincoln,[1] was that of public enemies. The only evidence of a different status was the fact of having taken the amnesty oath, or of having received a special pardon from the President. By the final order of Mr.

[1] McPherson, Rebellion, pp. 149, 150.

Johnson, however, the liability of all civilians in the United States to the President's military authority ceased, and no legal effect of the war remained upon the private citizen in the Southern states, save that a rapidly diminishing number of unpardoned individuals were still responsible before the civil law for the crimes of treason and rebellion.

Such was the condition of affairs that was claimed to have been brought about, by the autumn of 1866, through executive action. As far as the judiciary was concerned, the restoration seemed to be fully accepted. The district courts of the United States resumed their work under the direction of the President as fast as the provisional organizations were effected. Chief Justice Chase declined to sit on the circuit bench while military authority was maintained in the circuit, on the ground that it was not becoming to the dignity of the highest judicial officers of the government to act under even the least shadow of subjection to armed force. He did not object, however, to the holding of a circuit court by the district judge sitting alone.[1] As early as the December term of 1865, the Supreme Court ordered the cases on its docket from the Southern states to be called and disposed of.[2] Upon the proclamations by the President of the end of the insurrection, the regular sessions of all the courts were resumed.

[1] Letter to the President, Annual Cyclopedia for 1866, p. 514.
[2] 3 Wallace, viii.

This action indicated a judicial belief that normal conditions had been restored in the South. The rebel states, at all events, were not reduced to the territorial status; for by the long-accepted principle laid down by Chief Justice Marshall in 1828, the jurisdiction of the constitutional courts of the United States did not extend to territories. In such regions it was for Congress to provide at will for the administration of justice.[1]

Great weight cannot be attached, however, to the attitude of the judiciary in this matter. Its duty was to follow the decisions of the political departments on questions of political status. But as regards the status of the Southern states, it early became evident that no harmony of views could be reached between the executive and the legislative. Already before the meeting of Congress Mr. Johnson's course had provoked sharp criticism, and threats of undoing his too hasty work of restoration had not been wanting. Even the friends of his general policy felt aggrieved that so important a matter had been determined without any reference whatever to the legislature. They thought that an extra session of Congress should have been called after the collapse of the Confederacy. In the opposition on principle to the President's policy three chief elements were distinguishable: first, the extreme negrophiles, who, on abstract grounds of human equality and natural

[1] American Ins. Co. *vs.* Canter, 1 Peters, 546.

rights, demanded full civil and political privileges for the freedmen ; second, the partisan politicians, who viewed the elevation of the blacks mainly as a means of humbling the Democrats and maintaining the existing supremacy of the Republican Party ; and third, the representatives of an exalted statesmanship, who saw in the existing situation an opportunity for decisively fixing in our system a broader and more national principle of civil rights and political privilege. It was this last element that controlled the proceedings during the earlier months of the Thirty-ninth Congress. Later the more radical elements assumed the lead.

The President, as we have seen, had prepared to push his theory before Congress at its very opening. Credentials were promptly presented by members elect from the restored states. But Congress declined to be hurried into committing itself to any doctrine on the great subject. Instead of the customary reference of the credentials of the claimants to the committees on elections in the respective houses, a joint committee of fifteen was constituted to inquire into the condition of the rebellious states and their title to representation ; and it was agreed that all papers relating to those states should be referred to this committee. Thus was provided a convenient limbo to which might be relegated any question that should threaten to interfere with the placid progress of Congressional deliberation. The next step was to unfold a scheme by which the ends of the conservative Republicans might be attained by simple legislation.

III. *Nationalization of Civil Rights*

Despite the strong opposition to Mr. Johnson's policy among the Republicans in Congress, there was at the same time a disinclination to an open rupture with the President. It was in obedience to this latter feeling that the joint committee on reconstruction was so heartily agreed to. Through this the main issue—the recognition of the Southern state governments — was deferred until it could be ascertained whether a substantial protection for the freedmen might not be obtained without coming to open hostility with the President. In accordance with this plan the aggressive spirit of the radicals was repressed, and a series of measures was devised, of which the Freedmen's Bureau Bill was the first to be presented.

By this bill[1] the bureau which had been organized during the preceding session[2] was enlarged as to both the duration and the territorial extent of its powers. The limit of one year after the end of the war was abolished, and the bureau's operations were to extend to "refugees and freedmen in all parts of the United States." The powers of the officials were of the vaguest character imagina-

---

[1] McPherson, Reconstruction, p. 72. [2] See *ante*, p. 73.

ble, involving practically absolute discretion in the regulation of matters in which the freedmen were interested. Provisions, clothing and fuel were to be furnished to destitute blacks, land was to be set apart for their use, and schools and asylums to be erected for their benefit. But the central point of the bill was in the seventh and eighth sections. Here it was made the duty of the President to extend the military protection of the bureau to all cases in which the civil rights and immunities of white persons were denied to others on account of race, color or any previous condition of slavery or involuntary servitude. Further, any person who should, under color of any state law, ordinance or custom, subject the negro to the deprivation of equal civil rights with the white man, should be guilty of a misdemeanor, and the jurisdiction of such cases was conferred upon the officials of the bureau. Such jurisdiction was limited, however, to states in which the ordinary course of judicial proceedings had been interrupted by rebellion, and was to cease there when those states should be fully restored to all their constitutional relations to the United States.

The grave questions of constitutionality involved in the details of this bill were modified in their bearing by the general basis on which the whole legislation rested. It was, according to Senator Trumbull, who had charge of it in the Senate, a war measure, and inapplicable, by its

terms, to any other state of affairs.[1] Under the
"necessity" which the existing insurrection had
made the supreme law of the land, the forcible
displacement of a state's authority over matters
of civil jurisdiction normally under its control, was
fully justified.

But the President, in vetoing the bill, protested
against "declaring to the American people and
to the world, that the United States are still in
a condition of civil war." He asserted that the
rebellion was, in fact, at an end.[2] Mr. Johnson
was in rather a difficult position here; for the
habeas corpus was still suspended in the Southern
states, and even while he was writing his veto
message a military order had gone forth looking
to the suppression of disloyal papers there.[3] It
was reasonably asked upon what authority such
executive acts could be performed if a state of
peace prevailed. The President's real grievance
was evidently that which he referred to last in
his veto message. He complained that the bill
regarded certain states as "not fully restored in
all their constitutional relations to the United
States," and announced that in his judgment most
of the states were fully restored, and were entitled to all their constitutional rights as members
of the Union. Congress was censured with repressed severity for refusing to accord to those

[1] Cong. Globe, 1st sess., 39th Cong., p. 320.
[2] McPherson, Reconstruction, p. 68 *et seq.*   [3] *Ibid.*, p. 123.

states the right imperatively required by the constitution, of representation in the two houses.

The President's veto, made effective by the failure to override it in the Senate, strengthened the extremists in Congress; for many who desired the success of the conservative plan were indignant that it should be thwarted at the outset. A concurrent resolution was passed declaring that no member from any of the insurrectionary states should be admitted to either house till Congress should declare such state entitled to representation.[1] This was a formal declaration of war upon the executive policy. It notified the President that Congress intended to form its own judgment upon the status of the states, irrespective of any extraneous decision. It precipitated the conflict that had been impending since the amnesty proclamation of 1863, and which Lincoln's tact had been successful, and might afterwards have been successful, in avoiding. And finally, it indicated a strengthening of the feeling that some guaranty for the rights of the freedmen should be secured before the rights of the states should be conceded. A great silence and mystery hung about the committee whose report was to embody the views of

---

[1] McPherson, Reconstruction, p. 72. This declaration had been proposed as part of the resolution providing for the joint committee on reconstruction, but had been rejected by the Senate. According to Mr. Blaine the immediate occasion of its passage now was the pressure of Tennessee for admission. Twenty Years of Congress, II, 203.

Congress on the condition of the states. No one doubted that the enveloping clouds would continue until a satisfactory solution of the negro question should be discovered.

As the next step in the direction of such a solution, the Civil Rights Bill was presented to the Senate by its judiciary committee. The Freedmen's Bureau Bill had been confessedly in the nature of a temporary expedient. It had aimed to secure the protection of the blacks by military authority for a period that Congress should deem sufficient. By the second measure, however, the protection was to be incorporated permanently into the law of the land, and to be entrusted to the civil authorities of the nation. As the bill passed,[1] it provided first a broad foundation for rights in the declaration that "all persons born in the United States, and not subject to any foreign power, excluding Indians not taxed, are . . . citizens of the United States." It then secured to all such citizens of every race and color the same rights as were enjoyed by white citizens in respect to making and enforcing contracts, appearing in the courts, receiving, holding and transferring property, and enjoying the benefit of all laws for the security of person and property. Section second made it a misdemeanor to subject any inhabitant of any state or territory to the deprivation of any right secured by the act, or to different pun-

[1] McPherson, Reconstruction, p. 78.

ishment, by reason of race, color or previous condition of servitude, from that prescribed for white
persons.   The remainder of the bill was occupied
with provisions in great detail for the enforcement
of the first two sections.   Cognizance of all cases
arising under the act was given exclusively to
United States courts, and the machinery for its
strict execution was borrowed, with grim satisfaction, from the Fugitive Slave Act.[1]

At the time the Civil Rights Bill was proposed,
it had become a well-grounded conviction that the
Southern states would not yield to the negroes any
appreciable share of the rights which Northern
sentiment demanded for them.   The legislatures
of the reorganized governments, under cover of
police regulations and vagrancy laws, had enacted
severe discriminations against the freedmen in all
the common civil rights.[2]   In several states the
tendency of these enactments toward a system of
peonage had appeared so pronounced as to induce
the military commanders to order that they be disregarded.   This situation strengthened the resolution, already well defined, to remove the possibility
of a system of modified slavery under state sanction.
It was feared that Congress would be unable to
effect this purpose after the admission of the South-

[1] Trumbull; Globe, 1st sess., 39th Cong., p. 475.
[2] For a summary of this legislation, see McPherson, Reconstruction, p. 29 *et seq.*   For a Southern defence of the laws, see Herbert,
Why the Solid South (Baltimore, 1890), p. 31 *et seq.*

ern representatives. The end must be achieved
before extending recognition to the new governments, and acquiescence in the result could then
be made a condition of the erring states' return.

At first glance, the provisions of the bill appeared
out of all relation to our constitutional system.
Never before had Congress been known to arrogate
to itself the power to regulate the civil status of
the inhabitants of a state. The proposition that
United States courts should assume jurisdiction of
disputes relating to property and contracts, and
even of criminal actions down to common assault
and battery, seemed like a complete revelation of
that diabolical spirit of centralization, of which only
the cloven hoof had been manifested heretofore.
But the supporters of the bill showed a clear
appreciation of the change that the great conflict
had wrought. They found a constitutional basis for
the law in the Thirteenth Amendment. Slavery
and involuntary servitude were by that article prohibited; and, by the second section, Congress, and
not the state legislatures, was authorized to enforce
the prohibition. What constituted slavery and involuntary servitude, in the sense of the amendment?
Slavery and liberty, it was answered, are contradictory terms. If slavery is prohibited, civil liberty
must exist. But civil liberty consists in natural liberty, as restrained by human laws for the advantage
of all, provided that these restraints be equal to
all. A statute which is not equal to all is an en-

croachment on the liberty of the deprived persons, and subjects them to a degree of servitude. It is the duty of Congress, therefore, to counteract the effects of any such state laws. Thus the constitutionality of the bill was maintained. The essence of the plea was a wide construction of the terms "slavery" and "involuntary servitude." Broadly speaking, it was the practical application of what had heretofore been in the United States a mere theory, the idea of "equality" as an essential principle of "liberty." There was involved in this construction also a definite recognition of the national government as the protector of individuals against state oppression.

The far-reaching consequences of this view of the Thirteenth Amendment filled the friends of the old system with dismay. They insisted that the only effect of the new article was to destroy the relation of master and slave. Beyond this no action of the central authority was contemplated. The second clause gave no power to Congress that was not already conferred by the old constitution.[1] It was merely added to authorize the extension of the privilege of *habeas corpus* to a negro in case the master persisted in holding him.[2] Upon the dissolution of the old bond the freedman became subject to the laws of his state, like any other inhabitant. The idea that the amendment carried with it an

[1] Art. 1, sec. 8, last clause.
[2] Cowan, of Pennsylvania; Globe, 1st sess., 39th Cong., p. 499.

enormous centralization of power in the general government had never been heard of during the long discussion of the resolution in Congress. It was a recently devised scheme of the consolidationists to change the whole foundation of the government by interpretation. "Will anybody undertake to say," asked Cowan, "that that [amendment] was to prevent the involuntary servitude of my child to me, of my apprentice to me, or the *quasi*-servitude which the wife to some extent owes to her husband?" Nothing but African slavery was referred to, and only its various modifications were included in "involuntary servitude"; the broad question of civil liberty was not affected.

Whatever may have been the intention of the framers of the Thirteenth Amendment, the construction put upon it by Congress in the Civil Rights Bill was promptly adopted by the judiciary. The bill was vetoed by the President on the same general line of reasoning that was employed with respect to the Freedmen's Bureau Bill, but was immediately passed over the veto. Cases under its provisions came speedily before the circuit courts, where its constitutionality was questioned. Justice Swayne, in United States *vs.* Rhodes,[1] sustained the act, saying:

The amendment reversed and annulled the original policy of the constitution, which left it to each state to decide ex-

---

[1] 1 Abbot's U. S. Reports, 56.

clusively for itself whether slavery should or should not exist as a local institution, and what disabilities should attach to those of the servile race within its limits.

Chief Justice Chase also took a similar position, holding that Maryland's apprentice laws, discriminating between white and black apprentices, were in violation of the clause prohibiting involuntary servitude.[1] The later amendments, however, relieved the courts of the heavy burden which hung upon them in basing equality in all civil rights upon the thirteenth alone. The construction of this amendment has been narrowed in later opinions, or rather, the tendency to widen it has been checked.[2]

In addition to the definition of "slavery" and "involuntary servitude," the Civil Rights Bill undertook to fix the precise meaning of the phrase "citizen of the United States." The matter had been involved, up to this time, in hopeless confusion. No positive legal definition had been authoritatively given. For general practical purposes, exact determination of the scope of citizenship had not been found necessary. Where any opinion at all had been pronounced, it had in most cases been in relation to the status of the free negroes. The weight of authority on this point was adverse to the claim of citizenship for the blacks. "No per-

[1] Turner's Case, 1 Abbot's U. S. Reports, 84.

[2] *Cf.* Blyew *vs.* U. S., 13 Wallace, 581; Slaughter House Cases, 16 Wallace, 69; Civil Rights Cases, 109 U. S. 3.

son," said Attorney-General Wirt in 1821, "is included in the description of citizen of the United States, who has not the full rights of a citizen in the state of his residence."[1] This principle had been in general the basis of the government's practice in all the departments. For native-born persons living within a state, citizenship of the state was the prerequisite for citizenship of the United States; for persons of foreign birth, naturalization alone was necessary. The Dred Scott decision limited this rule by determining that state citizens of African descent could not be citizens of the United States. During the war, however, the old view was entirely overthrown in practice. Mr. Lincoln's attorney-general argued away all the precedents, and gave it as his official opinion that a free negro, born within the United States, was *ipso facto* a citizen thereof.[2] He assumed nativity as the broad basis of citizenship, universally recognized as such by public law. With that assumption the status of United States citizenship was placed entirely beyond the reach of any state influence whatever, and a purely national conception was attained.

This view was the one incorporated into the Civil Rights Bill. The declaration thus made by law was designed to end the uncertainty due to

[1] 1 Opinions of Attorneys-General, 507. *Cf.* Taney and Curtis in the Dred Scott Case.

[2] McPherson, Rebellion, 378.

[handwritten marginal note:] places the start of economic concentration + an increased centralism. In the very act of war, the US prepared for the corporate era; vi: the cap-

[handwritten note at bottom:] italists consolidated. WD argues that the Constitution itself was greatly altered during C.W.— becoming less federal + more central. Thus the period of the 1870–1900 is prefigured—

conflicting authorities. Its abstract principle did
not excite remonstrance so much as the deduc-
tions drawn from it in the remainder of the bill.
For while the immediate effect of the definition was to make the freedmen citizens of the
United States, the practical end of the other provisions of the bill was to make them also citizens
of the several states in which they resided. This
result was not stated in terms in the law, but was
considered as a necessary corollary of the main
proposition. The act gave to all citizens of the
United States, in every state and territory, the
same civil rights as were enjoyed by white citizens; or, practically, declared to the states that,
however they might widen the scope of their citizenship, they should never contract it so as to
embrace less than the whole number of citizens
of the United States residing within their respective borders.

To justify this sweeping enactment, the special
conception of citizenship which the history of our
institutions had developed was discarded, and the
broad principle of public law was adopted in its
place. All authorities agreed that the status of
citizen implied the reciprocal duties of allegiance
and protection.[1] A citizen of the United States,

---

[1] *Cf.* opinion of Attorney-General Bates; McPherson, Rebellion,
p. 379. The employment of this relation as a basis from which to
infer unlimited power to "protect," is discountenanced by the
Supreme Court in U. S. *vs.* Cruikshank *et al.*, 92 U. S. 549: "In

then, was entitled to the protection of that government to which allegiance was owed. But this protection was to operate against all sources of oppression, and if a state government happened to come in this category, it too must succumb.

IV. *Theories as to the Status of the States*

The intense opposition which the Civil Rights Bill had excited permitted little hope that its provisions could remain permanently upon the statute book. Hence arose the movement to incorporate the principles of the bill in the constitution.

The struggle for the passage of the law had involved the widest discussion of all the questions connected with reconstruction. Mr. Johnson had not only separated from the Republican leaders, but had placed himself in a position that rendered reconciliation inconceivable. Under such circumstances, the conservative plan of dealing with the situation in the South, which could only be successful through the President's support, had to be abandoned. Congress found itself obliged to formulate a theory of state status upon which it could rest for support in a decisive struggle with the execu-

the formation of a government, the people may confer upon it such powers as they choose. The government, when so formed, may exercise all the powers it has for the protection of the rights of its citizens and the people within its jurisdiction; but it can exercise no other."

tive. To the joint committee on reconstruction was entrusted the presentation of such a theory, and from this committee emanated the plan of reorganization which finally triumphed. Before considering the committee's report, however, it will be profitable to examine the various theories in respect to reconstruction which had become prominent since 1863. While varying infinitely in detail, these theories may be summarized, as to their fundamental principles, in five classes, which may be denominated: the Southern theory, the Presidential theory, the theory of forfeited rights, the theory of state suicide, and the conquered-province theory. Of these the first two were based on the idea of the indestructibility of a state in our system, the last two on the contradictory assumption, while the third was in the nature of a compromise on this question.

As preliminary to an examination of these theories it is necessary to determine as nearly as may be, what constituted the essence of the concept "state," under the *ante bellum* constitution. No attempt will be made, however, to discuss the question of sovereignty, or any other attribute held to exist outside of the organic law. "The word state," said Marshall, "is used in the constitution as designating a member of the Union, and excludes from the term the signification attached to it by writers on the law of nations."[1] What can

---

[1] Hepburn and Dundas *vs*. Ellzey, 2 Cranch, 452.

be derived from the constitution itself as to the meaning of the term? Three distinct uses of the word may be found in the supreme law. First, it designates a mere territorial division with definite boundaries; second, it denotes the people, politically associated, who inhabit the same region; and third, it refers to the body politic within a defined region, involving the threefold notion of territory, people and government. This last sense of the word is by far the most frequent in the constitution, and accordingly the Supreme Court has framed the definition of a state thus:

A political community of free citizens, occupying a territory of defined boundaries, and organized under a government sanctioned and limited by a written constitution, and established by the consent of the governed.[1]

The theories to be examined may be viewed in the light afforded by this definition. The three essential elements of a state were held to be a geographical locality with determined limits, a community inhabiting it, and a government organized by that people. At the close of the war, two principal questions arose as to the insurrectionary districts: first, did states exist in those districts; and second, what was the relation of those states or districts to the government of the United States?

To the first of these questions the Southern

---

[1] Texas *vs.* White, 7 Wall. 721. *Cf.* Hunt, dissenting, in U. S. *vs.* Reese, 2 Otto, 250.

theory, as has been stated, gave an affirmative answer. All the essentials of state-being remained unchanged by the war. Territory, people and government conformed to the definition. The war had been waged by the North for the avowed purpose of suppressing an insurrection of individuals, and with no idea of interfering with the rights of the states. On individuals, then, all the consequences of the defeat must fall. But the states, it was admitted, were out of their constitutional relation to the general government. Their officers had taken no oath to support the constitution of the United States. No senators or representatives were acting for the states at Washington. The authority of the United States judiciary and revenue officials was not recognized by the state governments. But the result of the war had established the nullity of the acts upon which this severance of connection was based. The supposed separation was therefore unreal, and it became the duty of the officers to take the oath required by the constitution, of the legislature to provide for the despatch of congressmen to Washington, and of the people of the state to submit to the authority of the courts and officials of the national government. These steps having been taken, the Union would stand under the constitution as before the war.

It was upon this theory that the celebrated agreement between Sherman and Johnston was

made after the surrender of Lee.[1]   On the same
principle, the rebel governors in most of the states
convoked the legislatures to take action on the
situation after the collapse of the Confederacy.
It was the prevailing opinion throughout the
South that the restoration would proceed on the
lines of this theory.[2] But the repudiation of General Sherman's agreement by the administration,
and the overthrow of the rebel state governments
by the military commanders, dissipated the hopes
of so simple an operation in readjustment, and
finally disposed of any possible realization of the
Southern idea.

The Presidential theory of state status has been
pretty clearly indicated in the discussion of its
practical application. Its cardinal doctrine was
the indestructibility of a state, either by its own
act or by act of the United States government.
At no time, either during actual conflict, or when
the Southern arms had been laid down, did the
United States consist of less component states
than before the first secession. To assert the
contrary was to admit the dissolution of the
Union. The territorial and popular conditions
of the constitutional state remained unchanged
in every case. As to the state government, however, a defect existed, brought about indirectly
through the immediate relation of the people to

---

[1] McPherson, Reconstruction, 121.
[2] Pollard, The Lost Cause Regained, p. 51.

the national government.   All the officers as well as the constituents of the rebel organizations were insurgents, and hence incapable of political recognition by the United States authorities.   With the removal of this disability, the *ante-bellum* status returned.   But until such removal, the vitality of the state was suspended through the incapacity of its organs to fulfil their functions.   The President's pardon was the healing agent.   Restored by it to normal relations with the general government, the people of the states became immediately invested with the *right* to establish their own will in organized form, and with the *right* to assume the former relation with the Union.

In these two theories, the Southern and the Presidential, the ultimate principle is obviously the resolution in favor of the states of all doubts arising out of the anomalous condition of affairs. Both alike relied for support upon the sentiment which the Republican platform of 1860 expressed in these words: "The maintenance inviolate of the rights of the states is essential to the balance of power on which the prosperity and endurance of our political fabric depend,"[1] and both alike adopted that view of the consequences of the war which corresponded to the statement of its object in the Crittenden resolution in Congress, in July, 1861, namely, "to defend and maintain the supremacy of the constitution, and to preserve the Union,

[1] Tribune Almanac for 1861, p. 30.

with all the dignity, equality and rights of the several states unimpaired."

Charles Sumner's famous theory of state suicide was the first of those which maintained that no state as known to the constitution existed on Southern soil at the close of the war. The enunciation of the theory was originally embodied in a series of resolutions offered in the Senate in 1862.[1] The basis of the series is contained in the declaration that any act by which a state may undertake to put an end to the supremacy of the constitution within its territory is void, and, if sustained by force, such act is a practical abdication by the state of all rights under the constitution. Further, the treason involved in this resistance works instant forfeiture of the powers essential to the continued existence of the state as a body politic, and the state is, in the language of the law, *felo de se.* But the territory of the extinct commonwealth belongs irrevocably to the United States, and consequently becomes henceforth subject to the exclusive jurisdiction of Congress, like other territory of the nation. The immediate consequence of these principles, was, of course, the termination of all peculiar local institutions, based solely on state authority. Slavery ceased to exist, and all the inhabitants of the territory, since they owed allegiance to the United States, must look to the national government for protection.

[1] McPherson, Rebellion, p. 322.

In Mr. Sumner's view, the three attributes involved in the definition mentioned above do not constitute the state known to the constitution. A fulfilment of the duties imposed by the fundamental law is indispensable to the conception. There can be no such an entity as a state out of practical relations with the United States. A state exists only by virtue of the maintenance of these relations. Certain obligations are imposed by the constitution upon the states, and certain privileges are accorded to them. Refusal to acknowledge the obligations works *ipso facto* a forfeiture of the privileges. Among the obligations is that fundamental one of recognizing the supremacy of the constitution and laws of the United States; among the privileges is the enjoyment of governmental rights not attributed to the central organization. Rejection of the former works forfeiture of the latter. But the immediate relation between the people and the general government is not at all affected. This government, therefore, becomes the sole authority for the regulation of their concerns. The inhabitants may organize themselves for admission as states, but Congress may impose its conditions upon them before granting their application. It may fix their boundaries at its pleasure and thus destroy every vestige of the former states. In short, where once existed sovereign states, only the territorial status survived the ordinance of secession.

The ultimate principle of this theory is that the United States is a nation, of which the constitution is the sovereign law. By the nation, through the constitution, certain powers are conferred upon people living in a given district. In these powers consists the essence of a "state." "A state under the American system," says an able advocate of the suicide doctrine, "is not in the domain and population fixed to it, nor yet in its exterior organization, but solely in the political powers, rights and franchises which it holds from the United States, or as one of the United States." [1] It was by an act of free will on the part of the communities that they assumed these rights, and, by the permission of Congress, became states. A similar act of free will is sufficient to resign these rights, and to revert to that condition which preceded their assumption. "Nothing hinders a state from committing suicide if she chooses, any more than there was something which compelled the territory to become a state in the Union against its will." But however frequent may be the shuffling on and off of the state form, the United States, as territorial sovereign by virtue of natural laws far beyond the reach of local action, remains unaffected.

The conquered-province theory, which was held chiefly by Thaddeus Stevens, coincided with that of Mr. Sumner in respect to the effect upon the states of their own acts. They became non-exist-

[1] Brownson, The American Republic, p. 290.

ent as states. But Stevens maintained that the course of the United States government had made it impossible to concede that they possessed, after their subjection, even the attributes of territories under the constitution. On Sumner's principle, the people of the South, upon submission to the national forces, became entitled to the rights of United States citizens, as guaranteed by the constitution and exercised prior to the erection of the state organization. They had been treated as belligerent enemies only so far as it was necessary in order to bring them under the power of the government as traitorous citizens. The government's right to treat them in either capacity had been affirmed by all departments, and acted upon by all. But Stevens regarded all the nice constructions of law by which this end was attained as forced and unreal. He appealed to the actual facts of the case, and asked if any one could look at the military rule controlling the South and say that it was not, in reality, the dominion of a conqueror. Neither during the war, nor at its close, had any constitutional limitation been regarded that stood in the way of making the Southern people subject to the absolute will of the United States government. Such had come to be their condition, and in no respect did it differ from that of a conquered foreign foe. By proclamation of the executive, by law of Congress and by decision of the judiciary, the people of all the states in insurrection had been declared public enemies; as such they had been subdued by the armies of the nation; by their own act they had rejected the authority of the constitution, and it was not for them now to claim any rights under that instrument. Whatever might be the technical pleadings of the lawyers, the plain facts of the situation were that the lives, the liberty and the property of all the South were, by virtue of conquest, at the absolute disposal of the government. The principles of international law might guide the settlement, if the government chose, but no provision of the domestic constitution had any binding force whatever.

From the theories of Sumner and Stevens, as well as from those of the Southerners and the President, conclusions were deduced which were very unpalatable to the majority of thinking men of the day. The possibility of arguing away the existence of a state was an idea quite as offensive as that of immediately conceding autonomy to the recreant commonwealths. On the one hand the historic conception of the nation as a federal union seemed threatened with destruction; on the other hand, there appeared no guarantee of political results at all commensurate with the military triumph of the Unionists.

It was in consequence of this dilemma that the theory of forfeited rights was matured. Standing midway between the extreme doctrines, it embraced some feature of each of the rival theories, and like every compromise, it was deficient in a consistent relation of its parts. Its supporters would not concede that any state had been or could be out of the Union. But, they argued, the insurgent communities, while still integral parts of the nation, are not in the enjoyment of all the rights which, in a normal condition, a state may enjoy. That element of the state which is designated the people, should be in strictness called the political people. This political people has committed a political crime against the nation. But just as the individual who violates the civil law of society forfeits his civil rights in that society, so the community which offends against the political order of the nation may lose its political rights at the will of the sovereign. In no other way can the integrity of the nation be secure. Now the agent of the sovereign, in adjudging the extent and duration of the punishment to be visited upon the recreant commonwealths, is Congress. This is evident from the very nature of government; but it is also immediately sanctioned by the constitution. For the United States is directed by that instrument to guarantee to every state a republican form of government. The nation thus becomes the final arbiter as to the status of a state. But Congress is empowered to make all laws necessary and proper to carry into effect the granted powers. Congress, therefore, and not the President, is to direct the rehabilitation of the states. Finally, the constitution, and laws made in pursuance thereof, must be the supreme law of the land; under this clause the power of the legislature in the matter becomes indisputable. Neither the state nor the executive can claim any rights or authority as against the constitutional law-making organ of the government.

In many points the theory of forfeited rights approached very near to that of Sumner. It might be said, in general, that the only difference between them consisted in a mere abstraction. Sumner held that the states did not exist; the forfeited-rights theory refrained from stating the idea in that form, but held in fact that they should be considered, at the pleasure of Congress, in a condition of suspended animation. But on the hypothesis of state suicide, the very boundaries of a commonwealth might be obliterated, and its identity utterly destroyed; the rival theory drew the line here, and, while placing the vital principle of political rights at the mercy of Congress, made to conservative sentiment the cheap concession of territorial indestructibility.

The President's theory also seemed at some points to follow quite closely the lines of the forfeited-rights doctrine. Mr. Johnson himself described the condition of the rebel states in respect to the exercise of their governmental rights, as that of suspended animation.[1] But the condition was not

---

[1] See his remarks to citizens of Indiana; McPherson, Reconstruction, p. 46.

recognized as arising from the forfeiture of any of the rights they once possessed. Only in the retention of each and every one of such rights did he see the maintenance of the integrity of the states. The suspended animation was the consequence of a concrete state of affairs among the people of the state, and was not at all dependent upon the will of any political body outside of that community. Congress, in fine, the President held, had no power to deprive a state of any right as a penalty for the crimes of the people of the state. It was that power, however, which the national legislature, supported by the great mass of the Northern people, finally determined to exercise.

V. *The Congressional Plan of Restoration*

From the theories just outlined, and the multitude of views by which opinion shaded imperceptibly from one to the other of the definite doctrines, the reconstruction committee was called upon to formulate a creed upon which the majority in Congress could stand united. Concession had to be made to all the various shades of opinion among Republicans. The report, therefore, embodied some feature of nearly all the theories, but the combination was such as to bring into clearest definition the doctrine of forfeited rights.[1]

[1] For the report, see McPherson, Reconstruction, p. 84.

In the first place, the committee adopted the view which the President had once proclaimed, that, at the close of the war, the people of the rebellious states were found "deprived of all civil government." The *de facto* governments set up during the rebellion were illegal, so far as the United States government was concerned, and the attempt to legalize them by force had failed. At the cessation of hostilities, then, the Southern states were disorganized communities, and subject only to military dominion. The President, in his capacity as commander-in-chief of the army, however, had no authority to deal with the restoration of civil government. He appointed provisional governors, who were, however, mere military officials. Through these officials the people of the disorganized communities adopted certain systems of government; but these were nothing more than phases of the President's military sway. There was nothing of a permanent nature in them, and their establishment had no effect as against any regulation that should be adopted by the law-making power in reference to the final adjustment of relations with the states.

We cannot regard the various acts of the President in relation to the formation of local governments in the insurrectionary states . . . in any other light than as intimations to the people that as commander-in-chief of the army, he would consent to withdraw military rule, just in proportion as they should by their acts manifest a disposition to preserve order among themselves, establish governments denoting loyalty to the Union, and exhibit a settled determination to return to their allegiance ; leaving with the law-making power to fix the terms of their final restoration to all their rights and privileges as states of the Union.

In meeting the conservative proposition that a state, under the constitution, must be either in the Union, with all rights absolutely recognized, or out of it, with no rights whatever, the committee's principle denied the completeness of the disjunction, and rested on the conception of a state with full rights, but with those rights in abeyance by virtue of circumstances demanding recognition by the supreme national government.

This view of the condition of the states was evidently that of the forfeited-rights theory. In deference to the conquered-province idea, however, the committee reminded the states that, "whether legally and constitutionally or not, they did, in fact, withdraw from the Union, and made themselves subject to another government of their own creation." The moral of this was that from one point of view "the conquered rebels are at the mercy of the conquerors." In such a situation, it was held to follow that the government had a right to exact indemnity for the injuries done, and to take security against the recurrence of such outrages. The concession to Stevens was thus utilized as a basis for the great maxim of the forfeited-rights school, "indemnity for the past and security for the future." Sumner's doctrine was also deferred to with much respect. The territorial unity of the nation was insisted upon, and it was denied that any portion of the people of the nation had the right, while remaining on its soil, to withdraw from or reject the authority of the United States. They might destroy their state governments, and "cease to exist in an organized form," but this in no way relieved them from their obligations under the constitution and the laws. The distinction was marked between the destruction of the states and the overthrow of the state governments. "The states," it was held, "may cease to exist in an organized form"; so far, but no farther, was the possibility of state destruction conceded. The constitution acts upon the people directly, and not upon the states as such; only by act of the people, therefore, may the states become amenable to the disciplinary power of the national government.

The conclusion of the committee, accordingly, was that the so-called Confederate states, having forfeited all civil and political privileges under the constitution, were not entitled to representation. Before allowing it, security for future peace and safety should be required. This could be obtained only by changes in the organic law with a view to determine the civil rights and privileges of citizens in all parts of the republic, to place representation on an equitable basis, to fix a stigma upon treason, to protect loyal people against future claims for the losses sustained in support of rebellion and by the emancipation of slaves, and to grant express power to Congress to enforce these provisions.

There is manifest in the view thus set forth the same tendency to blend purely constitutional conceptions with the broader notions of international law that is seen in the theory of the war power employed during hostilities. It is only through this tendency that the exaction of indemnity becomes prominent. The general sentiment against the infliction of penalties for treason upon individuals, together with the conviction that punishment should be visited upon something, resulted in a transfer of the consequences of rebellion from the individual to the state. Any difficulties in the way of such a transfer were readily avoided by the resort to precedents of international warfare.

A month previous to the presentation of the committee's report, the measures necessary to the application of its principles had been submitted to Congress. The conditions which were regarded as necessary to be imposed upon the South were embodied in a proposition for a fourteenth amendment to the constitution. Accompanying the resolution were two bills to supplement it in carrying out the committee's plan. By one it was provided that whenever any state lately in insurrection should ratify the proposed amendment to the constitution, and should modify its constitution and

laws in conformity therewith, the members from
that state might be admitted into Congress as such.
The companion bill declared ineligible to any office
under the United States government all persons
included in five specified classes, substantially the
same as those exempted from amnesty by the
President's early proclamation.[1]

In its general features this plan announced by
Congress resembled that by which the President
had effected restoration.   A constitutional amendment was proposed, the adoption of which was the
prime condition of recognition.   But it was not
deemed necessary to provide for governments
through which state action should be taken.   The
Johnson organizations, while stigmatized as mere
military concerns, were yet recognized as sufficiently representative in their character to express
the will of the states.   Such recognition constituted a vital flaw in the consistency of the Congressional plan.   If those governments were competent
to ratify an amendment to the constitution of the
United States, it was insisted that the states which
organized them were entitled to representation in
the national Congress.   The Thirteenth Amendment had become of effect through its adoption
by the Johnson governments.[2]   Much abuse was
heaped upon Mr. Seward for his action in recognizing the right of the rebel states to vote on

[1] For the bills, see McPherson, Reconstruction, p. 103.

[2] See proclamation by Seward; McPherson, Reconstruction, p. 6.

this matter,[1] but his method was found worthy of adoption.

The content of the proposed Fourteenth Amendment marks very accurately the progress that had been made by the spring of 1866 in ideas as to the extent to which reconstruction should go. In the first section, the desire of the conservative Republicans to put the civil rights of the negroes under the protection of the United States was gratified. The fourth guaranteed the financial integrity of the government, and thus satisfied those who feared some assertion of state rights that might legalize debts incurred in opposition to the national authority. These two provisions constituted the limitations upon the powers of the states that were generally recognized as unavoidable consequences of the war. The second section of the amendment dealt with matters upon which opinion in the dominant party was far from certain and harmonious. It embodied a very clumsy and artificial solution of the suffrage problem. The alternative presented to the states, of enfranchising the blacks or losing proportionally in representation, was a mere temporary compromise between two party factions. It was the most that the friends of negro suffrage could secure at this stage of the process; but there was no indication that they would be satisfied with this. The third section of the amendment was merely incidental to

---

[1] *E.g.*, Scofield, of Pa.; Globe, 2d sess., 39th Cong., p. 598.

the conflict between Congress and President Johnson. The President's very free exercise of the pardoning power interfered with the progress of the legislature's policy, and no method of checking this interference seemed so feasible as a constitutional amendment. As a whole, the amendment was tentative. It betokened a longing for a definite settlement of the two great questions of the day, tempered by dread of an adverse public sentiment.

The bills which accompanied the resolution containing the amendment were not acted upon during the first session of the Thirty-ninth Congress, and the full inauguration of the committee's plan, therefore, was not accomplished. The first steps having been taken, it was considered well to await the action which the Southern states should take in the matter, and especially to ascertain the result of the autumn elections in the North, before making any further advances.

Only in the case of Tennessee was this policy departed from. In that state the radical Union Party had in the previous year secured firm control of the government, and had adopted measures rigorously excluding their opponents from any share in its organization. The Fourteenth Amendment was promptly ratified by the legislature, though not without some doubts as to the regularity of the proceedings,[1] and Congress not less

[1] Ann. Cyclopedia, 1866, p. 729.

promptly declared Tennessee restored to the
Union.   In the preamble to the resolution restoring the state, the ground of the act was explained
in accordance with the theory that Congress had
adopted.   The conditions considered necessary,
it was stated, had been fulfilled, and, moreover,
acts "proclaiming and denoting loyalty" had
been performed by the new state government.
These acts, not named in the law, were in fact
the disfranchisement of all partisans of the
Confederacy and various steps looking to negro
suffrage.

It was to the attainment of these ends — disfranchisement and enfranchisement, in some degree — that a steadily growing sentiment had
been directed from the beginning.   Scruples as to
the constitutionality of any interference by Congress with the hitherto sacred right of a state to
regulate the qualifications for voting within its
boundaries, had alone prevented the requirement
of negro suffrage, at least, as a condition of restoration.   The moderate Republicans desired that this
regulation should be made by the voluntary act of
the Johnson organizations.   Till every hope of such
a consummation was exhausted, the forfeited-rights
school of thinkers preferred to lean toward the
conservative theories of state status.   Two events
converted this tendency into an unmistakable
swerve toward the opposite extreme.   These were,
the rejection of the Fourteenth Amendment by

the legislatures of the ten states still unrestored, and the overwhelming defeat of the President's supporters in the Congressional elections.

VI. *Military Reconstruction*

An exhaustive discussion of the further progress of reconstruction in its relation to the constitution would involve an examination in more or less detail of the conflict between Congress and the other great departments of the government. Such examination, however, is without the scope of this essay. The fruitless impeachment of President Johnson was the climax of the legislature's struggle with the executive. As to the judiciary, a hostility to the radical tendency of Congress was unmistakably manifested in the cases of Milligan,[1] Cummings and Garland.[2] The conservative character of these decisions aroused a feeling of intense bitterness against the Supreme Court. Many laws were proposed looking to a curtailment of its appellate jurisdiction, and the suggestion was not wanting that even the original jurisdiction in cer-

---

[1] Discussed *supra*, p. 45 *et seq.* Thaddeus Stevens regarded this decision as scarcely less infamous than that in the Dred Scott Case, and as much more dangerous to liberty. Globe, 2d sess., 39th Cong., p. 251.

[2] 4 Wallace. In these two cases a state and a federal test oath, designed to exclude rebels from exercising the functions of clergyman and attorney respectively, were held unconstitutional, as *ex post facto* laws.

tain cases secured to it by the constitution might be taken away by an amendment.[1] Whether the menaces directed against the judiciary had some effect, or whether adherence to the traditional policy of the court to avoid conflict on political questions with the legislature was sufficient, it is certain that the will of Congress met with no adverse opinion during the remainder of the reconstruction era.

The further and final action of Congress in bringing about the reorganization of the Southern commonwealths, is marked by a gradual but certain relinquishment in fact of the theory of state status which had been previously adopted and which was still adhered to in name. Each successive step rendered more and more obscure the connection with the forfeited-rights idea. Hitherto, by this theory, the will of the states, as expressed by the historical constituency of the states, had been recognized as entitled to at least the consideration involved in its assent to the conditions of restoration imposed by the national authority. Henceforth, the will of the nation is asserted without reference to that of the state. The process of military reconstruction, in its leading features, follows closely the lines of the theory of state suicide.

Through the rejection of the Fourteenth Amendment by the Southern states, the process of res-

Bingham; Globe, 2d sess., 39th Cong., p. 502.

toration proposed in the committee's report was brought to a standstill. It was evident that the Southern whites would not consent to the admission of the blacks to the polls. In the North, the hot campaign in the fall elections of 1866 resulted very favorably to the friends of negro suffrage. Supported by a strong and growing public sentiment, the radicals now devoted their energies to the task of making the black vote the basis of reconstruction. This involved of necessity the subordination of the old political people of the various states to a new political people created by Congress. In this fact lay the practical triumph of the Sumner theory.

The law which finally inaugurated the work of military reconstruction was passed, over the President's veto, March 2, 1867. It declared that no legal state governments existed in ten states of the Union, and no adequate protection for life or property. The deficiency was made good by placing the said states under the military authority of the United States, and dividing them into five military districts with an officer of rank not less than brigadier-general at the head of each. The existing state governments were not abolished, but the sixth section of the bill enacted that any civil government which might exist in any of the states before its representatives were admitted to Congress should be deemed provisional only, and in all respects subject to the paramount authority

of the United States.   In the fifth section of the
act were stated the conditions on which representatives would be admitted and military government withdrawn.   Here the triumph of the
radicals was manifest; in addition to the ratification of the Fourteenth Amendment, it was required that a state constitution should have been
framed by a convention chosen by all male citizens of the state of proper age, "of whatever race,
color or previous condition," and that, in that
constitution, the same qualifications for the electoral franchise should be ordained.   The act itself
disfranchised and declared ineligible to the convention all who were excluded from office by the
proposed Fourteenth Amendment.   In short, full
enfranchisement of the blacks and disfranchisement
of the leading whites were required as conditions
precedent to the enjoyment of the rights of a state.

The theory of a voluntary acceptance of these
terms by the states was still nominally adhered
to; but no provision appeared in the act for the
initiation of any movement for the fulfilment of
the conditions.   Such a movement could scarcely
be expected of the existing governments, which
had rejected the Fourteenth Amendment, and
which were by the act declared illegal.   On the
23d of March, 1867, the Fortieth Congress, by
the supplementary reconstruction act of that date,
took into its own hands the whole process of
reorganizing the recalcitrant districts.   To the

military commander of each district was assigned the duty of causing to be made a registration of voters qualified under the act of March 2, and of holding elections for delegates to a constitutional convention in each state. The work of the convention was afterward to be submitted to the voters for ratification, all under the immediate control of the military commanders.

To overcome the conservative constructions of the law which were adopted by the administration, still another supplementary act was passed on the 19th of July. Attorney-General Stanbery, in construing the first two laws, had declared that the military authority was to be used only as auxiliary to the existing civil governments in the rebel states. The new act declared that those governments, if continued, were to be subject in all respects to the military commanders. Their officers could be removed at the will of the officer in command of the district. Further, practically unlimited discretion was conferred upon the registering officers as to who should be put upon the lists of voters. And finally, to thwart effectually the hostile influence of the administration, the General of the Army was invested with the final authority in the removal and suspension of officers, and no commander concerned in carrying out the acts was to be bound by any opinion of any civil officer of the United States. This last provision was aimed at the attorney-general.

The three acts just outlined contain all the essential principles of the process by which reconstruction was actually accomplished. The chief features of the process were: first, the overthrow of ten state governments that had been organized under the Presidential proclamations; second, the establishment of military government in the disorganized districts; and third, the determination by Congress of the qualifications of voters, not only for the immediate purpose of reorganization, but also for all the future existence of the commonwealths.

As to the first point, the action of Congress was entirely consistent with the ground it had taken at the beginning of its struggle with the President. It had steadily declined to recognize the organizations set up under Mr. Johnson's guidance as anything more than provisional. The status of a state that had forfeited its rights precluded the exercise of self-government until those rights had been restored. Under the radical tendency imparted to the legislature by the autumn elections of 1866, Stevens succeeded in embodying his conquered-province theory in the preamble to the first military bill as it passed the House.[1] The Senate, however, toned down the clause so as to avoid declaring the states extinct. In its final form, the act stigmatized them as "rebel states." Exactly what a "rebel state" is was not stated.

[1] Globe, 2d sess., 39th Cong., p. 1037.

By the radicals, the expression was regarded as conceding their claim that a state, as a corporate entity, could commit the insurrectionary act, and so draw upon itself the penalty of forfeiting its rights. The more moderate school, on the other hand, maintaining that rebellion was a crime of which only the individual could be guilty, construed the phrase as signifying a state whose inhabitants were wholly or chiefly rebels. But whether the state was extinct or merely without rights, the authority of the national government over its territory and people was equally indisputable. And of this national government, Congress was the responsible directing agency.

The second feature of the process gave rise to vehement discussion in Congress. What was the ground of justification for the imposition of purely military government on the rebel states? Assuming that the whole question was extra-constitutional, and that only the law of nations controlled Congress, there was no difficulty. Stevens and his followers had plain sailing. But if the rebel districts were still states, and their people citizens of the United States, how could the proclamation of martial law and the substitution of the military commission for the jury court be reconciled with the Bill of Rights? The most obvious answer was that the act assumed the existence of one of those cases of rebellion or invasion in which the constitution authorizes Congress to suspend the ordinary safeguards of civil liberty. All admitted that the judgment of the legislature as to when such a case had arisen was final. But as a mere question of fact, the existence of rebellion or invasion in 1867 was far from being clearly demonstrable. In spite of reports of outrages upon freedmen and Unionists in various parts of the South, which partisan zeal magnified *ad libitum*, it could not be made to appear that the situation was such as in itself to involve rebellion. The moderates were therefore compelled to fall back upon the assumption that the old war had not yet technically ended. For the benefit of this class, the radicals, though troubled with no scruples themselves, resurrected an ancient Latin phrase, *bello non flagrante sed nondum cessante,* and pointed out that *bello nondum cessante* was recognized in international law as one phase of warfare. Such was the situation now in the Southern states.[1] "A rebellion," said Shellabarger, "is simply crushed by war, by the arms of the republic, but is still sufficiently strong to overthrow and defy the courts in nearly half the territories of the republic. That is a state of things contemplated by your constitution." The war power, in all its completeness, was therefore in the hands of Congress, and would continue to be until state governments were recognized.

[1] Globe, 2d sess., 39th Cong., p. 1083.

The difficulty with this theory was that it put the legislature in distinct contradiction to both itself and the other two departments of the government. For by proclamations of April 2 and August 20, 1866, the President had announced that the insurrection once existing in the eleven specified states was at an end.[1] His right to decide this, as a mere military fact, was never seriously questioned. Congress itself, in at least one instance, recognized the date of the last proclamation as ending the war.[2] The Supreme Court, in its first opinion on the question,[3] expressly declined to discuss whether the rebellion could be considered as suppressed for one purpose and not for another, but in the case before it, accepted the date of the President's final proclamation. Later, Chief Justice Chase, on the ground that some act of a political department must be regarded as conclusive, decided, without reservation, that the executive must be followed.[4]

There is but one theory on which the setting up of military government in the Southern states by Congress can be made to harmonize with the view of the other departments as to the termination of the rebellion, and that is, that the alleged inade-

[1] McPherson, Reconstruction, pp. 15 and 194.
[2] Public Acts, 39th Cong., 2d sess., ch. cxlv, sec. 2.
[3] U. S. *vs.* Anderson, 9 Wallace, 56.
[4] The Protector, 12 Wallace, 700. *Cf.* Brown *vs.* Hiatts, 15 Wallace, 184, and Balesville Inst. *vs.* Kauffman, 18 Wallace, 155.

quate protection for life or property in the rebel states in 1867 constituted a new "case of rebellion or invasion," which justified the establishment of martial law. But on this supposition there would be a direct collision between Congress and the judiciary at another point. In the case of Milligan the Supreme Court declared with unmistakable emphasis that "martial rule can never exist where the courts are open, and in the proper and un-obstructed exercise of their jurisdiction." Yet in the states which were relegated by Congress to the unlimited dominion of officers "not below the rank of brigadier-general," the ordinary courts, both local and federal, had transacted their regular business for nearly two years.

In reference to the third and perhaps the most important feature of the Reconstruction Acts, the legislature and the judiciary are in harmony, though the difficulty of reconciling their doctrine with the earlier interpretations of the constitution is in-superable. Congress enacted that new state gov-ernments should be organized by a political people differing *in toto* from that which had formerly been recognized as the basis of the commonwealths. The leaders of the Southern whites were excluded from any part in the reconstruction ; the freedmen were awarded the ballot, and were relied upon to accomplish the formation of state governments. Two questions arose in connection with these acts: first, by what authority did the national legislature direct the organization of new governments in the rebel states; second, by what authority did Congress prescribe the qualifications of electors for the operation? The answer to both questions was: By virtue of the guarantee clause of the constitution. Forfeited-rights, state-suicide and conquered-province theories all agreed that Congress was the proper organ to provide for the re-establishment of state governments. By only the first, however, was an indefinite continuance of the existing condition of affairs considered anomalous. Sumner and Stevens saw no states existing in the South, and therefore felt no need of haste in the erection of states there. The less radical thinkers saw states without governments, and insisted upon the speediest termination of such a paradox.

It is declared by the constitution that "the United States shall guarantee to every state in this Union a republican form of government." The intention of the framers of the constitution in this clause was precisely stated by Madison in *The Federalist*, number 43: "The authority extends no further than a guaranty of a republican form of government, which supposes a pre-existing government of the form which is to be guaranteed." [1] A practical application of the clause had been demanded in connection with the Dorr rebellion in Rhode Island. The malcontents sought to secure interference by the general gov-

[1] *Cf.* also Elliott's Debates, V, 128, 182, 333.

ernment on the ground that the limitation of the franchise under the old charter organization was unrepublican.   President Tyler, however, wrote to Governor King: " It will be my duty to respect that government which has been recognized as the existing government of the state through all time past." [1]   In other words, the term "guarantee" was understood to express a corrective and not a creative power.   As Webster put it before the Supreme Court in 1848 :

The law and the constitution go on the idea that the states are all republican, that they are all representative in their forms, and that these popular governments in each state, the annually created creatures of the people, will give all proper facilities and necessary aids to bring about changes which the people may judge necessary in their constitutions.[2]

There can be no doubt that the construction of the guarantee clause embodied in these passages was the recognized principle of the law prior to 1867.   Only by a complete rejection of the old interpretation could the moderates derive from the constitution the power of Congress to organize a government for a state.   To maintain themselves in their somewhat unsteady position that a state could not perish, they wrenched the guarantee clause wholly away from its history.   Nor was their violence successful.   For to the impartial reader, the act of March 23, 1867, is much more

[1] *North American Review*, vol. 58, p. 398.
[2] Works, VI, 231.

suggestive of an enabling act for a territory than of a guaranteeing act for a state.

As the power to organize new governments in the rebel states was based upon an interpretation of the word "guarantee," so the right to determine the suffrage was evolved from the expression "a republican form of government." No authoritative definition of such a form exists in our law. The Supreme Court has ascribed the determination of its characteristics to Congress.[1] It was held by the negro-suffragists that the emancipation of the blacks and their admission to the enjoyment of civil rights had effected a modification in the conception of a "republican form." This doctrine was adopted by all the supporters of military reconstruction. "The new freemen," said Chief Justice Chase, in Texas *vs.* White, "necessarily became part of the people, and the people still constituted the state. . . . And it was the state, thus constituted, which was now entitled to the benefit of the constitutional guaranty." The implication was that a republican form under the new circumstances must include negroes among the bearers of the suffrage. It cannot be doubted that the decision of Congress as to when a state has a republican form of government is final. But a decision which runs counter to the facts of history as well as to the previous

---

[1] Luther *vs.* Borden, 7 Howard, 42; Texas *vs.* White, 7 Wallace, 730.

interpretation of our fundamental law may well be regarded as revolutionary. The principle of the reconstructionists was that impartial manhood suffrage, without respect to color, was a characteristic feature of a republican form of state government. In contradiction to this doctrine stood, first, the historical fact that at the formation of the constitution as well as at the era of the reconstruction many if not most of the states excluded negroes from the polls; and second, the universally recognized legal principle that, by the plainest inference from the words of the constitution,[1] the states were authorized to fix the qualifications of electors absolutely at their discretion. Sumner met both these obstacles boldly. He declared that the whole history of the negro in this country gave the lie to any claim that our state governments were or had been republican, and he argued with all the power of his learning that color was in no sense a "qualification" of electors. The majority of the reconstructionists declined to follow him into such radical paths. They preferred to bridge the abyss that yawned between the old system and the new with a series of disjointed quibbles.

The doctrine of forfeited rights has been adopted, as a theory of constitutional law, by the Supreme Court,[2] and for a long time, probably, the legal re-

---

[1] Article i, section 2.

[2] Texas *vs.* White, 7 Wallace, 700; *cf.* also 1 Chase's Decisions, 139, and Gunn *vs.* Barry, 15 Wallace, 623.

lations of the civil war and reconstruction will be construed in accordance with this theory. With its political bearings, however, the court has rightly disclaimed all connection. The question as presented to the judiciary was: Has such and such a state ever ceased to be a state of the Union? For answer to this interrogation, the court declared its obligation to follow the political departments of the government. A review of the acts of these departments failed to reveal an express declaration that any state had ceased to exist. The process of reconstruction presented many situations which could be explained as readily by assuming a revolution to have occurred as by strained constructions of the constitution. It was the duty of the judiciary, however, to preserve above all things the continuity of legal development. This duty was fulfilled, notably, in the elaborate argument, but very doubtful logic, of Texas *vs.* White. Private rights must be determined, then, on the theory that a state cannot perish. With political relations the case is different. Only the tension of a great national crisis is likely to call for a review of the Reconstruction Acts by the legislature; yet in such an emergency these precedents of political action may and probably will be regarded as much more consistent with the views of Sumner and Stevens than with the theory of forfeited rights.

MILITARY GOVERNMENT DURING
RECONSTRUCTION

By the acts of March 2 and March 23, 1867, Congress laid down the lines on which the process of reconstruction was finally to be carried through. This legislation, supported by the public sentiment of the North, practically settled the constitutional issues of the war. Not that efforts were not made to break the hold of the national military power on the South. Sanguine lawyers of both sections hastened to Washington to invoke the aid of the Supreme Court in overthrowing what seemed palpably unconstitutional proceedings under the Reconstruction Acts. Mississippi applied through counsel for an injunction to restrain the President from enforcing those acts,[1] but in vain; "government by injunction" in this particular aspect failed to win the favor of the court. Nor was any better success attained when Georgia moved against Stanton, the subordinate,[2] rather than Johnson, the chief. The court wisely recognized a sphere in

---

[1] Miss. *vs.* Johnson, 4 Wall. 475.
[2] Georgia *vs.* Stanton, 6 Wall. 51.

which it would not intrude upon the discretion of the executive. A more promising opportunity to test the obnoxious laws arose in connection with the writ of *habeas corpus*. For the better enforcement of the Civil Rights Act Congress in 1867 extended the appellate jurisdiction of the Supreme Court to all *habeas corpus* cases that involved United States laws. One McCardle, a Mississippi editor, availed himself of this law to bring before the court the question as to the legality of his arrest under the Reconstruction Acts. The supporters of these acts were very distrustful of the court, especially as to its possible opinion on the clauses establishing military government. When, therefore, the court denied a motion to dismiss McCardle's appeal and heard the case argued on its merits, the Congressional leaders were greatly alarmed. Before an opinion was rendered the House hurried through a repeal of so much of the act of 1867 as was involved in McCardle's case; the Senate concurred with unwonted celerity; and, though the scheme was detected in time to receive the President's veto, the bill became a law, and the court dismissed the case for want of jurisdiction.[1] The justices were no doubt greatly relieved to escape the responsibility of deciding this case. It was much better from every point of view that the fierce controversy of the times should be fought out entirely

[1] *Ex parte* McCardle, 6 Wall. 324; 7 Wall. 512.

by the distinctively political organs of the government. After the failure of the McCardle case the opposition to reconstruction found significant expression chiefly in the messages of the President and the platforms of the Democratic Party, neither of which carried much weight.

Meanwhile the process was carried to its conclusion by the military commanders to whom its execution was entrusted. The functions of these officers were, under the terms of the acts, of a twofold character. First, the "adequate protection to life and property," which was declared by the acts to be lacking, was to be furnished by the military; second, the organization of a new political people in each of ten[1] states was to be effected according to the method laid down in the acts. The purpose of this essay is to set forth the leading features of the military régime in the fulfilment of the first of these functions.

I

The chief end of the Reconstruction Acts was purely political. They were enacted for the purpose of giving the negro the ballot in the ten Southern states which had rejected the proposed Fourteenth Amendment. Their whole operation, therefore, must be regarded as incidental to this

[1] Tennessee had been restored to her normal relations in the summer of 1866. *Ante*, p. 119.

object. That the establishment of military government was a feature of the system they embodied, was due primarily to the fact that the introduction of negro suffrage was possible only by the strong hand. The act of March 2 did indeed allege that "no adequate protection for life or property" existed in the states concerned, and asserted the necessity of enforcing peace and good order therein. But these declarations were inseparably connected with the denunciation of the existing state governments as illegal; so that the lack of protection for life and property could be construed as arising from the illegality rather than from the inefficiency of the *de facto* civil authorities.

It was, indeed, contended by the more violent radicals in the debates on reconstruction that the actual conditions in the South were intolerable, and that military force was needed for the mere maintenance of peace, apart from political reorganization. But the weight of evidence pointed to the contrary. The reports of the army commanders and of the commissioners of the Freedmen's Bureau for 1866 were almost uniformly of a reassuring tone. Abuse of freedmen and Union men was not only becoming less common, but was also receiving adequate attention from the ordinary state courts. General Wood declared that in Mississippi substantial justice was administered by the local judiciary to all persons irrespective

of color or political opinions. General Sickles
thought the same to be true for most parts of
South Carolina. General Howard, the head of the
Freedmen's Bureau, drew from the reports of his
subordinates a similar conclusion as to the whole
region covered by their operations.[1] On the other
hand, General Sheridan found a good deal still to
be desired in Louisiana and Texas, and Sickles
admitted that certain specified counties of South
Carolina failed to afford a safe habitation for the
freedmen. The latter officer's explanation of the
existing disorder embodied a truth that was applicable very generally through the South. He declared that the outrages in the localities referred
to were not peculiar to that time.

> Personal encounters, assaults and difficulties between citi-
> zens, often resulting in serious wounds and death, have for
> years occurred without serious notice or action of the civil
> authorities; . . . where it has hitherto seemed officious to
> arrest and punish citizens for assault upon each other, they
> can hardly be expected to yield with any grace to arrests for
> assaults and outrages upon negroes.[2]

The general here touched upon a potent source of
evil to the South in the days of reconstruction.
Northern opinion tended to judge the rebel states
by social standards that never had been fairly
applicable to them. A laxity in the administration of criminal justice that had always prevailed

[1] See reports annexed to that of the secretary of war for 1866.
[2] Report of General Sickles for 1866.

was wrongly ascribed by the North to a mere *post-bellum* spirit of rebellion and race hatred.

The most striking evidence that affairs were assuming a normal condition in the South was afforded by the extent to which military authority and jurisdiction were withdrawn during the year 1866. The Freedmen's Bureau had been endowed with judicial authority in cases in which the freedmen were not assured of equal rights with the whites. But by the end of that year a gradual relinquishment of this authority was completed in most of the states. Only in parts of Virginia, Louisiana and Texas were the special courts still in existence at the time of the commissioner's report. The ordinary administration of civil and criminal justice for all citizens irrespective of race had thus been resigned to the state courts. This process had of course been rendered much more rapid by the enactment of the Civil Rights Act, which gave to the regular national judiciary jurisdiction over cases in which equal rights were denied. By action of the military authorities the "vagrancy laws" and other offensive statutes passed by the state legislatures for controlling the blacks had been rendered nugatory, and the United States courts manifested from the outset a resolution to give to the Civil Rights Act an interpretation that should effectively nullify any parts of the "black codes" that had escaped the military power. But all further labor by the judiciary on the problem of securing equal civil rights for the freedman was rendered for the time unnecessary by the resort to military power to secure him equal political rights.

In the spring of 1867, when the first Reconstruction Act went into effect, the general situation in the South was probably not as satisfactory as it had been at the beginning of the preceding winter. Two causes had contributed to a reaction. In the first place, the crops had in many parts of the South failed entirely in 1866. The pressure of famine began to be felt early in the winter, and by the beginning of the next spring the distribution of food through both public and private agencies had assumed large proportions.[1] Upon the relations between the races the crop failure had serious effects. Complaints arose in every direction from the freedmen that their wages were not being paid by their employers. The latter in too many cases were quite unable to pay, in others were disposed to take advantage of the situation to escape their liability. Much friction naturally arose out of the circumstances. To this was added the bad feeling generated by the discussion of negro suffrage in Congress and out during the winter. As the resolution of the dominant party

---

[1] By authority of a joint resolution of March 30, the Freedmen's Bureau devoted half a million dollars to the purchase and distribution of food in the South. — Report of Commissioner Howard for 1867.

to enfranchise the blacks by force became clear the disgust and despair of the whites tended toward expression in violence, especially wherever the freedmen manifested any consciousness of unwonted power. There is little room to doubt that the establishment of military government at the South was indispensable to the Congressional scheme of reconstruction; but that such government was necessary without reference to that scheme is hardly to be conceded.

II

By the act of March 2, 1867, the ten Southern states affected were divided into five military districts, each to be commanded by an officer not below the rank of brigadier-general. The primary duties of these officers were

to protect all persons in their rights of person and property, to suppress insurrection, disorder and violence, and to punish, or cause to be punished, all disturbers of the public peace and criminals.

For the execution of these duties the commanders could either allow the local civil tribunals to try offenders, or organize military tribunals for the purpose. In case the latter method were employed, the sentence of the tribunal was to be subject to approval by the district commander; and, if it involved the death penalty, to the approval of the President. Interference with the military under color of state authority was declared null and void, while the existing civil governments in the states were declared provisional only, and subject to the paramount authority of the United States, to abolish, modify, control or supersede. In these provisions were defined the functions of the commanders so far as the preservation of order and the conduct of civil administration were concerned. Their duties in the reorganization of the state governments were set forth in the supplementary act of March 23, and will be considered elsewhere.

On the 11th and 15th of March orders from army headquarters made the following assignments of commanders: First district, Virginia, General Schofield; second district, North Carolina and South Carolina, General Sickles; third district, Georgia, Florida and Alabama, General Pope; fourth district, Mississippi and Arkansas, General Ord; fifth district, Louisiana and Texas, General Sheridan.[1] All these officers had distinguished themselves in the war and had acquired reputations that guaranteed success in any military capacity. But the positions in which they now found themselves demanded other than purely

[1] None of these officers remained in command of his district till reconstruction was complete. The following is a list of their successors: First district, Stoneman, Webb, Canby; second district, Canby; third district, Meade; fourth district, Gillem, McDowell, Ames; fifth district, Griffin, Mower, Hancock, Buchanan, Reynolds, Canby.

military qualities. They were to carry out a great political policy, which was to be resisted not by armed force, but by political means. They were to act under a commander-in-chief who was a violent adversary of the policy, and under a General of the Army whose conscientious efforts to maintain an impartial attitude failed to conceal his disposition to favor the policy. They had to deal, moreover, with civil governments which their commander-in-chief insisted were constitutional organizations, but which Congress had declared destitute of legality. Though military officers are not supposed to have political opinions, the five generals could hardly fail to be influenced by their personal conclusions on the great issues of the day. It was generally known that Sheridan and Pope were in favor of strong measures in dealing with the South, and that Sickles would readily adopt a radical line of action.[1] If Schofield and Ord, from whatever motives, failed to conform to this example, it was inevitable that they should be displeasing to the extremists in Congress and should be sustained by the moderate Republicans and the Democrats. Political, rather than military, considerations would necessarily form the basis for

---

[1] *Cf.* Blaine, Twenty Years of Congress, II, 297, note. This note, satisfactory for the subject in connection with which I have cited it, contains, however, a number of those inaccuracies of statement and implication which mar every part of this useful but untrustworthy work.

judgment upon the conduct of the commanders; and in order to sustain their honorable reputations a degree of tact and discretion in civil affairs was essential that far exceeded anything that had been required of them before.

As to the mass of the whites — the people, in a political sense, of the South — no possible conduct of the military rulers could be expected to win their approval. The necessity of submission to force had been thoroughly learned, and no organized resistance was attempted to the few thousand troops that were scattered over the ten states.[1] But the loss of the self-government which had gradually been restored during the last two years caused deep indignation and resentment. Apart from the dread of approaching negro domination, the mere consciousness that the center of authority was at military headquarters, and not at the state capital, disheartened the most moderate and progressive classes. It soon appeared, moreover, that military government was not to be simply nominal; the orders of the commanders reached the commonest concerns of every-day life, and created the impression of a very real tyranny.

At the outset all five generals announced a pur-

---

[1] The adjutant-general's report of October 20, 1867, gives the total force in the ten states as 19,320, distributed among 134 posts. Richmond and New Orleans had about 1000 men each; but at no other post were there as many as 500. Of the total force, over 7000 were in the fifth district — Louisiana and Texas.

pose, and most of them a desire, to interfere as
little as possible with the ordinary civil administration.[1] Officials of the existing governments were
directed to continue in the performance of their
duties until duly superseded. All elections under
state laws were, however, forbidden, since the
negroes were to be clothed with the suffrage
before the popular will should again be consulted.
As to the administration of justice, whenever it
appeared to the military officers that the ordinary
courts were not sufficiently active or impartial in
their work, cases were transferred to the military
tribunals that were expressly authorized by the
Reconstruction Act. The punishment of blacks
by whipping or maiming, which was provided for
by recent state acts, was prohibited at once, in
accordance with a rider in the Army Appropriation
Act of March 2, 1867. It was inevitable that the
summary overriding of the established order, on
however moderate a scale, should engender conflicts of authority and consequent friction; but the
only result was that the assertion of military control in the administration of both civil and criminal
law increased steadily in scope in all the districts
as the months rolled on. Each fresh recourse to
arbitrary authority aroused a great storm of re-
proach and denunciation from the Democratic

[1] The most important orders and correspondence relating to
military government in its initial and determining stages are embodied in Sen. Ex. Doc., No. 14, 1st sess., 40th Cong.

press both North and South, and in June the
administration itself, through a published opinion
of Attorney-General Stanbery, harshly disapproved
the policy adopted by most of the officers.   This
brought a crisis and Congress, hastily reassem-
bling, conclusively defined the scope of the military
power by the supplementary legislation of July 19.

III

The most harassing question that had to be
dealt with by the generals on assuming their com-
mands was that of their relation to the officers of
the existing state governments.   The act of March
2 declared these governments to be provisional
only and subject to the paramount authority of
the United States "to abolish, modify, control or
supersede the same," but did not expressly empower the district commanders to wield this paramount authority.   In pursuance of their express
power to maintain order the generals were, however, obliged to assume that a control over the
personnel of the state administration was implied.
Removals from office, accordingly, were made from
the beginning on grounds of inefficiency or of
obstruction to the work of registering the negroes.
As removals did not abolish the offices, but were
followed by appointments, military headquarters
tended to become the center of a keen struggle for
place and patronage.   The mutual recriminations

of the parties to such struggles were echoed throughout the land and contributed one more element to the embarrassment of the commanders.

The manner of filling vacancies caused by removal or otherwise also gave rise to serious discussion. Under military law there seemed no doubt that an officer or soldier could be detailed by the commander to perform the duties of any position. This method was employed in many cases; but the supply of troops was entirely inadequate to the demand for non-military services and resort had to be made to civilians. At this point, however, important questions of constitutional law arose. What was the legal status of a civilian appointed, for example, governor of Louisiana? Was he a state or a federal officer? Certainly not the former; for apart from the question as to whether any state in the constitutional sense existed in Louisiana, no officer of such a state could be conceived as deriving his tenure from the will of an army officer. But if the appointee was a federal officer, why should he not be subject to the constitutional requirement of appointment by the President, with the advice and consent of the Senate? Congress might, under the constitution, vest the appointment of inferior officers in "the President alone, in the courts of law or in the heads of departments";[1] but there seemed no basis for appointment by a major-general com-

[1] Constitution, art. ii, sec. 2.

manding a military district. As a matter of fact,
the attempt to define the precise status of civilian
appointees was never successful. The radicals in
Congress thought they should be designated rather
as "agents" of the district commanders than as
officers in any strict sense.[1] It was rather gratifying than otherwise to reflect that these "agents"
drew their salaries, not from the army appropriation or any other national funds, but from the
treasury of the state.

Serious as were the questions involved in the
policy, the commanders were forced by sheer necessity to make civilian appointments from the very
outset. In this practice the whole spirit of the reconstruction legislation required that only "loyal"
men receive preferment. Thus was begun, even
before reconstruction was effected, the process of
giving political position and power to a class which,
from the nature of the case, could have little influence with the masses of the Southern whites.
In the beginning the test of "loyalty" was a record
of opposition to secession and of positive hostility,
or at least lukewarmness, to the Confederate cause.
As the reconstruction proceeded the test was in-
sensibly transformed until, before the end was
reached, the prime qualification of the loyal man
was approval of the Reconstruction Acts and of
negro suffrage. Office-holding thus tended to become the prerogative of those few whites who pro-

---

[1] *Cf.* Wilson in Cong. Globe, 1st sess., 40th Cong., p. 527.

fessed allegiance to the Republican Party. Only in connection with the registration and after the enfranchisement was complete were the blacks admitted to important official positions.[1]

The actual practice of the commanders in respect to removals and appointments varied in the different districts. From Virginia to Texas the construction and application of the powers conferred by the act grew more radical with the progress southward. General Schofield, in Virginia, besieged headquarters with supplications for authoritative rulings upon his powers, and meanwhile exercised the powers with great moderation. Civil officers were not "removed," but were "suspended" from office and "prohibited from the exercise of the functions thereof until further orders."[2] Civilian appointments were made after consultation with local judicial officers, and the appointees were duly commissioned by the governor of the state. In the Carolinas General Sickles was obliged to assert his authority more freely. He was, however, able to maintain cordial relations with Governors Worth and Orr,[3] and this fact smoothed his path somewhat. Removals were made only for positive mis-

---

[1] Five negroes were appointed policemen in Galveston as early as June 10, and there may have been other instances of this kind. — Ann. Cyc., 1867, p. 715.

[2] *Cf.* Special Orders, No. 50 and No. 54, in reference to certain justices of the peace.

[3] Sickles to Grant, Sen. Ex. Doc., No. 14, 1st sess., 40th Cong., p. 56.

conduct in office, and were but twelve in number
for the first three months of the command.[1] Appointments were very numerous, a large number
of municipal offices falling vacant by expiration of
the incumbents' terms. The extent to which the
military power affected the most peaceful aspects of
social life is illustrated by the fact that a "trustee
of Newbern Academy" was among those who were
clothed with official authority by orders from headquarters.[2] In the third district General Pope assumed at once an extreme position as to the scope
of his authority, and proposed to exercise it by
deposing Governor Jenkins, of Georgia, for expressing hostility to the Reconstruction Acts. The
governor saved himself by a plea of ignorance as
to the commander's will, and escaped with nothing
worse than a severe scolding, administered in a
letter which manifested the same easy self-con-
fidence and fluency of expression that had made
its author a little ridiculous in the second Bull
Run campaign.[3] At the end of May the mayor,
chief of police and other municipal officers of
Mobile were summarily removed, and their places
were filled by "efficient Union men." The occasion for this was a disturbance that took place in
connection with a meeting at which Congressman
Kelley, of Pennsylvania, made an address. This
exercise of the power of removal and appointment

[1] Sickles to Grant, Sen. Ex. Doc., No. 14, 1st sess., 40th Cong.,
p. 58.   [2] *Ibid.*, p. 81.   [3] *Ibid.*, p. 102.

attracted very widespread attention, and controversy raged fiercely as to the justice and legality of the action. It was but a few days later that General Sheridan, at New Orleans, took the most decisive step of all in removing Governor Wells, of Louisiana, and appointing Mr. Flanders, a civilian, in his place. Removals and appointments in minor offices[1] had been very frequent in the fifth district, but this last action brought the whole question to a head. As department commander before the passage of the Reconstruction Acts, General Sheridan had conceived a very poor opinion of the leading politicians of both Louisiana and Texas, Governor Wells among them.[2] But Wells had influential friends in administration circles at Washington, where Sheridan was particularly disliked; and moreover, the extension of the discretionary power of a commander to a sphere where very important considerations of influence and emolument were involved excited vehement criticism.

President Johnson was now overwhelmed with demands that the acts of Sheridan and Pope should be overruled. Attorney-General Stanbery had been asked for an opinion on this and other points in the interpretation of the reconstruction laws. His opinion, rendered under the date of

[1] The attorney-general of the state and the mayor and city judge of New Orleans were removed March 27.

[2] *Cf.* Sheridan's report for 1866, in Report of Secretary of War, 2d sess., 39th Cong.

June 12, declared that these acts gave no authority whatever for either removal or appointment of executive or judicial officers of a state.[1]   But Congress sprang promptly into the breach, and by the supplementary act of July 19[2] gave to the commanders, in the most unqualified terms, power to remove at their discretion any state officer, and to fill vacancies either by the detail of an officer or soldier, or "by the appointment of some other person."   Under this authority there was no longer any room for doubt or ground for hesitation.   The act provided further that it should be the "duty" of the commanders to remove from office all persons "disloyal to the government of the United States," and required that new appointees should take the "iron-clad oath."[3]

Every facility was thus afforded for a complete control of the *personnel* of the civil administration by the commanding officers.   When the constitutional conventions under the new registration met in the various states strong pressure was put upon the generals and upon Congress to bring about a "clean sweep" of the existing officials, and a bill requiring such a proceeding was brought before

---

[1] The opinion is in Sen. Ex. Doc., No. 14, 1st sess., 40th Cong., p. 275.

[2] Given in McPherson, History of the Reconstruction, p. 335.

[3] The stringent oath required from officers of the United States, by act of July 2, 1862.   It could not be taken by any one who had given "voluntary support" to any rebel government, state or Confederate.   See *infra*, p. 184, note.

the House of Representatives. But General Schofield and other officers declared that the adoption
of this policy would render government impossible,
as there were not available enough competent persons to fill the places vacated, if the iron-clad oath
should be required. Until reconstruction was nearly
completed, therefore, the commanders were permitted to retain their discretion in the matter, and
changes were made, as a rule, only for good cause.[1]
Governor Throckmorton, of Texas, was removed
July 30 for having made himself an "impediment
to the execution of" the Reconstruction Acts, and
was succeeded by a civilian named Pease.[2] Governor Jenkins, of Georgia, who had escaped the
power of General Pope, fell quickly before that
of General Meade, who succeeded Pope at the
beginning of 1868. The governor, having refused
to execute warrants on the state treasury for the
payment of the expenses of the constitutional
convention, was summarily deposed, and his functions were assigned to General Ruger.[3] Governor

[1] By law of Feb. 6, 1869, the commanders were required to remove all officers who could not take the iron-clad oath. But at
that time military government prevailed only in Virginia, Mississippi and Texas.

[2] The unsuccessful candidate in the election at which Throckmorton had been chosen governor.

[3] The treasury officials, sympathizing with Jenkins, concealed
and spirited away the books of the treasury, whereupon the suspected persons were brought before a military commission for
punishment. But General Meade's financial path was very thorny.
— See his report for 1868.

Humphreys, of Mississippi, was deposed in June, 1868, as an obstacle to reconstruction, and was succeeded by General Ames. In other states governors were removed, but only to facilitate the transition from the military régime to the permanent system under the new constitutions. Of the lesser state officials the changes in *personnel* were naturally the most extensive in the larger towns and cities. It was there that partisan zeal tended to find its most heated expression; and there also were to be found in the greatest numbers the Union men who could qualify for office under the new law. Before reconstruction was completed, therefore, the municipal administration in all the principal cities was remanned by military authority. The list in which this was wholly or partially the case includes Wilmington, Atlanta, Mobile, Vicksburg, New Orleans, Galveston and Richmond.

IV

In respect to the relation of the district commanders to the laws of the states subjected to their authority, there was room for a difference of opinion similar to that which we have seen in respect to the *personnel* of the governments. Power to modify or set aside existing laws was not expressly bestowed upon the commanders; and the recognition of civil governments of a provisional character gave room for the implication that the legislation of these governments was to have permanent force. But a different view was acted upon by most of the generals from the beginning. Assuming that they were endowed with all the powers incident to "the military authority of the United States," and that their duty to "protect all persons in their rights of person and property" required the unlimited use of such powers, they refused to regard the state laws as of any significance save as auxiliary to the military government. Whatever validity attached to such laws was due to their tacit or express approval by the commander. General Schofield, in giving to military commissioners the powers of county or police magistrates, directed them to be "governed in the discharge of their duties by the laws of Virginia," so far as these did not conflict with national laws "or orders issued from these headquarters."[1] General Sickles specifically proclaimed in force "local laws and municipal regulations not inconsistent with the constitution and laws of the United States or the proclamations of the President, or with . . . regulations . . . prescribed in the orders of the commanding general."[2] The implication from these illustrations is clear that existing law could be superseded by the military order — that the district commander had legislative authority.

Against this interpretation of the Reconstruc-

[1] First district, General Orders, No. 31, May 28, 1867.

[2] Second district, General Orders, No. 1, March 21, 1867.

tion Act Attorney-General Stanbery argued most earnestly in his opinion of June 12. No power whatever, he declared, was conferred on the commanders in the field of legislation. They were to protect persons and property, but the sole means for this purpose that the law gave them was the power to try offenders by military commission; save where such procedure was deemed necessary the jurisdiction and laws of the old state organization remained intact. But the ingenuity of Mr. Stanbery was of no avail. In the supplementary act of July 19 Congress declared explicitly that the ten state governments, at the time the Reconstruction Act was passed, "were not legal state governments; and that thereafter said governments, if continued, were to be subject in all respects to the military commanders of the respective districts, and to the paramount authority of Congress." This phraseology assured to the generals the same free hand in respect to state laws as was assured in respect to state officers by other parts of the act.

So far as the criminal law was concerned, the failures of justice which had been alleged as justifying the establishment of military government were attributed to the administration rather than to the content of the law. The military commissions which were constituted with various degrees of system and permanency by the district commanders served very effectively to supplement the regular judiciary in the application of the ordinary state law. No extensive modifications of the law itself, therefore, were considered necessary. When policemen or sheriffs failed to arrest suspected or notorious offenders the troops did the work; when district-attorneys failed to prosecute vigorously, or judges to hold or adequately to punish offenders, the latter were taken into military custody; when juries failed to convict, they were supplanted by the military courts. It was fully realized from the outset that, in the condition of public opinion in the South, trial by jury could not be expected to give strict justice to Union men or, in general, to the freedmen. As an alternative, however, for the general establishment of military commissions a remodeling of the jury laws was an obvious expedient. If juries could be empaneled from blacks and whites indiscriminately, the influence of the rebel sentiment would be neutralized. It seemed axiomatic, moreover, that, if the freedmen were qualified to vote, they were qualified for jury service. Accordingly, we find that the more radical commanders — Sickles, Pope and Sheridan — used their authority to decree that the blacks should be accepted as jurors. With the completion of the registration of voters, the attainment of the end sought was simple; court officers were directed to make up the jury panels from the registration lists.[1] General Schofield, in Virginia,

[1] *Cf.* Report of Secretary of War for 1867, vol. i, pp. 304 ss, 331 ss.

with his usual wise conservatism, concluded that this method of solving the problem would not be satisfactory, and confined himself, therefore, to the use of military commissions.[1]

Before the completion of the registration made feasible the method finally employed, the commander in Texas had sought to attain the end by requiring jurors to take the "iron-clad oath." But this was bitterly resented by the Southerners on the ground that it practically excluded native whites from the juries.[2] Even the final method caused great friction between the courts and the commanders in Louisiana and Texas. The vast extent and sparse population of the region included in these states made the fifth district altogether the most difficult to deal with in every phase of the reconstruction process. When General Hancock, succeeding Sheridan, assumed command in November, 1867, he formally revoked the order requiring that jurors be chosen from the registered voters, and put the old state laws in operation. This action was an incident of the new commander's general policy, which, as embodied in his famous

---

[1] "After full consideration I became satisfied that any rule of organization of juries, under laws which require a unanimous verdict to convict . . . must afford a very inadequate protection . . . in a society where a strong prejudice of class or caste exists." — Report of General Schofield in Report of Secretary of War, 1867, vol. i, p. 240.

[2] For the correspondence on this matter, see Sen. Ex. Doc., 1st sess., 40th Cong., No. 14, pp. 208–210.

General Orders, No. 40, reversed that of his predecessor. " Crimes and offenses," he declared, "must be left to the consideration and judgment of the regular civil authorities "; and in Special Orders, No. 203, after reciting that Sheridan's order as to jurors was acting as a clog on justice, he asserted that in determining the qualifications for jurors it was best to carry out the will of the people as expressed in the last legislative act upon the subject.[1] The reluctance of General Hancock to interpose, either through military courts or through modification of the jury laws, in the ordinary administration of justice, gave great offense to the loyalists in the South and to the radicals throughout the Union, and was held to have resulted in a widespread revival of crime in the fifth district.[2]

The changes in the jury laws by military authority affected, of course, both civil and criminal law. Of like scope was the summary abrogation by General Sheridan of a Texas act of 1866 by which the judicial districts of the state were rearranged, the commander holding that the act had been passed for the purpose of legislating two Union judges out of office.[3] Of the modifications of

---

[1] For the whole subject see Hancock's report in Report of Secretary of War for 1868; also Ann. Cyc., 1867, pp. 463-4.

[2] See his report for a sharp correspondence with Governor Pease, of Texas.

[3] Sen. Ex. Doc., 1st sess., 40th Cong., No. 14, p. **218** *et seq.*

criminal law pure and simple, conspicuous examples are found in Sickles' General Orders,
No. 10, in which the carrying of deadly weapons
was forbidden, the death penalty for certain cases
of burglary and larceny was abolished, and the
governors of North and South Carolina were endowed with the powers of reprieve and pardon.[1]
This last provision was probably suggested by a
case in which the military power had been effectively invoked by the civil in the interest of mercy.
A negro in North Carolina had been convicted of
burglary and sentenced to death. The governor
believed that the case called for clemency; but
under the state laws he had the power only to
pardon and not to commute. As a pardon was
not desirable, the case was laid before the district
commander, who then, by his paramount military
authority, commuted the sentence to imprisonment
for ten years.[2]

The operation of military government in connection with the general police power of the states
is illustrated by General Sickles' prohibition of
the manufacture of whiskey, on the ground that
the grain was needed for food; by his prohibition
of the sale of intoxicating liquor except by inn-
keepers; by General Ord's command that illicit
stills and their product be sold for the benefit of
the poor, on the ground "that poverty increases

[1] Sen. Ex. Doc., 1st sess., 40th Cong., No. 14, p. 62.
[2] *Ibid.*, p. 76.

where whiskey abounds"; and by General Sheridan's summary abolition of the Louisiana levee board and the assignment of its duties to commissioners of his own appointment, "in order to have the money distributed for the best interests of the overflowed districts of the state."[1]

V

As to the administration of justice in the field of private law, interference by the district commanders was for the most part confined to action in special cases where the proceedings of the courts seemed inequitable or contrary to public policy. Under the latter head fall a variety of instances in which the circumstances of the war and of emancipation were involved. Thus we find General Schofield ordering a Virginia court to

[1] The full reason assigned in the commander's order was: "To relieve the state of Louisiana from the incubus of the quarrel which now exists between his excellency the governor and the state legislature as to which political party shall have the disbursement of the four million dollars of 'levee bonds' authorized by the last legislature, and in order," *etc.*, as above. — Sen. Ex. Doc., 1st sess., 40th Cong., No. 14, p. 250. General Sheridan's orders and correspondence afford copious evidence that his temper was sorely tried by the Louisiana politicians. In several of his dispatches to General Grant his language in reference to the President's policy was perilously near the line of insubordination; but it won for him the enthusiastic support of the radicals in the North, and the House of Representatives passed a special vote of thanks to him for his services in Louisiana.

suspend proceedings for collecting a judgment in a case of assault committed in 1863.[1] General Sickles set aside a decree of the South Carolina court of chancery which ordered that a fund, raised to remount a Confederate cavalry force in 1865, but left unused in a Charleston bank, should be returned to the contributors. The general held that the money belonged to the United States.[2] Again, a Charleston savings bank was obliged by military order to pay, with interest, sums due to certain soldiers who were in the garrisons of Forts Sumter and Moultrie in 1860, and who had demanded their money, but in vain, just before the beginning of hostilities.[3] General Ord suspended proceedings looking to the sale of an estate on account of a deed of trust for money due for the purchase of negroes.[4]

Such examples of intervention by special orders are numerous; a far-reaching modification of law and procedure was attempted only by General Sickles in the second district. His General Orders, No. 10, of April 11, 1867, with the later supplementary decrees, assumed, as Attorney-General Stanbery complained, "the dimensions of a code."[5] The basis of this policy was the wide-

---

[1] Sen. Ex. Doc., 1st sess., 40th Cong., No. 14, p. 47.
[2] Ann. Cyc. for 1867, art. "South Carolina."
[3] Sen. Ex. Doc., 1st sess., 40th Cong., No. 14, p. 86.
[4] *Ibid.*, p. 152.
[5] Opinion of June 12, *ibid.*, p. 281.

spread destitution among the people and the general's conviction that extraordinary measures were necessary to enable them to develop their resources. There was no room for doubt that the Southern states were all in a condition of economic demoralization. As usual under such circumstances, the complaints of debtors, based generally on real hardship, were loud and widespread. Not in the Carolinas alone, but all through the South, the demand for stay laws was heard. It would hardly have been surprising if all the district commanders, in the plenitude of their powers and the benevolence of their hearts, had sought to bring prompt relief by decreeing new tables. General Sickles, after describing the distress due to crop failure and debt, and the " general disposition shown by creditors to enforce upon an impoverished people the immediate collection of all claims," declared that "to suffer all this to go on without restraint or remedy is to sacrifice the general good." Accordingly, he announced the following regulations, among others, to remain in force until the reconstructed governments should be established: Imprisonment for debt was prohibited. The institution or continuance of suits, or the execution of judgments, for the payment of money on causes of action arising between December 19,[1] 1860, and May 15, 1865,

[1] South Carolina passed its ordinance of secession Dec. 20, 1860.

was forbidden. The sale of property upon execution for liabilities contracted before December 19, 1860, or by foreclosure of mortgage was suspended for one year. Advances of capital, required "for the purpose of aiding the agricultural pursuits of the people," were assured of protection by the most efficient remedies contained in existing law; and wages of agricultural labor were made a lien on the crop. A homestead exemption, not to be waived, was established for any defendant having a family dependent upon his labor. The currency of the United States was ordered to be recognized as legal tender. Property of an absent debtor was exempted from attachment by the usual process; and the demand for bail in suits brought to recover ordinary debts, "known as actions *ex contractu*," was forbidden.

These sweeping enactments were followed by others of a similar character. Having prohibited the manufacture and regulated the sale of whiskey within the district, General Sickles further decreed that no action should be entertained in any court for the enforcement of contracts made for the manufacture, sale, transportation, storage or insurance of intoxicating liquors. Having prohibited discrimination in public conveyances between citizens "because of color or caste," he gave to any one injured by such discrimination a right of action for damages. Finally, he abolished distress for rent, and ordered that the crops should be subject to a first lien for labor and a second lien for rent of the land.[1]

This interpretation of military authority as the basis of a benevolent despotism called forth a vigorous protest from Attorney-General Stanbery in his opinion of June 12. But nothing was done to interfere with the commander's proceedings until he came in rude conflict with the national judiciary. On the theory on which his decrees were based they were valid against any authority save Congress. Chief Justice Chase sat in the circuit court at Raleigh in June, 1867, and proceeded in due course to decide cases and issue process of execution to enforce judgments. A marshal who undertook to execute in Wilmington a judgment that fell within the stay decrees of General Orders, No. 10, was prevented by the commander of the post, who was sustained by General Sickles. This action raised an issue of a much more serious character than was involved in the interference with merely state judicial procedure. Protests were made to the administration that the military authority established to enforce the laws of the United States was being employed to obstruct them. Steps were taken by the federal district attorney in North Carolina to proceed against the commander for resisting the process of the federal courts. General Grant wrote

[1] Gen. Orders, No. 32, May 30, 1867, Sen. Ex. Doc., 1st sess., 40th Cong., No. 14, p. 71.

to Sickles that "the authority conferred on district commanders does not extend in any respect over the acts of courts of the United States." Still Sickles asked for time to explain; but before his explanation was completed, the President performed the executive duty which Mr. Stanbery had in June assured him could not safely be avoided or delayed;[1] for on August 26 General Sickles was, by order of the President, relieved of his command. His successor, General Canby, promptly instructed the commander at Wilmington not to oppose the execution of the circuit court's judgment. Thus it was settled that, though a debtor was protected against a creditor who was a citizen of the same state, a foreign creditor was assured of the customary relief. This situation was only another example of the anomalies that characterized the whole process of reconstruction. To any protest against the injustice of such a condition the ready response was: Hasten the work of reconstruction, secure the admission of the states to full rights, and all irregularities will cease.

In other districts than the second the apparent necessity of relieving distress produced a few instances of paternal modification of private law. In June, 1867, General Ord, "with a view to secure to labor . . . its hire or just share of the crops, as well as to protect the interests alike of

[1] Opinion of June 12.

debtors and creditors from sacrifices of property by forced sales," suspended till the end of the year the judgment sale of lands under cultivation, crops or agricultural implements, on actions arising before January 1, 1866.[1] But this decree was explicitly declared to be not applicable so far as the United States courts were concerned. In Virginia, also, sales of property under deeds of trust were suspended where the result would be to sacrifice the property or to leave families or infirm persons destitute of support.[2] Radical action on behalf of debtors was strongly favored by many in the South; and this sentiment found expression in the constitutional conventions when they assembled in the various states. In Mississippi the convention petitioned General Gillem, Ord's successor, to stay executions for debt by military order; but the general refused.[3] Hancock, in the fifth district, when asked if he would enforce an ordinance for the relief of debtors, replied that he regarded such an ordinance as beyond the scope of the convention's authority.[4] Pope, in the third district, referring to suggestions that had been publicly made, said: "I know of no conceivable circumstance that would induce me to

[1] Gen. Orders, No. 12, Sen. Ex. Doc., 1st sess., 40th Cong., No. 14, p. 146.
[2] Ann. Cyc., 1868, p. 760.   [3] *Ibid.*, p. 508.
[4] Report annexed to Report of Secretary of War, 1868, vol. i, p. 249.

interfere by military orders . . . with the relation
of debtor and creditor under state laws."[1]   The
conventions in Georgia and Alabama, however,
adopted ordinances prohibiting various proceedings "oppressive" to debtors and abolishing certain debts, to take effect with the new constitution.
General Meade, who had succeeded Pope, became
aware that great hardships were being caused by
the eagerness of creditors to press for executions,
in order to anticipate the operation of the ordinances.   As the only method of meeting this difficulty, he proclaimed the ordinances in force at
once as a military order.[2]   Thus Georgia and Alabama were for a time on the same plane with the
Carolinas in this particular matter.

VI

In the administration of state finances the same
arbitrary authority was exercised as in the matters
already considered.   By the act of March 23 Congress provided for the payment out of the treasury
of the United States of "all expenses incurred by
the several commanding generals, or by virtue of
any orders issued or appointments made by them
under or by virtue of this act."   But the "fees,
salary and compensation to be paid to all delegates

[1] Ann. Cyc., 1867, p. 365.
[2] Report annexed to Report of Secretary of War, 1868.

and other officers . . . not herein otherwise provided for" were to be prescribed by the respective
conventions, which were authorized by the act to
levy and collect taxes for the purpose. A method
of interpretation no more liberal than that which
was applied by Congress to other provisions of the
act would have availed, if applied to these, to throw
the entire burden of state administration on the
national treasury.[1] In practice, however, the Congressional appropriations were employed only for
the expenses of the registration and of the elections, both for delegates to the conventions and
for ratification of the constitutions. The running
expenses of the state governments were paid from
the respective state treasuries. The condition of
the finances in most of the states was anything but
reassuring; and the feeling of the property owners
toward reconstruction did not conduce to more than
usual promptness in the payment of taxes. Considerable friction developed also in adapting the
administrative machinery of assessment, collection
and disbursement of moneys to the requirements of
military rule. Most of the difficulties were removed
through the generals' control over the *personnel*
of the administration. Their legislative authority
became necessary, however, in a number of cases

---

[1] President Johnson, employing this method, rolled up an appal-
ling total ($16,000,000, certainly, and "hundreds of millions," prob-
ably) as his estimate of the sum necessary to carry out the Reconstruction Acts. — Message of July 15, 1867.

through expiration of the laws regulating tax levies
and appropriations. The assembling of the legislatures was, of course, forbidden ; and the prolongation of the laws beyond the term fixed by their
provisions was effected by orders from headquarters.[1] At the same time advantage was taken of
the opportunity to effect such changes in taxation
and expenditure as seemed desirable under the
changed circumstances. General Pope directed
that no payments should be made from the state
treasuries of his district, except on his approval,
in order that he might prevent further expenditures
for "bounties to soldiers in the rebel army for support to their families; pay of civil officers under
the Confederacy; providing wooden legs, *etc.*, for
rebel soldiers; educating rebel soldiers, *etc.*, *etc.*,"
few of which he thought likely to be authorized by
the reconstructed state governments.[2] In South
Carolina General Canby decreed in December material reductions in several kinds of taxes; he had
previously suspended the collection of a tax on
sales which, having been imposed by the last legislature, had given rise to complaints because of its
retroactive effect.[3]

When the conventions met in the various states,
the military authority was required to settle vari-

---

[1] *E.g.*, Hancock's Special Orders, No. 40, of February 22, 1868.
Report of Secretary of War, p. 232.

[2] Pope's report, annexed to Report of Secretary of War for 1867.

[3] Ann. Cyc. for 1867, p. 699.

ous questions connected with their financial operations. As we have seen, the conventions were
authorized by law to levy and collect taxes on
property for the payment of the delegates and for
other expenses. One of the first acts in each convention was to fix the salary of delegates — at a
figure generally that aroused much enthusiasm
among the negro members. But to await the
levy and collection of a tax before enjoying the
emolument of office was a possibility that seriously
damped the ardor of the constitution-makers: in
fact, in view of the poverty of the people in general and the antagonism of the whole tax-paying
class to the convention, such delay threatened
the further process of reconstruction with failure.
Hence recourse was had at once to the expedient
of an advance from the state treasury for immediate expenses on the security of the tax that was
levied by the convention. Such advance was
ordered by the commanders,[1] as no authority of
state law for this appropriation of funds could be
found. But the power of the commanders was
called upon to restrain as well as to promote the
activity of the conventions. There was a marked
tendency on the part of these bodies to arrogate
to themselves governmental as well as constituent
functions, and to exceed the limits of the task pre-

---

[1] It was for refusing to issue the warrants in conformity to this
order that the governor and financial officers of Georgia were removed by General Meade. — *Ante*, p. 155.

scribed by the terms of the Reconstruction Acts. This tendency the commanders firmly repressed. In Mississippi, among other manifestations of this spirit, the ordinance for the levy and collection of the tax to cover the convention's expenses was cast in a form that General Gillem refused to approve. His refusal to enforce it caused the convention to repeal it and pass another that was satisfactory to the general.[1] This episode illustrates the fact that, in the plenitude of their powers as absolute rulers, the generals were above the constituent assemblies of the inchoate new states as distinctly as they were above the governmental organs of the expiring old states.

The foregoing review reveals how far-reaching was the authority of the military commanders in the practical operations of state government. It would be hard to deny that, so far as the ordinary civil administration was concerned, the rule of the generals was as just and efficient as it was far-reaching. Criticism and denunciation of their acts were bitter and continuous; but no very profound research is necessary in order to discover that the animus of these attacks was chiefly political. The instincts and traditions of popular government

---

[1] Report in Report of Secretary of War, 1868, p. 585 *et seq.* One clause of the second ordinance, which imposed a tax on railroads contrary to an exemption in their charters, was annulled by General Gillem.

would permit no recognition of excellence in any feature of arbitrary one-man rule; and the whole system, moreover, was, in the eyes of the critics, hopelessly corrupted by the main end of its establishment — negro enfranchisement. The influence of this end was, in truth, so all-pervading that a judgment on the merits of the administration of the generals apart from it is almost impracticable. Yet equity and sound judgment are sufficiently discernible in their conduct of civil affairs to afford a basis for the view that military government, pure and simple, unaccompanied by the measures for the institution of negro suffrage, might have proved for a time a useful aid to social readjustment in the South, as preliminary to the final solution of the political problems. But the opportunity for the most profitable employment of such government had passed when, through President Johnson's policy, civil functions had been definitely assumed by representative organizations in the states. There would have been, indeed, substantial merit in the consistent application of either the Presidential or the Congressional policy in reconstruction; but there was only disaster in the application of first the one and then the other.

THE PROCESS OF RECONSTRUCTION

MILITARY government in the South, 1867–70, was merely incidental to reconstruction proper. The maintenance of order was but a negative function of the district commander under the Reconstruction Acts; his positive and most characteristic duty was that of creating in each state subject to him a political people. Having given to such a people a definite existence, he was furthermore to communicate to it the initial impulse toward the organization of a government for itself, and then to retire into the background, maintaining an attitude of benevolent support until Congress should decree that the new structure could stand alone. The purpose of this essay is to sketch the proceedings incident to the performance of these duties.

I

The creation of a people in each state was to be effected by a registration of those citizens whom Congress had declared qualified to perform political functions. The Reconstruction Acts contemplated both additions to, and subtractions from, the people of the states as hitherto defined. Enfranchisement of the blacks was to be accompanied by disfranchisement of the whites. Not that distinctions of color were embodied by express terms in the laws ; nothing so invidious would have been tolerated at that date, and nothing of the kind was necessary.

The enfranchisement of the blacks was fully provided for in the single clause of the act of March 23, 1867, requiring each commander to "cause a registration to be made of the male citizens of the United States, twenty-one years of age and upwards, resident in each county or parish in the state or states included in his district," so far as such citizens were qualified to vote under the act of March 2. The latter act had contemplated a convention in each state " elected by the male citizens of said state, twenty-one years old and upward, of whatever race, color or previous condition." Under these clauses the inclusion of the blacks as a part of the political people in the South was as complete and unqualified as language could make it.

When, on the other hand, the disfranchisement of whites is considered, the Reconstruction Acts were far less exact; their language reflected the marked differences of opinion that existed in the dominant party on this subject. The feeling that prominent rebels should not be allowed to resume at once the political leadership they had formerly enjoyed had been very strong, and had been expressed in the proposed fourteenth amendment to the constitution. But with the definite adoption

of negro suffrage many Republicans manifested a
reaction from the earlier feeling. It was thought
that the anticipated evils of the black vote might
perhaps be mitigated by giving all the whites an
equal part in politics ; and doubtless some felt that
the imposition of negro suffrage and the prospect
of negro domination constituted a sufficient punishment for the leaders in rebellion. Others, again,
among them some of the most extreme radicals,
found a certain doctrinaire satisfaction in coupling
with "universal suffrage" the principle of "universal amnesty." By the first Reconstruction Act
all were excluded from taking part in the elections
who "may be disfranchised for participation in the
rebellion, or for felony at common law." By the
supplementary act of March 23 the oath prescribed
to be taken by every applicant for registration embodied an additional and much more definite disqualification. Among other requirements, each was
obliged to swear or affirm as follows :

That I have never been a member of any state legislature,
nor held any executive or judicial office in any state, and
afterwards engaged in an insurrection or rebellion against
the United States, or given aid or comfort to the enemies
thereof; that I have never taken an oath as a member of
Congress of the United States, or as an officer of the United
States, or as a member of any state legislature, or as an
executive or judicial officer of any state, to support the constitution of the United States, and afterwards engaged in
insurrection or rebellion against the United States, or given
aid or comfort to the enemies thereof.

The general purpose of these provisions is clear. As against the two classes of extremists in Congress, who on the one hand wished to disfranchise all who had participated in the rebellion, and on the other would give the ballot to all, a middle opinion prevailed, and the same test was applied in the matter of voting that had been embodied in the proposed fourteenth amendment as to holding office. A stigma was put upon those who had led the mass of the Southern people astray. But while the disfranchisement of rebels who, before becoming such, had held office was obviously the general purpose of the laws, the application of the provisions in practice gave rise to a host of difficulties in detail. Who were to be regarded as "disfranchised for participation in the rebellion"? Was a man's word to be taken on the subject, or was some other evidence to be sought for? Could the phrase be construed to exclude all who had taken part in the rebellion? Again, were all rebels disqualified who before engaging in insurrection had held state office, or only such as had, in connection with such office, taken the oath to support the constitution of the United States? And what was the scope of the phrase "executive or judicial office in any state"? Did it include municipal offices, and all the petty administrative and judicial positions? Further, what was meant by "engaging in rebellion" and by giving "aid or comfort" to enemies of the United States? Had the

Confederate conscript engaged in rebellion as well as the Confederate volunteer? And did the giving of food and drink and clothing to the Confederate soldiers constitute giving aid or comfort to the enemies of the United States? All these and many other questions confronted the district commanders as soon as preparations for the registration were begun. Appeals for an authoritative construction of the law on these points came to Washington from all the districts.[1] Under date of May 24 the attorney-general submitted an elaborate opinion on the whole subject, a summary of which was afterwards transmitted to the district commanders.

In most respects Mr. Stanbery's interpretation as to disfranchisement was unexceptionable. While tending, as in his views on military government, to strict restraint of the commander's discretion, he found few questions upon which he could fairly devise a construction that differed from that of the radicals. As subject to disfranchisement he included all officers of the United States, civil and military, and all civil officers of any state who had, prior to rebellion, taken the oath to support the constitution of the United States. But neither municipal officers, like mayors, aldermen and policemen, nor persons

---

[1] For formal applications for such construction by Generals Schofield, Ord and Sheridan, see Sen. Ex. Doc., 1st sess., 40th Cong., No. 14, pp. 15, 140, 193.

who exercised mere agencies or employments under state authority, like commissioners of public works, bank examiners and notaries public, were disqualified for registration. As to engaging in rebellion, Mr. Stanbery absolved from responsibility for such an offense all conscripts who would not voluntarily have joined the army, and all officials who, during the rebellion, discharged functions not incident to war, but merely necessary to the preservation of order and the administration of law. And again, "aid or comfort to the enemy" he held was not involved in mere acts of charity, where the intent was rather to relieve the individual than to aid the cause. But organized contributions of food and clothing for the benefit of all persons concerned in insurrection would subject contributors to disfranchisement. So also forced payments of taxes or assessments would not disqualify those who paid; but voluntary loans to the Confederate government, or the purchase of its securities, would disqualify.

On most of these points the attorney-general's interpretation had been anticipated in provisional regulations prescribed by the various commanders. There were some statements in the opinion, however, which excited almost as much dissent in Congress as the administration's view on the relation of the military commanders to the civil authorities.[1] Chief of these was Mr. Stanbery's declaration that

[1] *Cf.* the preceding essay, *passim.*

the taking of the prescribed oath by the applicant was conclusive upon the registering officers as to his right to be placed upon the list of voters. No authority was given to the board of registration, said the attorney-general, to make any further investigation of the applicant's qualifications. If he swore falsely, he was liable to prosecution for perjury, and that was the end of the matter. It was easy to perceive that, in the existing condition of public sentiment in the South, a prosecution for perjury afforded a very slight guarantee against illegal registration. Again, Mr. Stanbery's opinion was stoutly assailed where he held subject to disfranchisement only such state officers as had taken the oath to support the constitution of the United States. This rule, like other features of his opinion, seemed likely to admit too freely to the franchise.

The perversity of the administration in respect to registration was checked, like that in respect to the military government's authority, by the supplementary act of July 19. By this Congress declared explicitly that the registering officers had the power and the duty, in considering an applicant for registration,

to ascertain, upon such facts or information as they can obtain, whether such person is entitled to be registered . . . ; and the oath required by said act [act of March 2] shall not be conclusive on such question . . . ; and such board [of registration] shall also have power to examine under oath . . . any one touching the qualification of any person claiming registration.

The act further provided that disfranchisement should extend to every one who had been in the legislature or who had held executive or judicial office in any state "whether he has taken an oath to support the constitution of the United States or not"; and construed the words "executive or judicial office in any state" to include "all civil offices created by law for the administration of any general law of a state or for the administration of justice." And finally, in order to exclude all possibility of Presidential extension of the franchise, it was enacted that no person should acquire the right to registration through any pardon or amnesty.

Through this legislation the rules of disfranchisement were fully determined. There was obviously much room left for construction by the registering officers in application of the rules to particular cases. Where, as in the determination whether a man had "engaged in rebellion," the whole question might be made to turn on the subjective motive of a given act, there was abundant room for discretion. A much-discussed case was that of a hypothetical parent who sent food and clothing to his son, serving in the Confederate army,[1] but who had in no other way given aid or comfort to enemies of the United States. He must be disfranchised or not according as the

---

[1] Generals Schofield and Pope held that giving food or clothing would not disfranchise, but that giving a horse would. — Reports for 1867.

chief motive was regard for the son or regard for the cause. A trained casuist would be troubled to deal with the case; the boards of registration had as a rule a very small proportion of trained casuists among them.

As a matter of fact the boards of registry had been carefully constituted with a view to prevent evasions of the disfranchising clauses. By the act of March 23 the registration and elections were to be conducted by boards of three, appointed by the district commanders and consisting of "loyal officers or persons"; and loyalty was insured by the requirement that all officers of registry should take the oath prescribed by the act of July 2, 1862 — the famous "iron-clad oath." [1] The utmost care was taken in every district that the purpose of this provision should be fulfilled. General Schofield, in selecting registration officers, gave preference, first, to officers of the army and of the Freedmen's Bureau; second, to honorably dis-

---

[1] "I . . . do solemnly swear that I have never voluntarily borne arms against the United States since I have been a citizen thereof; that I have voluntarily given no aid, countenance, counsel or encouragement to persons engaged in armed hostility thereto; that I have never sought nor accepted nor attempted to exercise the functions of any office whatever, under any authority or pretended authority in hostility to the United States; that I have not yielded a voluntary support to any pretended government, authority, power or constitution within the United States, hostile or inimical thereto; and . . . that . . . I will support and defend the constitution of the United States against all enemies, foreign and domestic," *etc., etc.*

charged Union soldiers; and third, to loyal citizens of the particular locality.[1] General Pope
deemed it inadvisable to employ soldiers in this
work, but constituted the boards exclusively of
citizens, including in every case one negro. This
bold recourse to the employment of the blacks, in
addition to the influence it exerted in stimulating
a large registration of the race, had the further
advantage of overcoming the difficulties of scant
material. Especially in the fourth and fifth districts the number of white men who could take
the test oath was very small. In some localities
it was practically impossible to find three such
persons to constitute the registration board. For,
besides the ability to take the oath, there was
necessary also the willingness to take it and the
intelligence to perform the duties of office. The
state of public sentiment in the South was not
such as to encourage timid men to proclaim publicly that their sympathies during the war had
been with the North;[2] nor, where this difficulty
might be overcome, was the intellectual equip-
ment of the candidate apt to be on a par with
his courage. That the registration was effected,
under the circumstances, in any tolerable form

---

[1] Report for 1867.

[2] *Cf.* Ord, in his report for 1867: " In the majority of counties in
my district there are but very few men who can take the test oath,
and these are not disposed to defy public opinion by accepting
office."

whatever, is in itself a tribute to the efficiency of the military authorities. Like the practice adopted in appointments to office under the existing governments, the use of the test oath in the registration and election boards tended to elevate into political prominence a class which lacked the moral authority to conduct government in the Southern states.[1] The organization and activity of these boards gave coherence and dignity to the element of Northern sympathizers of which they were composed, and contributed very greatly to the development of the Republican Party, already started on its career in the South. There can be no doubt that, for the ends in view, the provisions of the Reconstruction Acts requiring the test oath for members of the registry boards were necessary. There is just as little doubt that the exclusion of the dominant element of the white population from active and official part in the reconstruction added much to the bad feeling which, without this particular stimulus, would have been serious enough.

The process of registration occupied the summer of 1867. By the act of March 23 it was to have been completed by September 1 ; but the difficulties and delays that arose in the fourth and fifth districts led to an extension of the time to October 1, by the act of July 19. After the completion of the registration the next duty of the

[1] *Supra*, p. 150.

commanders was to provide for an election in each state, at which the registered voters should express their will, first on the question as to whether a constitutional convention should be held, and second, on the choice of delegates to such convention. The number of delegates was fixed by the act of March 23, but the details of apportionment were left to the commanders.

At the outset the impulse of the disfranchised leaders in the South had been to throw all their influence against any participation by their followers in the reorganization of the states. "Refuse to register," was the cry raised in many quarters; "have no concern in the establishment of black rule!" Military government was declared to be preferable to negro domination : better the tyranny of the intelligent one than that of the ignorant many. But as a matter of policy it was soon discerned that abstention from registration would be less effective than participation therein. In discussing the Reconstruction Acts the radicals in Congress had manifested much sensitiveness to possible charges that they aimed to establish at the South minority governments, supported by bayonets. It was less important, they held, that new governments should be established, than that these governments should be fully representative of the whole people, white as well as black.[1] That the new state constitutions, therefore, should cer-

[1] *Cf.* Cong. Globe, 1st sess., 40th Cong., pp. 143–151.

tainly be based upon the action of a majority, it
was provided by the act of March 23 that in the
elections, both on the calling of a convention and
on the ratification of the constitution, the vote
should be valid in the affirmative only if at least
half of the registered voters took part. In view
of these provisions the effective way in which to
thwart reconstruction was to register but refrain
from voting.   This accordingly became the policy
of the extremists in the South.   As a consequence
the registration proved very successful as to numbers; the subsequent voting proved far less so.
The following table exhibits some features of the
result:[1]

	REGISTERED		VOTE ON HOLDING CONVENTION	
	WHITE	COLORED	FOR	AGAINST
Virginia	120,101	105,832	107,342	61,887
North Carolina	106,721	72,932	93,006	32,961
South Carolina	46,882	80,550	68,768	2,278
Georgia	96,333	95,168	102,283	4,127
Alabama	61,295	104,518	90,283	5,583
Florida	11,914	16,089	14,300	203
Mississippi [2]	TOTAL: 139,690		69,739	6,277
Arkansas [2]	" 66,831		27,576	13,558
Louisiana	45,218	84,436	75,083	4,006
Texas	59,633	49,497	44,689	11,440

From this it appears that in four of the states —
South Carolina, Alabama, Florida and Louisiana

[1] Compiled from House Ex. Doc., No. 53, 2d sess., 40th Cong.
[2] No distinction by color made in registering.

—the new electorates embodied pronounced negro majorities: in three — Virginia, North Carolina and Texas — the whites were in more or less considerable excess; and in one, Georgia, the races were very evenly balanced. Of the two states in the fourth district, where General Ord felt that the spirit of the reconstruction policy was opposed to any distinction of voters by color, Mississippi belonged notoriously to the class in which the blacks were in the majority, and Arkansas to that in which they were in the minority.[1] As to the number of persons disfranchised by the operation of the laws, no trustworthy figures were attainable. By various methods of estimate, more ingenious than convincing, the commanders arrived at hypothetical results in some states: *e.g.*, Virginia, 17,000; North Carolina, 12,000; South Carolina, 9000; Georgia, 10,500; but no especial validity was attached to the figures.

As to the attitude of the whites on the holding of conventions, the insignificant negative vote in most of the states is eloquent. The policy of abstention was not, however, successful in any state at this time.[2] It happened, indeed, that just at the time of the voting a hopeful feeling pre-

[1] In 1860 the population stood as follows:

	WHITE	BLACK		WHITE	BLACK
Mississippi	353,899	437,404	Arkansas	324,143	111,259

[2] It will be seen by the table that the excess of the vote over half the registration was small in most of the states, and particularly so in Florida and Texas.

vailed in the South, due to general Democratic gains in Northern state elections in the autumn, and especially to the rejection of a negro-suffrage amendment in Ohio by 50,000 majority. Under the influence of these events many Southern whites who had resolved upon abstention actually voted, trusting to be saved by the Democracy from the most dreaded consequences of black rule. Moreover, the whole influence of the military authorities was directed toward securing a large vote, and various devices of the Conservatives for keeping the negroes from the polls were met by orders from headquarters that were hardly compatible with accepted ideas as to regularity at elections. As in the registration, so in the voting, the generals assumed with the most unconventional frankness that their duty required them to insure the participation of the newly enfranchised citizens. Not the passive possession, but the active exercise, of political rights by the negroes was held to be the essential principle of the Reconstruction Acts. The limits of time set for the registration were repeatedly extended, to secure a full enrollment of the blacks ; and when the elections came the same expedient was employed to secure a full vote. General Schofield, in Richmond, finding at the time set for closing the polls that in certain precincts many blacks had failed to vote, forthwith issued an order extending the time and permitted votes to be received for twenty-four

hours longer.   The result was to reverse the
choice of delegates to the convention from one
district.[1]   In Georgia also two additional days
were, after the voting had begun, added to the
three fixed for the elections in the original order.
These measures, it will be perceived, affected not
only the issue as to whether a convention should
be held, but also the membership of that body if
the vote resulted in favor of its assembling ; for
both matters were voted upon at the same time.
As party organization then stood, a large negro
vote meant a Radical majority in the convention.

The measures just noticed were designed to
counteract the effects of the negroes' own ignorance or lack of experience at the polls.   In the
orders regulating the elections, the commanders
had embodied very explicit injunctions to prevent
the whites from interfering with the other race.
Not only force and intimidation, but also threats
of discharge from employment and other like
methods of " discouraging " the participation of
the blacks, were made offenses subject to military
jurisdiction.[2]   Moreover, from the beginning of
their authority the commanders had contributed
much to disorganize opposition to reconstruction

---

[1] For the protest of candidates and the general's reply, see Report
of Secretary of War for 1867, p. 389 *et seq*.   The general's justification is clever but somewhat sophistical, as it evades the most
serious element in the case of the protestants.

[2] *Cf.* Pope, Gen. Orders, No. 59, Ann. Cyc. 1867, p. 27.

by requiring office-holders, on penalty of dismissal, to abstain from all share in such opposition. It was in the office-holding class that the natural and customary leaders of the old political people were to be found. General Pope had gone even further in direct promotion of the new policy by decreeing that the printing patronage of the state should be given to such newspapers only as should not oppose reconstruction.[1] The general's own report concedes that the effect of this order in silencing the press was not all that might have been desired; but it must have had some influence in developing support for the policy he represented. Much complaint was made in the South and elsewhere that the orders just mentioned involved a policy of arbitrary restriction upon freedom of speech and of the press. No such general policy was adopted by any commander. The requirement upon office-holders was no more restrictive of free speech than the orders of modern days in respect to "offensive partisanship" and "pernicious activity," and may fairly be regarded as indispensable to the performance by the commanders of their official duties. General Pope's newspaper order was perhaps less defensible; but it merely adopted in the open the policy which was quietly but consistently pursued by legislative bodies, both state and national, of assuring an official subsidy to that part of the press that

[1] Report for 1867.

was in sympathy with the dominant party in the government.[1] As a whole, while the military authorities gave much positive support to the developing party of reconstruction in the South, and while a surveillance was exercised over press and platform to prevent incitations to violence, it cannot fairly be said that freedom of speech and the press was interfered with. Indeed, the latitude permitted by the commanders was perhaps accountable for many of the difficulties met with in bringing reconstruction to its conclusion. The policy of the generals, in fact, is strongly suggestive of the ancient maxim of benevolent despotism : "Let my subjects say what they like, so long as I may do what I like."[2]

II

The constitutional conventions determined upon by this first election were in session during the winter of 1867–68, and most of them had fulfilled their function by the middle of the ensuing spring. As required by the Reconstruction Acts, the time and place of the conventions were set by orders from the military headquarters of the respective

[1] *Cf.* the Sundry Civil Appropriation Act of March 2, 1867, sec. 7, designed to assure federal patronage in the South to papers supporting reconstruction.

[2] For two incidents illustrating the relation of the military authorities to the press, see Ann. Cyc., 1867, pp. 51 and 520.

districts. Naturally, there was an ostentatious exchange of civilities between each convention and the district commander, as well as a less public but very powerful current of influence running from headquarters to the convention hall. The opponents of reconstruction denounced with great severity the subservience of the constitution-makers of a "sovereign state" to a "military satrap." As a matter of fact, however, the generals did stalwart service for the cause of conservatism, and hence for the interests of the class by whom they were abused. It was inevitable, under all the circumstances of the situation, that radical ideas, social and economic as well as political, should be strongly represented among the members of the conventions. Southern Unionists, in whom rankled the memories of long oppression and ostracism, ambitious Northerners, filled with ideals of a new South modeled on the lines of New England, and negroes[1] less than three years out of slavery, were the classes numerically most important in the conventions. Moderation was hardly to be anticipated from any of these. There was, however, an element of sober

[1] The following was the division of delegates on the color line, so far as figures have been obtainable:

	WHITE	BLACK		WHITE	BLACK
Virginia	80	25	Georgia	133	33
North Carolina	107	13	Florida	28	18
South Carolina	34	63	Alabama	92	16
			Texas	81	9

Compare with table p. 184

and substantial Southerners — representatives, for the most part, of the professional and business classes who had voluntarily withdrawn from politics when the Whig Party disappeared — cn whom it now devolved to wield a decisive influence against radicalism. It was to the judicious policy of this class, supported by the moral force of the military commanders, that was due the moderate character, as a rule, of the new constitutions.

No influence, however, was strong enough to keep in the background the many non-political questions involved in the relations of the races. Debates were long and vehement on a variety of propositions which ultimately failed of adoption in most states. Among the mooted points were the expediency of giving freedmen a claim against their masters for services rendered in slavery after the date of the Proclamation of Emancipation; the admission of blacks and whites to the same schools; the freedom of intermarriage between the races;[1] and the recognition of equal rights in public places and conveyances as incidental to equality in civil rights. On the last point the Radicals were to a great extent successful. It was

---

[1] In almost every convention the Conservatives proposed a constitutional prohibition upon intermarriage. In several cases the negroes, with a certain grim humor, agreed to accept the proposition on condition that an additional clause should provide that any white man cohabiting with a negro woman should be punishable by death.

upon the question of the suffrage, however, that differences of opinion were most obstinate; and here also the Radicals in a number of states pre-vailed over all restraining forces.

By section five of the first Reconstruction Act Congress had in effect required that the new constitutions should secure the franchise to all male citizens twenty-one years of age and "not disfranchised for rebellion or felony." No option was left as to the enfranchisement of the negroes; as to disfranchisement of the whites the quoted phrase left the conventions with free hands. In six of the states this liberty resulted in a proscription of the late secessionists.[1] Alabama, Arkansas, Mississippi, Texas and Virginia denied the franchise to those whom the proposed fourteenth amendment disqualified for office, *i.e.*, those who, after having taken the official oath to support the constitution, had gone into rebellion.[2] Alabama and Arkansas added to the disfranchised any who had "violated the rules of civilized warfare,"—a provision directed chiefly at those who had refused to accord to negro soldiers the customary military treatment.

[1] The constitutions are all in Poore's collection. Abstracts, giving the franchise clauses, may be found in McPherson, Reconstruction, p. 326 *et seq.*

[2] This section of the Virginia convention's draft failed of ratification. On the other hand, in the first three of the states enumerated the disqualification was made somewhat more severe by applying it to all who were excluded from registration under the Reconstruction Acts.

Louisiana, whose provisions were perhaps the most severe of all, disqualified all who had held military or civil office for as long as a year in the Confederacy, all who wrote or published newspaper articles or preached sermons "in advocacy of treason," and all who voted for or signed the ordinance of secession. Eligibility to office was in most states denied on the same grounds as the right to vote. Mississippi, however, made ineligible all who voted for secession and all who held office under the Confederacy, together with every one who voluntarily gave aid or encouragement to the Confederates;[1] and Virginia achieved the same purpose by requiring the iron-clad oath of every officer.[2]

These proscriptive provisions of the new constitutions were for the most part not absolute in their terms. Recourse was had in Louisiana to that expedient, common in the political and religious commotions of recent centuries, which puts a premium on self-stultification: the removal of his disabilities was offered to any man who would

[1] This provision contained a clause the motive of which seems somewhat obscure: "Provided, that nothing in this section, except voting for or signing the ordinance of secession, shall be so construed as to exclude from office the private soldier of the late so-called Confederate states army." This probably reflects the familiar sentiment, that maintenance of one's convictions by physical force is essentially nobler than by moral or intellectual activity.

[2] This was carried in convention against a very energetic protest by General Schofield. *Cf.* Ann. Cyc. for 1868, p. 759.

publicly acknowledge that the late rebellion was morally and politically wrong and express regret for his participation therein.[1]   In Alabama, Arkansas and Mississippi works rather than professions were assumed as the proper test of political regeneration, and relief from disabilities was *ipso facto* secured to any one who had "openly advocated" or "voted for" or "aided in" the reconstruction and who accepted the equality of all men.   Most of the constitutions also authorized the legislatures, generally by extraordinary majority, to remove disabilities. The incorporation in the office-holder's oath of a clause expressing acceptance of "the civil and political equality of all men before the law" was a common feature of the new constitutions.   There was of course nothing of a proscriptive or stultifying character in this : for the phrase denoted legal obligation, not moral conviction, on the part of one who adopted it.

Alabama was the first of the states in which the work of the constitutional convention was concluded.   Between November 5, 1867, when the Alabama convention adjourned *sine die*, and May 15, 1868, when the draft of Mississippi's constitution was completed, all the other states save

---

[1] This adaptation of the theological doctrine of repentance and confession to the exigencies of political life need not be taken to signify a peculiarly keen moral and religious sense in Louisiana, as the history of her politics in the years immediately following very clearly shows.

Texas reached a like stage in the process of re-organization. The next step required by the Reconstruction Acts was the submission of each draft constitution to the registered voters of the state for ratification. For the purposes of this election the qualification of voters and the authority of the commanders [1] were the same as in the previous election. The contest throughout the South assumed a distinctly fiercer form during this second canvass. Race and class animosity had been whetted by the discussions centering about the conventions; the provisions of the new constitutions afforded definite issues on which party organizations, hitherto inchoate, were molded into efficiency; and the bearing of the results of the elections on national issues and on the outcome of the approaching Presidential canvass brought into play influences from without that in no way tended to allay the bitterness within the states.

Party lines, so far as they were drawn at all in the rebel states under the Presidential régime, followed *ante-bellum* prejudices. Though very energetic efforts were made in 1865–66 by the leaders of the National Republican Party to extend their organization throughout the South, the results were not satisfactory. Few Southern whites ventured to identify themselves with a name of such evil

[1] Except as to the date of the vote, which was fixed by the convention itself.

repute in their section, and so far as it achieved coherence at all the party consisted mainly of Northerners. The Democratic Party also failed to attract into full fellowship the leading Southerners. The white Unionists, who were most conspicuous in the political people and the state governments established under Presidential auspices, were mostly of Whiggish antecedents, and had supported Bell and Everett in 1860. To them Democracy meant in the South secessionism and in the North economic and political heresy. On the vital and pressing questions touching the status and the future of the freedmen opinion in the South was commonly classified as "radical" and "conservative," and these terms were assumed as the official titles of various organizations in the elections of 1866. In some states the name "Constitutional Union Party" was employed by the conservatives, suggesting the consciousness of affinity with the ideas represented by Bell and Everett in 1860. But upon the adoption by Congress of the policy expressed in the Reconstruction Acts a readjustment of opinion and organization began. Conservatives and Radicals at once put forth every effort to draw into their respective camps the freedmen, now the decisive factor in politics, but the success of the latter, prepared by the widespread formation of Union Leagues and by the teachings of the Freedmen's Bureau, was soon apparent to all. The Radical organizations, deserted by most of the Southern whites who had still clung to them, but swollen by the hosts of newly enfranchised freedmen, assumed everywhere the name of Republican and established relations with the national organization of that party. Among the Conservatives divided counsels for a time prevailed. Most were for opposing reconstruction *à l'outrance;* but some still hoped, by accepting negro suffrage, to preserve a control over the blacks, though without joining the Radical Party. This hope however, practically disappeared during the process of reconstruction, and the end of that process revealed in every state a coherent organization bearing the name and supporting the policy of the National Democratic Party. On the question of ratifying the constitutions framed by the conventions, party lines were perfectly clear, and party feeling was intensified in bitterness by the consciousness that the issue was indisputably that of race domination.

In view of the extreme feeling that prevailed, especially in the states whose new constitutions contained disfranchising provisions, the responsibility of the district commanders became exceedingly heavy as the elections approached. The letter of the law required that the military power should assure to every registered voter an opportunity to express his will. It was not difficult to construe the spirit of the law as requiring that the policy of Congress should not be allowed to fail

through the defeat of the constitutions.   Most of
the commanders maintained a rigorous adherence
to the letter of their authority, and in their regulations for the conduct of the elections displayed a
very high degree of practical wisdom.[1]   General
Pope, however, always inclined to radical measures,
infused into his orders for Alabama rather more of
the partisan spirit than the President was disposed
to put up with, and accordingly General Meade
was appointed to supersede him in January, 1868.
On two questions having an important partisan
bearing, General Pope had taken radical ground.
Election officers had been authorized to receive
the votes of persons who were not registered in
the precinct at which they offered to vote; and
voting for state officers was permitted at the same
time with the voting on the constitution.   Both
these expedients were in the interest of Republican success in the state, and both afforded great
facilities for fraud; but the first would enable very
many negroes to vote, who in the unsettled conditions of the time had changed their domicile since
registration, and the second would hasten the inauguration of the new régime.   The most serious
objection to the double elections lay in the fact

---

[1] *Cf.* especially the report of General Gillem on the election in
Mississippi, annexed to Report of Secretary of War for 1868.   The
excellent work in this case was the result of the lessons learned in
some very unfortunate experiences in Arkansas several months
earlier, on which, *cf.* same report.

that very many of the Republican candidates for office [1] were at the same time election officials, charged with the supervision of the vote in which they had so intimate an interest. [2] But General Pope had only anticipated a policy which was about to receive a high and conclusive endorsement.

The radical leaders in the Fortieth Congress were as watchful in the winter of 1867–68 as they had been in the preceding spring and summer for the promotion of their policy in the South. No point was to be lost that could contribute to the success of reconstruction. In view of recent successes of the Democrats in the North a Republican state more or less in the South might decide the next Presidential election. The chief uncertainty as to the outcome of the vote on ratifying the constitutions in the South turned upon the requirement that a majority of the registered voters should participate in the election in order that a result favorable to ratification should be valid. A bill to eliminate this requirement and make a majority of the persons voting sufficient to ratify, and also to authorize voting for state officers and congressmen at the same election, was passed by the House early in the session (Decem-

---

[1] The Republican state ticket was nominated by the constitutional convention, at the close of its official work.

[2] General Meade desired to separate the elections, but was discouraged by General Grant. *Cf.* correspondence, Report of Secretary of War, 1868, p. 84 *et seq.*

ber 18).   In the Senate the measure dragged
somewhat, apparently awaiting the outcome in
Alabama, where the election was set for February 4.   In that state the Conservative leaders
abandoned hope of defeating ratification by voting
against it, and adopted a formal policy of abstention.   An energetic campaign in this sense was successful.   The vote stood: for ratification, 70,812;
against ratification, 1005; total, 71,817, over 13,000
less than half the registration.[1]   The white vote
for the constitution was only 6702, as compared
with 18,553 in favor of the convention at the earlier
election.

The result in Alabama caused a real sensation
and much alarm among the friends of reconstruction.   There was no further delay in the Senate
as to the proposed modifications in the law.   The
bill was pressed with some vigor, in the hope that
it might become applicable to the election in Arkansas, which was fixed for March 13.   President
Johnson did not exhibit the same energy that
characterized Congress; he neither approved nor
vetoed the bill, and it only became law, by lapse
of time, on March 11.   At that date all the orders
for the Arkansas election had long been promulgated and the facilities for communication made
modifications impracticable.   Indeed the district

[1] Meade to Grant, Report of Secretary of War, 1868, p. 97.   A
revision of the registration in view of this election had afforded an
opportunity for material additions to the lists of qualified voters.

commander, General Gillem, was unaware of the
existence of the new law until after the election
had begun,[1] and accordingly the provision for voting in another precinct than that of registry was
not enforced. Elections for state officers, however, were held simultaneously, by ordinance of
the convention, the commander tolerating, but assuming no authority over them.[2] The result of
the vote on the constitution was close, the returns
showing a majority of 1316 for ratification, and a
total vote of 54,510 out of 73,784 registered voters.
The closeness of the vote gave great importance
to the somewhat startling fact that in one county
the vote exceeded the registration by 1195. Investigation revealed, however, that the registrars
in this and two other counties acted on unofficial
information that the act of March 11 had become
law, and received the votes of persons who claimed
to be registered in counties other than those in
which they offered to vote.

In the six other states which voted on their
constitutions during the spring and summer the
act of March 11 had full application, and in five of
them the results fulfilled the desires of those who
enacted it. During April and May the two Carolinas, Georgia, Louisiana and Florida ratified their

[1] Report of Secretary of War for 1868, p. 535.
[2] He declined to prohibit registrars from being candidates, on
the ground that he had nothing to do with state elections. Report
of Secretary of War, 1868, p. 548.

constitutions and simultaneously elected Republican state officers and congressmen. In Mississippi the Democrats entered upon a particularly
desperate campaign to defeat the constitution, and
though they were distinctly in a minority in the
registration,[1] they carried their point in the voting.
On June 22 the constitution was rejected by over
7000 majority, and at the same time the Democratic ticket for state offices was successful.

It is worthy of note that in all the states in
which the act of March 11 was operative at the
elections the vote for state officers and congressmen was cast, not by the electors qualified under
the new constitution, but by those registered under
the Reconstruction Acts.[2]   This was provided for
in the act of March 11.   The provision had dia-
metrically opposite effects according as the states
had or had not inserted severe disfranchising
clauses in their constitutions.   Where such disfranchisement existed, the effect was to install a
state government by vote of an electorate larger
than that under which the future government was
to be carried on.   Where there was no disfranchisement in the constitution, the smaller class of registered voters imposed their will at the outset on

[1] Address of Democratic Associations to the People. — Ann. Cyc.,
1868, p. 513.

[2] In some states this end was secured by the requirement that
the vote for state officers should be on the same ballot as that on
ratification.   *Cf.* constitution of Arkansas, schedule, secs. 2 and 3.
Poore, Charters and Constitutions, I, 152.

the larger class of citizens. It probably did not escape the notice of the framers of the act that the tendency of this provision would be to secure for the first official period and for the first Presidential election Republican control of such states as North Carolina and Georgia, where the very fact of a liberal suffrage clause created a presumption that the Democrats would normally rule.

Texas and Virginia failed to reach the conclusion of the process of reconstruction during the second session of the Fortieth Congress. In Virginia the convention completed the draft of a constitution early in April; but the Congressional appropriation had been exhausted and the commander possessed no funds with which to meet the expenses of the election on ratification. The convention set the third of June as the day for the election, but Congress only made the appropriation after that date had passed. Matters were thus at a standstill, as the only authority empowered by law to fix another date was the convention, which had gone out of existence. The commander referred the situation to Congress, but no action was taken.[1] In Texas the session of the convention was long and stormy. By the middle of August the $100,000 that had been advanced from the state treasury was spent, but the constitution was not completed. Any additional advance was refused by the district

[1] Report of Secretary of War, 1868, p. 320.

commander, on the ground that the "state of the treasury, the rate at which money is coming in, and the prospective current wants of the state" would not warrant it.[1] The convention accordingly took a recess, to await developments in connection with the special tax which it had levied.

As the net result of the first year's full operation of the Reconstruction Acts but six states out the ten were qualified for restoration to normal relations to the national government. In view of the manifestations of public opinion in the North against both military government and negro suffrage, the Republican leaders were anxious to have the whole matter off their hands before the Presidential election. By resort to methods of questionable regularity they were able to increase the number of restored states to seven, and on this record to go before the people. The triumph in the elections relieved the pressure for prompt action, and it was only after two additional years of military rule that the reconstruction of the remaining three states was complete.

III

Upon the ratification of constitutions in the rebel states the next step contemplated by the Reconstruction Acts was the approval of these constitutions by Congress and the formal declara-

[1] Ann. Cyc., 1868, p. 730.

tion by that body that the states concerned were entitled to representation. Section five of the act of March 23, 1867, was so worded as elaborately to safeguard the full discretion of· Congress at this decisive point. After declaring the duty of the President to transmit the ratified constitution to Congress, it continued :

And if it shall, moreover, appear to Congress that the election was one at which all the registered and qualified electors in the state had an opportunity to vote freely and without restraint, fear or the influence of fraud, and if the Congress shall be satisfied that such constitution meets the approval of a majority of all the qualified electors in the state, and if the said constitution shall be declared by Congress to be in conformity with the provisions of the act to which this is supplementary, and the other provisions of said act shall have been complied with, and the said constitution shall be approved by Congress, the state shall be declared entitled to representation, and senators and representatives shall be admitted therefrom as therein provided.

It is clear that to the framer of this section the danger to be particularly guarded against was that of overhasty admission. No mere perfunctory compliance with the Reconstruction Acts, but a substantial conformity to the policy they expressed, was to be exacted before the states were to be restored to full rights. In the spring of 1868, however, it was not haste but delay in restoration that was feared by the Republican leaders. The result of the vote on ratification in Alabama was a severe blow to their projects. It likewise gave much distress to the successful candidates for state offices who, through the failure of ratification, were debarred from assuming authority.   Complaints and petitions from the local leaders and consultations with the extremists in the House of Representatives led to the introduction of a bill by Mr. Stevens, March 10, 1868, providing for the admission of Alabama to full rights as a state.[1]   The bill merely declared that the constitution was satisfactory and had been voted for by a large majority of the legal voters voting at the election.   No reference was made to the requirement of the Reconstruction Acts that a majority of the registered voters should participate in the election.   No importance was assigned, in fact, to any of the elaborate conditions embodied in preceding legislation save one — that "Congress shall be satisfied that such constitution meets the approval of a majority of all the qualified electors in the state." Such approval was not demonstrated by the returns of the election; for the majority of the electors had expressed no opinion at all.   But the supporters of the bill contended that the failure of a majority to vote was satisfactorily accounted for by the intimidation of negroes by white employers, by frauds in registration and irregularities in the election, and particularly by the fact that a heavy storm on some of the days during which the election continued prevented many who wished to vote

---

[1] Cong. Globe, 2d sess., 40th Cong., p. 1790.

from going to the polls.[1] These allegations of intimidation and fraud, if not regarded as adequately
met by counter-allegations by the Democrats, obviously cast much discredit on the efficiency of the
military authorities;[2] and the argument from the
weather could hardly be taken seriously. It proved
impossible, therefore, at this time to get a majority
of the Republicans in the House to throw over-
board their earlier legislation, and the bill failed.[3]

Meanwhile the constitution of Arkansas had
been voted upon, with the result stated above.[4]
The irregularities connected with the voting there
were sufficient to prevent General Gillem from
making any announcement as to whether the ratification was or was not accomplished. His report
merely presented the facts and showed that the
number of votes tainted with irregularity was considerably greater than the majority for ratification.
Under the existing pressure for speedy restoration
it was not to be expected that Congress would
attach much importance to the doubts raised, es-

[1] Globe, 2d sess., 40th Cong., p. 1818 *et seq.*

[2] General Meade insisted, after " the most thorough investigation," that the constitution was fairly rejected under the law requiring a majority of the electors to vote. Report of Secretary of War,
1868, p. 76.

[3] It was transformed by the adoption of a substitute installing
the Republican state ticket voted for at the election, as a provisional
government for Alabama pending revision and resubmission of the
constitution. Globe, 2d sess., 40th Cong., p. 2216.

[4] *Supra,* p. 205.

pecially as, through the refusal of the Democrats to recognize the ordinance proclaiming elections for state officers, the Republican candidates had been returned as elected with but little opposition. A bill to restore Arkansas was passed by the House of Representatives on the eighth of May. The Senate proceeded with some deliberation, owing to suspicions that certain manifestations of haste were prompted by a desire for two additional votes on the pending impeachment trial.[1] After the conclusion of the trial progress was easy and the bill became law, over the President's veto, June 22. The provisions of the act included, first, a preamble declaring that the people of the state had adopted a constitution " which is republican," and that the legislature had ratified the proposed Fourteenth Amendment; second, a declaration that Arkansas " is entitled and admitted to representation as one of the states of the Union"; and third, a qualification of the foregoing declaration by this " fundamental condition " :

That the constitution of Arkansas shall never be so amended or changed as to deprive any citizen or class of citizens of the United States of the right to vote who are entitled to vote by the constitution herein recognized, except as a punishment for such crimes as are now felonies at common law, under laws equally applicable to all the inhabitants of said state; provided, that any alteration of said constitution prospective in its effect may be made in regard to the time and place of residence of voters.

[1] Cong. Globe, 2d sess., 40th Cong., p. 2437.

By virtue of this act Arkansas became at once a member of the Union in full standing. Her senators and representatives qualified on the following day,[1] and reconstruction was complete in one of the ten states. That the friends of negro suffrage felt little confidence in the permanency of their work, needs no stronger evidence than the drastic and unprecedented condition under which the first of the errant states was restored to the Union.

Only three days after the passage of the Arkansas bill Congress acted finally upon the other six states which had voted upon their constitutions. The bill for this purpose was reported from the House committee on reconstruction early in May. It was quite characteristic of that committee and its leader, Mr. Stevens, that with the other states to which the bill referred should be included Alabama, whose restoration the House had refused to sanction only six weeks earlier. Nothing whatever had occurred in the state itself to modify the reasoning on which the former action had been taken; but the parliamentary device of winning reluctant support for an obnoxious proposition by coupling it with a popular one was too well-tried and efficient to be omitted on an occasion like that at hand. The desired end was attained. After much debate, in which the circumstances of the elections in Alabama were

[1] McPherson, Reconstruction, pp. 347, 348.

threshed over again and again, the argument prevailed that that state should come in at the same
time with the rest, and that the allegation of
breach of faith ought not to carry much weight
when only rebels and traitors were aggrieved.   In
both House and Senate the motion to strike out
Alabama from the bill was lost.   Florida, also,
where the vote on ratification was later, was ultimately included in the bill, and it became law on
June 25.   The declaration of restoration and the
fundamental condition were identical with the
terms of the Arkansas bill.   In the preamble,
however, a difference was necessary : it could
not be declared that the legislatures had ratified
the Fourteenth Amendment; and the inclusion
of Alabama made impossible the simple affirmation that republican constitutions had been
adopted.[1]   Moreover, instead of going into effect
at once, the restoration was only to ensue upon
the ratification of the Fourteenth Amendment by
the legislatures ; and in the case of Georgia
upon the approval by its legislature of an additional fundamental condition, namely, that specified

---

[1] They were declared to have been adopted "by large majorities
of the votes cast at the elections held for the ratification or rejection
of the same."   This wording reflects the rather ridiculous tendency of
the extremists to ignore the notorious in the Alabama case, and to
declaim about the huge majority in that state for the constitution,
as if the size of the majority really expressed the triumph of those
who voted rather than that of those who abstained.

clauses of her new constitution, abolishing certain debts, should be null and void. The bill provided further that meetings of the legislatures should be promptly held to act upon the amendment.

By this legislation Congress was presumed to have completed its part in the reconstruction of six states, namely, North Carolina, South Carolina, Georgia, Florida, Alabama and Louisiana. It will be observed that the action of the national legislature did not correspond exactly with the requirements of the first Reconstruction Act. In this it was declared that admission to representation should only take place after the Fourteenth Amendment "shall have become a part of the constitution of the United States."[1] This requirement was dropped in the act of March 23, 1867, for the reason that the lawyers were unwilling or unable to agree as to whether the ratifications of the reconstructed states were necessary to the validity of that amendment. All agreed that those states should be obliged to ratify it, as a visible pledge and token of their reconstruction; but many held that the amendment became operative when approved by three-fourths of the states exclusive of those under military government. This vexatious point became of much importance at the conclusion of the process of reconstruction, through the bearing of that clause of the amendment which disqualified certain persons for

[1] Act of March 2, 1867, sec. 5.

state office.   The act restoring the six states contained a clause distinctly providing that no one
disqualified by the proposed amendment should
hold office under the states concerned.   The feeling which dictated this provision is made clear in
the incidents connected with the transition from
the military to the representative régime in the
various states.

IV

When once the elections had been held and a
body of Republican claimants for the state offices
had thereby been created, a readjustment of relations took place among the various elements of
authority in each state.   In their impatience to
assume power the Republicans tended to regard
the military as hostile to them, and to be somewhat captious in their judgments upon the conduct of the commanders.   On the other hand the
Democrats, who still had some shadow of official
power through the lingering remnants of the
Johnson governments, were disposed to regard
the prolongation of the military régime with much
complacency.   The commanders, for their part,
might well have conceived that the spirit of the
Reconstruction Acts justified the concession of
authority to the chosen representatives of the new
electors, but the letter of the law was explicit, that
military power should be supreme until an act of
Congress should declare the state entitled to rep-

resentation. In Alabama and Arkansas, where there was a long interval between the elections and action by Congress, the situation was particularly trying. The Republican members-elect of the respective legislatures assembled[1] and went through the form of organization. As their only claim to official character rested upon the new constitutions, which the commanders refused to consider as ratified, it was of course impossible for the commanders to recognize these assemblies. Under such circumstances it was not to be expected that the pretenders would receive much respect from the mass of the white citizens. In fact the existence of these pseudo-governments introduced a new element into the already serious problem of maintaining peace and order in the states. Ultimately the action of Congress validated the action of the Arkansas legislature in ratifying the Fourteenth Amendment;[2] but as to Alabama, all the proceedings of its legislature-elect antecedent to the act of June 25 were ignored.

The difficulties due to the cause just considered were of less importance in the other states, though they made themselves felt. In Louisiana, for instance, the eagerness of the new officials to begin

---

[1] In Alabama, they met in a newspaper office; in Arkansas, they broke into the legislative halls of the state capital. Ann. Cyc., 1868, pp. 16, 38.

[2] The preamble of the admitting act assumed that the amendment had been ratified.

their duties had to be sharply repressed by General Buchanan. But very troublesome to all the commanders were the questions that arose as to the qualifications and the method of installation of officers who were to assume power under the new constitutions. The situation was a very puzzling one. As prerequisite to restoration the legislature of each state must ratify the Fourteenth Amendment. The organization of the legislature must accord with the new constitution, which in some states required the participation of governor and lieutenant-governor; hence these officials must qualify. But the new constitution could not be considered as in force until after the action on the Fourteenth Amendment. Until such action was complete, the Reconstruction Acts retained their full authority, and the military commander was paramount ruler.

The difficulty here indicated was overcome through that provision of the act of March 2, 1867, which declared that until the admission of representatives to Congress, any civil government existing in the rebel states should "be deemed provisional only." On the basis of this clause the policy was devised of regarding the legislature-elect and the executive officials necessary to its action as provisional in character, and as the creatures, so to speak, of the military commanders. By the orders of the generals the persons hitherto acting as governors in the two Carolinas and in Louisiana were removed, and the governors-elect were appointed in their places. The acts necessary to the transition from the military to the civil régime were thus performed by the holders of authority under both, and conflict was avoided.

But the more fundamental problem as to qualifications for office at once assumed formidable dimensions. Three conflicting factors entered into the situation — the state constitutions, the proposed Fourteenth Amendment and the Reconstruction Acts. The state constitutions required of legislators and officers various qualifications and oaths, some more rigorous than what was required by the Fourteenth Amendment. This latter disqualified for office in the states those who, after taking oath to support the constitution, had gone into rebellion. Normally, then, the new state officers and legislators would conform to the qualifications prescribed by the state constitutions, provided these excluded such persons as were excluded by the Fourteenth Amendment. But as we have seen, the officers and legislators installed before the full restoration had to be regarded as "provisional"; and section nine of the act of July 19, 1867, required that "all persons hereafter elected or appointed to office in said military districts" should take the iron-clad oath.[1] Relatively few of the officers-elect could honestly take this oath,[2] and it early

[1] *Ante*, p. 184, note.
[2] In practice it seems to have been assumed that every negro

became a serious question as to whether it or the oath prescribed by the state constitutions was to be exacted from those who took part in the proceedings preliminary to full restoration. The military commanders, after referring the matter to headquarters, proceeded on the more moderate theory that the officials elected under the new constitutions were not officials of " provisional governments" in the meaning of the Reconstruction Acts,[1] and therefore need not take the "iron-clad oath." This was probably an equitable interpretation of the law, but it was quite inconsistent with the theory on which was based the action of the legislature in transacting business before the restoration of the state.[2] The interpretation was rejected by the Republican officials in Louisiana, who, in spite of the orders of the commander, attempted to exclude the Democratic members of the legislature by requiring the test oath. A serious disturbance became imminent before the recalcitrant majority finally gave way.[3]

Another difficult question, related to the foregoing, was as to the authority of the commanders to pass upon the qualifications of the individual

could take this oath, though such an assumption was irreconcilable with notorious facts as to the conduct and sympathies of the blacks during hostilities.

[1] *Cf.* House Ex. Doc., No. 276, 2d sess., 40th Cong.

[2] General Meade distinguished between officers and legislators, and thought the latter might be required to take the test oath. *Ibid.*

[3] Ann. Cyc., 1868, p. 434.

members of a legislature when that body assembled. It was generally conceded that by force of either the Fourteenth Amendment or the provisions of the admission act of June 25, 1868, no person disqualified by the amendment was eligible to the state legislature. But much depended upon the ground chosen as the basis of ineligibility. If disqualification was based upon the amendment, the capacity of members must be determined by the normal methods of constitutional and parliamentary procedure; if upon the act of Congress, the military commander must determine the matter and, in pursuance of his duty to enforce the law, must, upon the assembling of the legislature, " purge " that body of disqualified persons. In several of the states, where the creation or increase of a Republican majority was deemed important, the newly elected state officers were eager for the use of the latter method. But grave doubts as to the policy of such a proceeding appeared on the surface. To set up a major-general as final judge of membership in a representative assembly whose electorate had been so carefully constructed and so elaborately protected in its action, would reflect seriously on the fundamental principles of reconstruction. The commanders themselves had no stomach for so invidious a duty. Accordingly, with the approval of leading members of the majority in Congress,[1] they confined themselves to pointing out the

[1] *Cf.* Report of Secretary of War, 1868, vol. i, p. 78.

test of eligibility to the legislatures and calling upon
the respective houses to apply this test in exercising their constitutional control over the elections,
qualifications and returns of their members.   This
solution, again, was hardly to be reconciled with
any clear-cut theory of reconstruction.   It was the
outcome of expediency rather than logic.   In the
case of one state, Georgia, logic asserted itself later
in a somewhat startling manner.

For the six states affected by the act of June 25,
the month of July, 1868, brought the formal conclusion of the process of reconstruction.   Legislatures met and ratified the Fourteenth Amendment;
recently chosen governors and other officers were
installed with the usual ceremonies; and on receipt
of official notice that the amendment had been
ratified in each state, the respective district commanders issued orders declaring that military government under the Reconstruction Acts had ceased.
Legislative and administrative routine was at once
assumed by the regular organs of the states, and the
cases pending in the military tribunals were turned
over to the ordinary courts.   At the same time the
two houses of Congress fulfilled their duty by admitting to seats the representatives and senators from
the reconstructed states.   Before the close of the
session all the six states had members at work in
the House, and all but Georgia in the Senate.

The state last named had, as we have seen,
required exceptional treatment in the restoring

act of June 25. Circumstances conspired to continue the special character of her reconstruction. Of all the states she alone had returned a Conservative or Democratic majority [1] in her legislature; but the governor-elect, Bullock, was a Republican. In the prevailing condition of political feeling, friction between executive and legislative departments was inevitable. It made its appearance during the transition from military to regular government. The governor-elect had and expressed very strong convictions on the questions noticed above as to the qualifications of members of the legislature that performed the acts preliminary to restoration. He believed that the iron-clad oath was the legal test of eligibility, and he strongly urged General Meade to exclude at least certain members whom the governor considered ineligible under the Fourteenth Amendment.[2] As committees of the houses reported that all the members were eligible, and as Bullock's aspirations for a United States senatorship seemed to influence his opinions,[3] the general declined to act on the governor's suggestion. In consequence of this initial incident relations between the governor and the majority in the legislature were greatly strained after mili-

[1] The Senate was evenly divided between the parties, 22 members each; the lower house stood Democrats 102, Republicans 73. Ann. Cyc., 1868, p. 312.

[2] The correspondence is given in Sen. Ex. Doc., No. 13, 2d sess. 41st Cong., p. 69 *et seq.*

[3] Meade to Grant. Doc. last cited, p. 50.

tary rule was withdrawn. United States senators were elected July 29, after Congress had ceased work for the summer, but Bullock was not chosen.

Later in the session the legislature recurred to the question of eligibility of members, but from a new point of view. Taking advantage of a loophole left by the framers of the constitution, the majority decided that negroes were ineligible to any office in the state, and forthwith unseated all the blacks in both houses, twenty-seven in number. This proceeding was doubtless gratifying to the hot partisan spirit of the day, but it was not judicious. It gave to the governor a weapon that he was prompt to use. The Democratic leaders in the state had doubtless supposed that their immunity from further action by Congress was complete. But when the credentials of the Georgia senators were presented, at the meeting of Congress in December, objection was promptly made to their acceptance.[1] Radical senators declared that the act of the legislature in expelling the negro members was good ground for refusing to recognize the state as restored to normal relations. Governor Bullock submitted a paper reciting his views as to the qualifications of members of the legislature and assuming that his own tenure, as well as that of every other member of the state government, was still only provisional. Though moderate senators protested against delay, the desired

[1] Cong. Globe, 3d sess., 40th Cong., p. 2 *et seq.*

impression was made by the radicals and the formal act that would have made incontestable the full restoration of the state was prevented. The senators-elect were not permitted to take their seats, and thus a slight, but as circumstances proved a sufficient, foundation was secured for the theory that Georgia was still in the class of states in which the process of reconstruction was incomplete.

V

The point now reached marks an epoch in the process of reconstruction. A variety of events combined to change the conditions under which the process was to be completed in the four states that were still unrestored. In the first place, the Fourteenth Amendment had become formally a part of the constitution. On July 20, 1868, Secretary Seward, after receiving notice of ratification by the reconstructed legislatures,[1] issued his proclamation announcing that the amendment was in force. The secretary's document was a unique production, ingeniously devised to avoid recognition of the reconstructed legislatures as lawful,[2] and expressly reserving judgment as to the validity

[1] Except that of Georgia, which ratified later.
[2] It was declared that the article had been ratified by the legislatures of twenty-three specified states, and in six states by "newly constituted and newly established bodies avowing themselves to be, and acting as, the legislatures."

of rescinding acts passed after ratification in **New Jersey** and Ohio; but Congress immediately by concurrent resolution made short work of Mr. Seward's scruples and declared the new article part of the constitution.[1] In the second place, the issue of reconstruction had again been fought out in a general election, and the Republicans had decisively won. By the voting of November, 1868, the future control of the executive as well as the legislative department at Washington was assured to the friends of Congress' policy, and it was a source of much satisfaction that of Grant's 214 electoral votes, forty-one came from states lately in rebellion.[2] Harmonious relations and an identical policy on the part of President and Congress must necessarily modify the conduct of reconstruction after March 4, 1869; but probably quite as great a modifying influence was exerted by the fact that two of the reconstructed states, Louisiana and Georgia, chose Democratic electors in November.

A third element of novelty in the general situation was a change of attitude by the Republican Party as to negro suffrage. Certain manifestations of Northern sentiment on this topic had given much concern to the Republican leaders in the Presidential campaign. Four important states,

---

[1] McPherson, History of the Reconstruction, p. 380.

[2] Virginia, Mississippi and Texas of course did not take part in the election.

Ohio, Michigan, Minnesota and Kansas, had refused to extend the right of voting to the blacks, while manifesting entire sympathy with the Congressional policy of reconstruction. It was the condition of feeling thus indicated that found expression in the national platform:

The guarantee by Congress of equal suffrage to all loyal men at the South was demanded by every consideration of public safety, of gratitude and of justice, and must be maintained; while the question of suffrage in all the loyal states properly belongs to the people of these states.[1]

But the flush of victory actually achieved quickly banished from further consideration the policy foreshadowed by this declaration. That the permanency of what reconstruction had effected in the South was insecure, was made very obvious by the fact of Democratic victory in Georgia and Louisiana. The "fundamental conditions" which afforded the only basis for Congressional maintenance of negro suffrage in the restored states were regarded by a large majority of constitutional lawyers in both parties as of doubtful validity. Under the circumstances a further amendment to the constitution was the only resort that could be depended upon for the end desired. Hence the Fifteenth Amendment was, after a long and ardent discussion of the whole field of political phi-

[1] Ann. Cyc., 1868, p. 744.

losophy, sent to the state legislatures by resolution finally passed February 26, 1869. The pendency of this amendment had, as will soon appear, a most important influence on the conclusion of reconstruction in the last four states.

Finally, the actual working of the reconstructed governments during the first few months of their existence had suggested, if it had not clearly revealed, the inability of those governments to stand alone. The withdrawal of military government had been followed in most of the states by disturbances which, whatever their source and magnitude, — and both were the subject of vehement partisan dispute, — led to anxious appeals by the state authorities for military aid from the United States.[1] It was in connection with the elections that the disorders assumed the most serious character. The Ku Klux Klan, conspicuous for some time in Tennessee, had begun to manifest its terrorizing features in various other states. Louisiana was believed to have been carried by the Democrats in the Presidential election wholly through fraud and violence.[2] All these facts conspired to intensify the zeal of the Republicans for stringent methods in completing reconstruction. The obvious danger to party supremacy where *a priori* such supremacy was to be expected revived the flagging interest in the process. In-

---

[1] Report of Secretary of War, 1868, p. xviii *et seq.*
[2] Blaine, Twenty Years of Congress, II, 409.

stead of the mere eagerness to get rid of the whole
subject, which had been apparent in 1868, there
became conspicuous in the following year a resolute purpose to make every possible point for
effective and permanent Republican control in the
remaining states.

The final session of the Fortieth Congress, in
the winter of 1868–69, produced no legislation
designed to hasten the admission of the states
still unrestored. On the other hand the long-
standing demand of the Radicals for control of the
state offices was gratified by an act requiring the
commanders in Virginia, Mississippi and Texas to
remove all incumbents who could not take the
iron-clad oath and to replace them by persons who
could take it.[1] Moreover, the process of removing the disabilities imposed by the Fourteenth
Amendment began to appear prominently in the
work of Congress, and the methods by which the
grant of relief was carried on [2] left no doubt as
to the tendency of the process to aid the Radicals in both reconstructed and unreconstructed
states.

Meanwhile the problem as to the next steps to
be taken in the three states mentioned above had
been the subject of intense controversy both within

---

[1] Became law without the President's approval, Feb. 6, 1869.
Cong. Globe, 3d sess., 40th Cong., Appendix, p. 327.

[2] *Cf.* Globe, 3d sess., 40th Cong., p. 1712 *et seq.*, esp. remarks
of Tipton and Howard; also remarks of Beck, p. 1888.

the states themselves and in the room of the committee on reconstruction at the Capitol. In Mississippi and in Virginia the stringent disfranchising and test-oath clauses of the constitutions had caused a distinct split of the Republican state organizations. The radical wing in Mississippi demanded the admission of the state under the constitution as it stood, on the ground that its rejection in the previous election had been effected by fraud and violence. The conservative wing, on the other hand, were ready for resubmission of the constitution to the people, with a separate vote on the obnoxious disfranchising clauses, to which the previous failure of ratification seemed to be chiefly due. In Virginia the Republicans divided on similar lines; and in both states the Democrats abandoned a distinct policy and coalesced with the conservative Republicans in the movement for separate submission of the disabling clauses. The Texas convention reassembled and completed a constitution during the winter of 1868–69; but here also the Republicans were split into factions, and political conditions, like social conditions, in the state were chaotic.[1] Under all the circumstances the task of the military commanders in maintaining some semblance of governmental authority became increasingly burdensome, and their difficulties were enhanced by the require-

[1] *Cf.* Ann. Cyc., 1869, p. 671 *et seq.* Also Report of Secretary of War, 1868, p. 704.

ment of a "clean sweep" in the offices, which was imposed by the action of Congress in February.[1]

It was not until after the inauguration of the new administration that definitive action was taken to put an end to the existing situation. By act of April 10, 1869, Congress authorized the submission of the constitutions in the three states to popular vote. The change wrought by the installation of President Grant was manifested in the fact that the administration of the law was entrusted, not to the district commanders, as in previous acts, but to the President; and even more in the provision by which Congress evaded entirely the troublesome question as to a separate vote on test oath and disfranchisement, by leaving the matter to the President's discretion.[2] The passage of the act had indeed been due to a recommendation of the President in a special message of April 7,[3] in which he had indicated both his desire to promote the admission of Virginia and Mississippi, and his conviction that a separate vote on the obnoxious clauses should be permitted. By far the most striking innovation embodied in the act, however, was the requirement that, as a condition precedent to restoration, each state should

---

[1] In Virginia, 5176 offices were vacated under this law, of which 2814 were still vacant on October 1. Report of Secretary of War, 1869, p. 111; *cf.* for Texas, p. 145.

[2] The act is in McPherson, Reconstruction, p. 408.

[3] *Ibid.*, p. 417.

ratify the Fifteenth Amendment.   The fairness
and justice of imposing a new condition at this
late stage in reconstruction — a condition that
seven of the states had escaped — were seriously
doubted by many Republicans and were strenuously denied by the Democrats;[1] but the contest
over the amendment in Northern legislatures was
looming fierce and doubtful,[2] and the opportunity
to insure three states in the affirmative could not
be lost.   It was quite probable that these states
would have ratified the amendment voluntarily,
and the chief significance of the Congressional
action lay in the triumph of a radical program.
The strength secured to radical sentiment by the
admission of the states already reconstructed is
illustrated by the fact that in the Senate eight of
the members from those states voted for the new
condition and but one against it.

Under the authority of the act just considered
elections were held in Virginia July 6, and in Mississippi and Texas November 30.   In the first two
states the President exercised the discretion conferred upon him by submitting to separate votes
the disabling clauses.   The results justified the

---

[1] *Cf.* debate in Senate, Globe, 1st sess., 41st Cong., p. 654 *et seq.*

[2] In Indiana the Democratic members of the legislature, to prevent action by the Republican majority, resigned in a body and destroyed the quorum.   Ann. Cyc., 1869, p. 356 *et seq.*   The use of such
methods against the amendment was held to justify extraordinary
procedure in its favor.   *Cf.* Morton in Globe, 1st sess., 41st Cong.,
p. 654.

pledges made by the Conservatives; for in both states, while the rest of the constitutions were ratified almost without opposition, the obnoxious clauses were defeated by decisive majorities. The Texas convention had embodied no disfranchisement in the constitution, and the instrument as a whole was ratified. Elections were held in all three states for state officers and congressmen, and in all three the contest was between Radicals and Conservatives, the Democrats abandoning any distinctive organization. The result was victory for the Conservatives in Virginia and for the Radicals in the other two states. On the question of eligibility to the legislature in Virginia, General Canby, then commanding in the state, excited some commotion by arguing away the precedents established in the states earlier admitted [1] and ruling that the iron-clad oath must be taken by members before taking their seats. [2] President Grant, however, clung to the opinion which he had formed as General of the Army, that only the oath required by the state constitution was necessary, and this view was fortified by Attorney-General Hoar in a formal opinion. Though the act of July 19, 1867, forbade district commanders to be bound in their action by "any opinion of any civil officer of the United States,"

[1] *Ante*, p. 220.

[2] All the documents connected with this incident are in Sen. Ex. Doc., No. 13, 2d sess., 41st Cong.

the "spirit of the Reconstruction Acts" very clearly justified the interpretation of this clause as meaning President Johnson's attorney-general and not President Grant's. Accordingly the iron-clad oath was not required of the members of the legislature. The commanding general did, however, look very carefully after the qualification of members of the legislature under the Fourteenth Amendment, and excluded from their seats several persons whom he regarded as ineligible.

When Congress reassembled in December, 1869, it was informed by the President, in his annual message, that Virginia had conformed to all the requirements of the Reconstruction Acts and that her legislature had "abstained from all doubtful authority"; the prompt admission of her senators and representatives was therefore recommended. The President had committed himself definitely from the beginning of his term to the support of the Conservatives in Virginia, and their triumph in the election had pleased him. In Congress, however, a strong element of the Republicans sympathized with the Radicals, and regarded the result of the election as expressing the failure of the whole reconstruction. A vigorous opposition was made, therefore, to immediate action on Virginia. It was urged that the abuses of power which were alleged against the Conservatives in Georgia would be repeated by the Virginia Conservatives. The pressure of the administration,

however, meant much at this time: where Johnson's urging admission would have insured the
exclusion of the state, Grant's had a different
result. The bill for the restoration of Virginia
became law on the 26th of January, 1870. It
bore the impress of the opposition, however, in
the form of conditions, both precedent and subsequent, that considerably exceeded in severity those
imposed upon the states earlier restored. It was
first required that every member of the legislature
should, as a condition of taking his seat, subscribe
to an oath to the effect either that he was not disqualified by the Fourteenth Amendment, or that
his disability had been removed by Congress.
Then, as fundamental conditions upon the state's
admission, it was prescribed first, as in case of the
former states, that the constitution should never
be so amended as to deprive of the suffrage any
persons on whom it was bestowed therein; second,
that the state should never "deprive any citizen
of the United States, on account of his race, color
or previous condition of servitude, of the right to
hold office," or "upon any such ground" impose
discriminating qualifications for office; and third,
that the constitution should never be so amended
as to "deprive any citizen or class of citizens of
the United States of the school rights and privileges secured by the constitution of said state."
The second of these provisions very obviously bore
upon such proceedings as those of the Georgia

legislature in ousting its negro members; the last
condition was suggested by an issue that had
played a large part in the Virginia campaign, and
in connection with which the triumph of the Conservatives was alleged to forebode the denial of
free education to the blacks.   Both these new conditions were antagonized by many Republicans as
unconstitutional and as involving breach of the
faith pledged in the act laying down the terms of
restoration.   But the arguments once more prevailed that the guarantee of a republican form of
government involved Congressional control of both
qualifications for office and general education; and
that the breaking of faith, even if it were fairly
chargeable, need not signify much with a people
who had put rebels in power.

On the day after the approval by the President
of the act just described, orders were issued by
General Canby terminating military government
in Virginia and the reconstruction of the state was
formally complete.   Mississippi and Texas meanwhile had conformed to the transitional requirements, following closely the lines laid down in
Virginia, and Congress enacted their restoration in
terms identical with those of the Virginia act.
Some effort was made to relax the severity of the
fundamental conditions, on the ground that the
victory of the Radicals in the two states removed
all fear of improper proceedings, and that no issue
existed as to school privileges.   The extremists in

Congress persisted, however, in retaining the Virginia form, and in some cases made no concealment of a conscious and deliberate purpose to fix thus an interpretation upon the national constitution that should vastly enlarge the powers of Congress.[1] The Mississippi bill became law on the 23d of February, and the Texas bill on the 30th of March. Military rule was at once withdrawn and the states assumed their normal condition.

VI

At the beginning of April, 1870, of the ten commonwealths whose reconstruction had been undertaken by Congress Georgia alone was unrestored to the full enjoyment of state autonomy. The situation of the state in December, 1868, has already been described.[2] She had been by act of June 25 declared entitled to representation in Congress upon the performance of certain acts by her legislature; these acts had been performed, military government had been withdrawn from the state, and her representatives had been admitted to the lower house in Congress. On this condition of the facts the legal status of Georgia as a state of the Union appeared pretty well established.

[1] *Cf.* debates on Virginia and Mississippi bills, *passim*, in Globe, 2d sess., 41st Cong., esp. remarks of Morton, Howard, Drake and Sumner in the Senate.

[2] *Ante*, p. 224 *et seq.*

The Senate, however, had refused to admit her members to their seats. During the winter the question of her status required an answer in connection with the count of the electoral votes for President and Vice-President. Georgia had chosen Democratic electors, but the result of the election was not sufficiently close to be affected by their nine votes. Republican opinion in Congress as to the treatment of Georgia was as yet too indeterminate to warrant a solution of the whole problem at this time.[1] Accordingly the issue was avoided by the device of the "alternative count," the president of the Senate declaring the number of votes both including and excluding Georgia, and announcing the election of Grant and Colfax in either case.[2] But there was abundant evidence presented in the course of this session that the ultimate settlement of the state's condition would be on radical lines.

After the installation of the new administration the influences which have been described as affecting reconstruction worked with especial force in respect to Georgia. In the organization of the new House of Representatives a technical irregularity that was discovered in the credentials of her

[1] Remarks of Edmunds, Globe, 3d sess., 40th Cong., p. 976.

[2] It illustrates the anomaly of the general situation that in the House the names of the Georgia members appear in the votes bearing on the status of the state. Most of these members were Republicans, and voted against counting Georgia's electoral vote.

members afforded an opportunity for refusing to seat them.[1] The participation of members from the state in the determination of the state's right to have members was thus obviated. Soon afterward the radical plan for dealing with Georgia was revealed in a bill introduced by General Butler, the worthy successor of Thaddeus Stevens at the head of the committee on reconstruction. In the preamble to this bill the basis for Congressional action as to the state was laid in three leading assertions: first, that the legislature had violated the Fourteenth Amendment by failing to exclude persons disqualified thereunder; second, that the majority of the legislature had violated the constitution of the United States, the constitution of Georgia and the fundamental principles of the Reconstruction Acts by expelling the negro members; and third, that the local authorities of the state were unwilling or unable to protect loyal citizens from violence.[2] The bill then provided that the governor should re-convene the members of the legislature as originally elected, purge it of all who could not or would not subscribe to a designated oath, based on the Fourteenth Amendment, and retain the negroes; and that the military forces of the United States should be subject to the governor's call for aid in the administration of government and the protection of life and property.

[1] Globe, 1st sess., 41st Cong., p. 16 *et seq.*
[2] *Ibid.*, p. 591.

Republican sentiment, practically harmonious as to the necessity of some punishment of the Georgia Conservatives, was seriously divided as to the basis for the desired action by Congress. The record of acts, both legislative and executive, through which the national government had acknowledged to Georgia the full character and rights of a state seemed to many complete and unassailable; and under such circumstances the assumption by Congress of control over the organization of the legislature or over the administration of justice was wholly without constitutional warrant. On the other hand stood the fact that the Senate had not admitted the Georgians to their seats, and that, therefore, by the merest shade the restoration of the state might be regarded as not complete. Until every least step in the process laid down in the Reconstruction Acts had been taken, "any civil governments which may exist therein [in the several states] shall be deemed provisional only, and in all respects subject to the paramount authority of the United States."[1] Strictly considered, thus, the government of Georgia might still be held provisional. But so fine-spun a theory was not deemed necessary by all the Republicans. It was argued by some that the state of Georgia, whether the existing authorities were provisional or permanent, had not a republican form of government. This was evident not only in the exclusion

[1] Act of March 2, 1867, sec. 6.

of a large part of the population from the freeman's right to hold office, but also in the substantial denial of protection of life and property to an equally large class. It was the constitutional duty of Congress to see that a republican form of government existed in every state, and in fulfillment of that duty the assumption of control in Georgia was justifiable. But even more conclusive, if possible, was the right to enforce the Fourteenth Amendment in Georgia. There could be no pretense, it was held, that the disqualifications for office-holding imposed by that amendment were respected by the legislature, or that the equal protection of the laws was given to blacks as the amendment required. It was the duty of Congress to enforce the provisions of this amendment, and the purging of the legislature and the maintenance of order by the military power were necessary and proper means for the performance of this duty.

The House of Representatives did not act finally on General Butler's bill in the spring of 1869. Before the next meeting of Congress the supreme court of Georgia, on a test case brought before it, decided that under the constitution and laws of the state negroes had the right to hold office.[1] There had been a general understanding that the majority in the legislature would be guided by the opinion of the court, though there was of course no obligation upon them in this respect. In view

[1] The opinions are given in McPherson, Reconstruction, p. 466.

of what was threatened when Congress should meet, the Conservatives petitioned Governor Bullock to summon a special session of the legislature, and give it an opportunity to re-seat the colored members. The governor, however, refused. Meanwhile the President had caused General Terry to investigate thoroughly the stories of extensive outrages upon freedmen and white Republicans in the state. The general in his report [1] represented the conditions throughout the state to be most deplorable, chiefly through the activity of the Ku Klux Klans, and gave his opinion that the interposition of the national government was indispensable to the protection of life and property. The report of General Terry doubtless had considerable influence in neutralizing the effect produced by the decision of the court in the matter of office-holding; it strengthened the feeling that some action by Congress was imperative to break the spirit of the old rebel element in Georgia.

When Congress assembled in December, 1869, President Grant, in his annual message, suggested the prompt passage of an act requiring the reorganization of the Georgia legislature. Congress conformed to the suggestion, and an act " to promote the reconstruction of the state of Georgia " became law on the 22d. There was still much reluctance manifested by moderate Republicans as to supporting the measure, but among the con-

[1] Sen. Ex. Doc., No. 3, 2d sess., 41st Cong.

siderations of expediency which had been adduced, that of securing the ratification of the Fifteenth Amendment was now urged with especial insistency. It was perfectly understood that the immediate outcome of interference by Congress would be the substitution of a Republican for a Democratic majority in the legislature. The legislature had in March, 1869, rejected the Fifteenth Amendment; with a reversal of the majority the state could be transferred to the list of those ratifying. By December, 1869, twenty-two states had ratified; but of these there was doubt as to the validity of the act in Indiana and Missouri, and New York had since elected a Democratic legislature, which was likely to rescind the state's ratification. From this showing it could be argued that only nineteen ratifications were already sure. Twenty-eight were necessary. Of the additional nine Ohio's newly elected Republican legislature would doubtless reverse the action of its Democratic predecessor and ratify, and favorable action by Mississippi and Texas was insured by the terms of the act providing for their restoration. Beyond these but five states remained whose legislatures were Republican, and a sixth was obviously necessary.[1] Accordingly a clause was added to the bill dealing with Georgia requiring ratification of the Fifteenth Amendment

[1] As a matter of fact, Missouri healed the defect in her action by a subsequent vote, and that in Indiana was disregarded. *Cf.*, for the whole matter, McPherson, Reconstruction, pp. 488, 545, 557.

before her representatives should be admitted to Congress. With the addition of this provision and the omission of the preamble, the act as passed was substantially the same as the House bill described above.

In accordance with the provisions of this law the process of re-reconstruction of Georgia was carried through in the first half of 1870.[1] The governor proceeded in January to reorganize the legislature, but his methods excited such vigorous opposition that the military power had to be promptly called in. In view of the situation the orders of July, 1868, withdrawing military government from Georgia were countermanded, and General Terry was endowed with all the powers of commander of a military district under the Reconstruction Acts. The general assumed charge of the purging of the legislature. Disputed questions as to the eligibility of members-elect under the Fourteenth Amendment and the acts of Congress were decided by a committee of officers appointed by the commander,[2] and twenty-four Democrats were excluded from their seats. Following the example of the majority that excluded the negroes in 1868, the Republican majority now filled the vacant seats with the candidates who had been defeated in the elections, and by the end of

[1] A good sketch of the process is in Ann. Cyc., 1870, *sub voc.* "Georgia."

[2] *Cf.* House Ex. Doc., No. 82, 2d sess., 41st Cong.

January the legislature was pronounced good by General Terry. It then ratified the Fourteenth and Fifteenth Amendments (the former by way of special caution lest the earlier ratification should be tainted with the defects of the legislature that enacted it), elected Republicans to claim seats in the Senate at Washington, and then ceased further activity until Congress should declare the state restored.

The declaration by Congress was slow in forthcoming. The proceedings in the organization of the legislature had been of a character to disgust many of the strongest supporters in Congress of the act under which it had been effected. Discreditable personal motives had been either clearly revealed or strongly suggested in connection with official acts of the state administration, and the methods of commanding general, governor and majority in the legislature were all alike condemned as unlawful by the judiciary committee of the Senate.[1] The Republican majority in Congress was divided on the precise status of the state, one faction holding that the existing government was provisional and fully subject to the will of Congress, the other holding that since the restoring act of June 25, 1868, the state government thereby recognized had been a permanent and regular state government save as to the defect in membership of the legislature, which had been

[1] Sen. Rep., No. 58, 2d sess., 41st Cong.

corrected through the act of December 22, 1869.
An immediate practical importance was given to
the disputed point by the fact that its settlement
involved the continuance or cessation of Governor
Bullock's control of the state government in
Georgia. Party lines in the state had been so
affected by the governor's conduct of affairs that
the only division playing an important rôle was
that into "Bullock men" and "anti-Bullock men."
Under such circumstances the moderate Republicans in Congress thought it best to drop all interference with the state as quickly as possible, and in
such manner as not to appear to favor any personal
interest; the radicals were disposed to prolong to
the utmost the dominance of the "Bullock men,"
who were on the whole most likely to maintain
Republican party ideas. From February to July
the bill to pronounce Georgia restored was the subject of a most obstinate contest in both houses.
To the aid of the radical wing of the Republicans
came the increasing prominence of the Ku Klux
operations in Georgia and other Southern states.
But with Democratic aid the moderates held their
own, though the bill which at last became law on
July 15 contained no definite settlement of the
most hotly contested points.

This act merely recited the ratification of the
Fourteenth and Fifteenth Amendments, and declared Georgia entitled to representation in Congress. It left entirely undetermined the precise

status of the existing government in the state. An attempt on the part of the Bullock party to prolong its lease of power by assuming that the provisional character of the government only ceased after the passage of the act of July 15, was frowned upon by the national administration,[1] and was therefore abandoned. Members from Georgia were admitted to both House and Senate at the next session of Congress, the Senate fighting over again the issues of the state's status in connection with the credentials of her senators. By finally seating those who were elected in July, 1868, the one house of Congress seems to have declared that Georgia had been a state in full standing from before that date. The course of the executive in exercising military power in the state in 1870 cannot be reconciled with this view. But whatever the solution of the problem may be, from the seating of her members in the Forty-first Congress, there was no longer doubt that the reconstruction of Georgia was complete.

VII

The reconstruction of the Southern states, by the process which we have followed above, is one of the most remarkable achievements in the history of government. As a demonstration of political and administrative capacity, it is no less con-

---

[1] Ann. Cyc., 1870, p. 338.

vincing than the subjugation of the Confederate armies as an evidence of military capacity. The Congressional leaders — Trumbull, Fessenden, Stevens, Bingham and others — who practically directed the process of reconstruction, were men of as rugged a moral and intellectual fiber as Grant, Sherman and the other officers who crushed the material power of the South. The obstacles to success were as great for the one set of men as for the other. In the path of reconstruction lay a hostile white population in the South, a hostile executive at Washington, a doubtful if not decidedly hostile Supreme Court, a divided Northern sentiment in respect to negro suffrage and an active and skillfully directed Democratic Party. Yet the process as laid out in 1867 was carried through to its completion. With much the feelings of the prisoner of tradition who watched the walls of his cell close slowly in from day to day to crush him, the Southern whites saw in the successive developments of Congress' policy the remorseless approach of negro rule. The fate of the Southern whites, like that of the prisoner of tradition, may excite our commiseration; but the mechanism by which the end was achieved must command an appreciation on its merits.

From a constitutional point of view, the actual conduct of the reconstruction has no particular interest. The power of the national government to impose its will upon the rebel states, irrespective of any restriction as to means, was assumed when the first Reconstruction Act was passed, and this assumption was acted upon to the end. Only in connection with the relations between legislature and executive were important issues raised during the process, and these are not within the scope of this essay.

It is from the political point of view that the process of reconstruction is most interesting to the historical observer. Given the end, there is some-thing refreshingly efficient in the means employed to achieve it. Wide and deep divergencies of opin-ion there were in the Republican majority in Con-gress; but they were fought out and settled in the party caucus; the capacity for discipline, which is the surest evidence of political wisdom under party government, manifested itself in a high degree; and the measures that determined the fate of the South rolled inexorable as the decrees of Provi-dence from the two-thirds votes of House and Senate. Was a restrictive construction of a law devised by clever lawyers, new legislation promptly overruled it. Was the authority of the attorney-general invoked on the side of tradition and legal-ism, Congress ordered the commanders to disregard him. Were the ordinary methods of political cam-paigning resorted to by the whites to profit by the ignorance or stupidity of the blacks, general orders from headquarters nullified them. Did the Con-servatives win a success, as in Alabama, by exact conformity to the law, Congress ignored its own law and gave victory to the other side. Was an assurance embodied in law that admission of a state should follow ratification of one constitutional amendment, no hesitation was felt about postponing admission till the ratification of another. Such methods as these were not the methods common to political practice in republican governments. But no more were the circumstances under which they were employed common in republics. The methods were well adapted to the end, and the end was a huge social and political revolution under the forms of law. Another way of attaining the end would have been a simple decree by the majority in Congress to the effect that the freedmen and white Unionists in the rebel states should organize governments, and control those states indefinitely thereafter. Essentially that was the conscious practical purpose of reconstruction, and everything beyond that in the content and execution of the Reconstruction Acts was incidental. But the incidental testifies to the sagacity of those who directed the policy.

That the purpose of reconstruction evinced as much political wisdom as the methods by which it was attained, is not clear. To stand the social pyramid on its apex was not the surest way to restore the shattered equilibrium in the South. The enfranchisement of the freedmen and their enthronement in political power was as reckless a species of statecraft as that which marked "the blind hysterics of the Celt" in 1789–95. But the resort to negro suffrage was not determined to any great extent by abstract theories of equality. Though Charles Sumner and the lesser lights of his school solemnly proclaimed, in season and out, the trite generalities of the Rights of Man, it was a very practical dilemma that played the chief part in giving the ballot to the blacks. By 1867 it seemed clear that there were three ways available for settling the issues of the war in the South: first, to leave the Johnson governments in control and permit the Southern whites themselves, through the Democratic Party, to determine either chiefly or wholly the solution of existing problems; second, to maintain Northern and Republican control through military government; and third, to maintain Northern and Republican control through negro suffrage. The first expedient, however defensible as to social and economic readjustment in the South itself, was from the standpoint of the great national issues demanding settlement grotesquely impossible. The choice had to be made between indefinite military rule and negro suffrage. It was a cruel dilemma. The traditional antipathy of the English race toward military power determined resort to the second alternative. It was proved by the sequel that the choice was unwise. The enfranchisement of the blacks, so far from removing, only increased, the necessity for military power.   The two expedients were not alternative, but indissolubly united.   Months before the final restoration of Georgia this truth had begun to make itself manifest.   On March 30, 1870, the ratification of the Fifteenth Amendment had been proclaimed, and just two months later the first enforcement act became law.   By the policy thus expressed the issue was definitely made up which ended in the undoing of reconstruction.   Seven unwholesome years were required to demonstrate that not even the government which had quelled the greatest rebellion in history could maintain the freedmen in both security and comfort on the necks of their former masters.   The demonstration was slow, but it was effective and permanent.

You better believe it —

THE IMPEACHMENT AND TRIAL OF PRESIDENT JOHNSON

THE differences of opinion in the Republican Party as to the method of dealing with the states lately in rebellion resulted, in February of 1866, in a definite declaration of war between President Johnson and the radical leaders in Congress.[1] It was not long before the bad judgment and worse taste [2] of the President drove over to his enemies nearly the whole body of Republican congress, men, and compelled him to look for support to an insignificant minority consisting chiefly of Demo, crats. By midsummer the contest had shaped itself into a pitched battle between the executive and the legislative departments of the government. Mr. Johnson claimed that the policy proposed by Congress involved the destruction of the constitution; his opponents charged that his course had been one of usurpation, and that his purpose was to establish a despotism based on rebel dominion. Each side professed to represent the people, and

[1] *Ante*, p. 90.
[2] Especially exhibited in his public speeches. See McPherson, Reconstruction, pp. 58, 127 *et seq*.

each bent all its energies to securing a favorable verdict in the Congressional elections in the autumn. The contest was an intensely bitter one. The canvass was as thorough as the importance of the issues demanded, and the result was an overwhelming defeat for the President. A majority almost as great as that in the Thirty-ninth was secured to oppose him in the Fortieth Congress. It was made certain that his vetoes could be overridden, and that, accordingly, reconstruction could proceed on the lines laid down by the legislature.

But it was hardly to be expected that President Johnson would quietly accept such a view of the situation. The asperities of the campaign had not tended to mitigate his hostility to his radical enemies, and his historic feat in "swinging round the circle"[1] had stimulated his enemies even more perhaps than it had his friends. He felt his duty to sustain the constitution not in any way affected by the determination of any number of persons that the constitution should not be sustained. The radicals in Congress looked forward to the same opposition that had so seriously interfered with their progress in the last session. Moreover, Mr. Johnson's control of the official patronage was a source of the deepest concern to many Republican parti-

---

[1] For the origin of this phrase, so famous in the campaign literature of the period, see his Cleveland speech, McPherson, Reconstruction, p. 135.

sans.[1] From the circumstances of the war, the patronage in the hands of the President at this time was more extensive than probably at any other period in the history of the nation. Mr. Johnson was no civil-service reformer, and the steadfastness with which he employed this great weapon for the purposes of his policy gave bitter offence to the Congressional majority, whose members found themselves cut off from the spoils. Mr. Wade, of Ohio, who was also notoriously free from any taint of reform principles, was president *pro tem.* of the Senate, and hence was only one step from the White House. Under such circumstances, with a majority in the House sufficient to overcome all obstacles to an accusation, and with an ample majority in the Senate to convict, it is not strange that attention was called to the grounds for impeachment of the President.

I

On December 17, 1866, about two weeks after the opening of the second session of the Thirty-ninth Congress, Representative Ashley, of Ohio, took the first formal step in the matter. He sought to get before the House a resolution for a select committee to inquire into the advisability of impeaching. His effort at this time failed. On

[1] *Cf.* Ingersoll, Life of Greeley, p. 424; also Blaine, Twenty Years of Congress, II, 267.

the 7th of January, however, he was successful in securing the passage of a resolution directing the judiciary committee to institute the inquiry.[1]   But March 4th came, and the Thirty-ninth Congress expired without further action.   The judiciary committee reported that it had been diligently at work in accordance with Ashley's resolution, but that it had not been able to accomplish enough to make any definite presentation to the House; the committee could only state that enough had been learned to warrant further investigation.[2]

Under the law passed by its predecessor, the Fortieth Congress met in its first session on the day the former adjourned *sine die*.   Three days later the impeachment inquiry was referred to the new judiciary committee.   The constitution of this committee had been carefully watched by the friends of impeachment, and, as appeared later, they were quite confident that it had been arranged to suit them.   Great was the disgust, therefore, of the radicals, especially Thaddeus Stevens and

[1] On this same day another resolution to impeach was offered, the preamble alleging that the purpose of the impeachment was "to give effect to the will of the people as expressed at the polls during the recent elections."   McPherson, Reconstruction, p. 187. In the debate on this resolution Johnson was charged with collusion with the rebels in Lincoln's assassination, for purposes of his own aggrandizement and their restoration to power (Globe, 2d sess., 39th Cong., p. 443).   This charge had been made before, and is characteristic of the spirit in which the conflict with the President was carried on.

[2] McPherson, Reconstruction, p. 188.

Benjamin F. Butler, when on July 10th the committee reported that its labor was completed, and that its members stood five against and four in favor of impeachment.[1]

There is no doubt that the House at this time was in sympathy with the majority of the committee. Mr. Pike, of Maine, expressed the prevalent feeling when he described the question as merely whether, after having killed the President politically, they should proceed to mangle the corpse. "It is one question," he said, "whether he has discharged the duties of his office acceptably, and quite another question whether, with him for a foot-ball, this house shall enter upon the game of President-making."[2] But the persons who were seeking to play that very game were not discouraged by their first failure. By sharp parliamentary practice they succeeded in getting the matter before the judiciary committee again, with orders to report in the autumn. And when autumn came their confidence was justified by the announcement that, by a vote of five to four, the committee had determined to report a resolution of impeachment. No new evidence had been secured, but through some instrumentality not disclosed, one member of the committee[3] had been brought to see the light. Mr. Boutwell, of Massachusetts, made the report, and for the first time

---

[1] Globe, 1st sess., 40th Cong., p. 565.   [2] *Ibid.*, p. 587.
[3] Churchill, of New York.

in the history of the United States, the House of Representatives was required to vote upon the direct question of impeaching the highest officer of the nation.

The consideration of the resolution was taken up at the opening of the second session of the Fortieth Congress, in December of 1867. It appeared from the committee's report and from the debate, that the points of variance between the Republican factions were two in number. The first was as to what constituted impeachable offences in our system. The constitution provides that the House may impeach any civil officer for "treason, bribery or other high crimes and misdemeanors." Treason and bribery were sufficiently accurate terms, but what should be regarded as the scope of "high crimes and misdemeanors"? By the radicals it was held that these words were employed in the widest and most extended sense known to jurisprudence, and included all cases of misbehavior in office, whether known to common or statute law or not. The moderate Republicans pretty generally adopted the view that these words limited the list of impeachable offences to such as were indictable either at common or by statute law. Otherwise, it was said, it would be in the competence of the Senate to define an offence as it proceeded with the trial, and the accused would have no legal certainty on which to base his defence. Another theory, maintained in this instance chiefly by the Democrats, held that the expression "high crimes and misdemeanors" was used generically in the constitution, and that it was left for Congress to declare by legislation what specific acts should be included in this designation. As Congress had taken no steps to define the offences, no impeachment could be based upon those words of the organic law.

But besides this diversity of opinion on the preliminary legal question, a very radical difference was manifested as to the sufficiency of the evidence collected by the committee as a basis for action against Mr. Johnson. Over a thousand quarto pages of printed testimony proved that no clue, however slight, had been left untraced. Never had the public life of a President been subjected to more searching investigation by more hostile investigators. Yet after all, Mr. Boutwell was obliged to acknowledge that no specific offence could be charged as a basis for action; only from a vast number of acts, related and individual, the general accusation was framed, that Mr. Johnson had used the power of the nation for the purpose of reconstructing the government in the interest of rebellion, and of restoring the old Democratic Party to power.[1] So vague a charge could scarcely be expected to entice the conscientious Republicans into the radical scheme. The deposition of a President seemed too serious a matter to rest for justification

[1] Globe, 2d sess., 40th Cong., Appendix, p. 60.

upon mere party apostasy.   On December 7, by a vote of one hundred and eighty to fifty-seven, the resolution was lost, and the first formal attempt to oust Mr. Johnson was proclaimed a failure.[1]

Much angry recrimination was indulged in by the two factions of Republicans as the result of this vote, but the radicals were forced to wait for some actual crime or misdemeanor before they could expect to carry their point.   Among the moderates was a very large body who believed that by means of the two-thirds majority in each house the policy they favored could be carried out, in spite of executive hostility, without proceeding to the extreme assertion of their power.   It is beyond doubt that the question of succession was more or less potent in forming opinion on this point; Senator Wade, who would succeed to the presidency in case of Johnson's removal, was not popular with the Eastern men.   But those who opposed impeachment were far from lagging behind in the work of tying the President's hands so as to render him harmless while still in office.   The impeachment, when it came, was the result and culmination of a series of assaults on the executive power which for a time carried the centre of gravity of our constitutional system as near to the revolution point on the legislative side as the exigencies of civil war had a few years before carried it on the executive side.   The President's pardoning power

[1] McPherson, Reconstruction, p. 264.

was limited;[1] his military authority as commander-in-chief was shorn of essential attributes;[2] and his civil prerogative received a terrible blow through the Tenure-of-Office Act passed March 2, 1867. It was in consequence of Mr. Johnson's struggles to tear away the meshes which Congress was so mercilessly weaving about him that a second and then a third and successful attempt at impeachment were made.

II

It had been understood, prior to the passage of the Tenure-of-Office Act, that Mr. Johnson's policy in regard to the South had the approval of all his cabinet save one member. The dissenter was Mr. Stanton, one of the four remaining members of Mr. Lincoln's cabinet.[3] Up to the inauguration of military rule in the Southern states, the difference between the President and his secretary of

[1] *Cf.* act of Jan. 17, 1867, repealing the clause of the Confiscation Act of July 17, 1862, which authorized the President to pardon by proclamation; and see Blaine, Twenty Years of Congress, II, 281. By the Reconstruction Act of July 19, 1867, it was specifically declared that no right to vote should result from " any executive pardon or amnesty"; and the Fourteenth Amendment conclusively divested the President's pardon of political significance by conferring the power to remove disabilities upon Congress.

[2] Army Appropriation Act, March 2, 1867. *Cf.* McPherson, Reconstruction, p. 178.

[3] The others were Messrs. Seward, McCullough and Welles. Three of Mr. Lincoln's secretaries, Messrs. Dennison, Speed and Harlan, had resigned in 1866, in consequence of the President's breach with Congress.

war had not occasioned any unpleasantness. But when the army was called upon for active participation in carrying out the policy of Congress, the fact that Stanton was in sympathy with that policy became immediately of the highest importance. The Tenure-of-Office Act, by which the President was deprived of the power of removal, also assumed great significance. In executing the Reconstruction Acts, the administration adopted the policy of conforming to the letter of the law with great exactness, while giving the least possible heed to what was deemed its revolutionary spirit. With what success this policy was carried out is indicated by the supplementary act of July 19, 1867, which Congress was obliged to add to its original enactment. But the secretary of war was no party to the devising and execution of this Presidential scheme. He became, on the contrary, altogether isolated from the rest of the administration, and, as his enemies charged, employed his position only to obstruct executive action and betray the secrets of the cabinet consultation room to the President's foes.

Stanton remained impervious to repeated intimations that his retirement would not be opposed by the President, till, on the fifth of August, 1867, Mr. Johnson formally called for his resignation. The secretary declined to resign before the next meeting of Congress. A week later the President sent a note in these words: "By virtue of the power and authority vested in me as President by the constitution and laws of the United States, you are hereby suspended from office as secretary of war." At the same time General Grant was authorized to act as secretary *ad interim*. Stanton replied, denying the President's right to suspend him "without the advice and consent of the Senate, and without legal cause"; but, in view of the appointment of the General of the Army, submitting, under protest, to superior force.[1]

It is important just at this point to consider under what authority this order of suspension was issued. Before the passage of the Tenure-of-Office Act, while the power of removal was recognized as belonging to the executive, obnoxious officers had been generally disposed of during a recess of the Senate by simple removal, and when the Senate was in session, by the appointment of a successor. Under this act, however, no removal was permitted during a recess. The second section provided that in case of incapacity or legal disqualification for the performance of his duties an officer might be suspended by the President; but the cause must be reported to the Senate within twenty days after the opening of the next session, and if that body refused to concur in the suspension, the officer should immediately resume his duties.[2] In his communication to Stanton, Johnson stated his

[1] For the whole correspondence, see McPherson, Reconstruction, p. 261.

[2] For text of bill, see McPherson, Reconstruction, p. 176.

authority to be "the constitution and the laws," but omitted to specify what laws, and especially whether the Tenure-of-Office Act was one of them. This omission, as afterward appeared, was far from unintentional.

On December 12 the President sent to the Senate a message setting forth his action in suspending Stanton, and stating at length the inharmonious situation which the secretary's presence in the cabinet had produced.[1] But here again no mention was made of the Tenure-of-Office Act as the authority for the suspension. The act was discussed, and its unconstitutionality asserted in terms similar to those of the veto message when the law passed, but no admission was made of its pertinence to the present case. The Senate debated the President's communication for about a month, and finally, on January 13, 1868, refused to concur in Stanton's suspension. This action was taken in accordance with the theory that the suspension was based on the Tenure-of-Office Act. Notice of the Senate's action was immediately served upon General Grant, who thereupon notified Mr. Stanton that, under the Tenure-of-Office Act, the functions of the *ad interim* incumbent had ceased. The general thus committed himself to the Senatorial view of the President's action. Stanton resumed possession of the War Department, but without any communication with, or

[1] See supplement to Cong. Globe, "Trial of the President," p. 51.

recognition by, the head of the administration.[1] The situation was anomalous. It could only be explained by an official announcement of Johnson's attitude toward the Tenure-of-Office Act. If he recognized that act as valid, Stanton must now be his secretary of war; if he did not recognize it, the War Department must be without a head.

On January 29 Mr. Johnson instructed General Grant not to obey any order from that depart, ment, assumed to be issued by the direction of the President, unless such order should be known by the general to have been authorized by the executive. Grant replied that under the law he should be obliged to regard orders coming from the secretary of war as authorized by the President. This response precipitated a correspondence of a somewhat acrimonious character between Johnson and Grant, in which the motives of the former in the course pursued in respect to Stanton were fully revealed.[2] The President, it appeared, had resolved to get rid of the secretary at all hazards. He refused to admit that the Tenure-of-Office Act covered Stanton's case, though he was aware that the latter held that it did. But even if the terms of the act did apply, the President was convinced that the law was a flagrant breach of his constitutional rights, and was deter-

[1] See Stanton's letter transmitting to the House the Grant-Johnson correspondence; McPherson, Reconstruction, p. 282.

[2] For the correspondence, see McPherson, Reconstruction, p. 283.

mined to bring the matter to a judicial decision. For this purpose, having once dispossessed Stanton, he proposed to make the secretary apply to the courts for reinstatement, and thus to test the question of constitutionality. In pursuance of this plan, General Grant had been requested to remain in possession of the department, whether the Senate should concur in the suspension or not. If the Senate should refuse to concur, Stanton would regard himself as entitled to immediate possession; but if Grant should hold on, the only method through which Stanton would be able to secure his office would be by resort to the courts. Grant manifested a disinclination to become involved in the political quarrels of the departments, and thereupon Johnson requested that if he should decide not to take the responsibility, he should let the President know before the Senate acted, in order that an incumbent might be secured who could be relied upon to carry out the executive's plan. As to the sequel, authorities differ. Mr. Johnson and five of his cabinet asserted that General Grant agreed to do as requested, and then, in deliberate violation of his promise, held on till the Senate's action relieved him. The general, on the other hand, denied having been a party to any such agreement. Whatever the truth of the case, however, it was certain that the President's plan had miscarried, and that, if the Tenure-of-Office Act was valid and applicable, the obnoxious Stanton was still an officer of the administration.

The correspondence between Johnson and Grant was called for by the House of Representatives, and formed the basis of a second attempt at impeachment. An effort was made to formulate an indictment on the President's instructions to Grant not to obey the orders of his superior in the War Department. The careful wording of the instructions, however, and their total lack of effect, proved too serious obstacles for even the hot-heads of the reconstruction committee to surmount. Only three out of the nine members of the committee favored action.[1]

It is to be noticed that the conflict between the executive and the legislature had now centred in a struggle for the control of the military department. This fact had the effect of throwing over the situation a sort of martial glamour, which was artfully utilized to stimulate the passions of parti-sans on both sides. Wars and rumors of wars were the topics of the times. The President's hostility to Secretary Stanton was treated as evidence of a design to employ the army in a repetition of "Pride's Purge." Congress was to be dissolved, and Andrew Johnson was to be king.[2] At the same time, the friends of Mr. Johnson pointed with alarm to the open strides of the radi-

---

[1] McPherson, Reconstruction, p. 265.

[2] Kelley, of Pennsylvania, drew a harrowing picture of the President in the rôle of the third Napoleon. — Globe, 2d sess., 40th Cong., p. 1348.

cals toward their object of converting the government, by force, from the balanced system of the fathers into the dominion of a party caucus. Submission to the dictates of this oligarchy was to be enforced through the army, against all efforts of the President to defend the rights conferred upon him by the constitution.

In the midst of such recriminations and in the extraordinary position of the War Department, a crisis must be reached soon. It came on the twenty-first of February. On that day the President issued two orders, one removing Stanton from office as secretary of war, and the other appointing Adjutant-General Lorenzo Thomas secretary *ad interim*, and directing him to assume immediately the duties of the position.[1] Thomas repaired to Stanton's office and communicated to him the President's will. Without indicating what course he should pursue with reference to the order of removal, Stanton asked until the next day to adjust his personal affairs in the office. His request was granted. Early the next morning Thomas was arrested by the District police on a charge of violating the Tenure-of-Office Act. He had been boasting that he would use force to eject Stanton in case of resistance, and the latter had sworn out a warrant for his arrest. Having been released on bail, the somewhat humbled secretary *ad interim* proceeded again to the War Department and

[1] McPherson, Reconstruction, p. 265.

formally demanded possession. Stanton formally refused to recognize the order of removal, and ordered Thomas to his duties as adjutant-general. The latter thereupon reported to the President, and affairs were left in *statu quo* pending the next move toward either judicial or forcible settlement of the dispute.[1] Mr. Johnson immediately took steps toward bringing the defiant secretary before the Supreme Court by a writ of *quo warranto*, but the arraignment of Thomas as a criminal, and the energetic action of Congress, soon to be narrated, quickly put the President on the defensive and interrupted all aggressive action. The lawyers who took charge of Thomas's defence did indeed devise a plan by which his arrest could be utilized to bring the whole subject before the Supreme Court by a writ of *habeas corpus;* but at the very first manifestation of such a purpose the ardor of the prosecution was seized with a sudden chill, and the culprit whose alleged crime had convulsed the whole nation was released from custody against the desire of his own counsel.[2] All interest then became centred in the steps which Congress was taking for the maintenance of its authority as vested in Stanton.

On the day of the removal Mr. Johnson sent a message to the Senate, transmitting copies of the orders issued, and basing his action, as in the case

[1] Testimony of Thomas, Trial of the President, pp. 136 *et seq.*
[2] Testimony of Cox, Trial, pp. 201 *et seq.*

of the suspension, on the "power and authority vested in the President by the constitution and laws of the United States." The Senate's reply was a resolution, passed by a party vote, that "under the constitution and laws of the United States, the President has no power to remove the secretary of war and designate any other officer to perform the duties of that office *ad interim*." On the same day, Mr. Stanton communicated the order of removal to the House of Representatives. It was referred to the reconstruction committee, and on the following day the committee reported a resolution, that "Andrew Johnson, President of the United States, be impeached of high crimes and misdemeanors in office." A continuous session of two days, devoted to debate, ended with the adoption of the resolution, 128 to 47, a strict party vote.[1] To those Republicans who had opposed the previous attempts on the ground that only a technical crime or misdemeanor could give good cause for impeachment, the President seemed to have deliberately removed the obstacle which their consciences had raised.[2] The Tenure-of-Office Act prohibited removal from office by the President except with the advice and consent of the Senate. In section six it was enacted that "every removal, appointment or employment made, had or exercised

[1] McPherson, Reconstruction, p. 266.
[2] See remarks of Wilson, of Iowa, Globe, 2d sess., 40th Cong., p. 1386.

contrary to the provisions of this act, and the making, signing, sealing, countersigning or issuing of any commission or letter of authority for or in respect to any such appointment or employment, shall be deemed, and are hereby declared to be, high misdemeanors." In the face of these provisions the President's action appeared to be a most gross violation of the laws he had sworn to maintain.

From the moment the resolution of impeachment was adopted the moderate wing of the Republicans in the House disappeared, and many of its leaders joined in the struggle for prominence in the great achievement of ousting a President. Under the special leadership of Messrs. Thaddeus Stevens, Benjamin F. Butler and George S. Boutwell, matters were pushed with the utmost diligence, and, on the second of March, nine articles were adopted by the House. The next day two others were added, and on the fourth the articles were formally exhibited to the Senate. The latter body met as a court of impeachment on the following day, with Chief Justice Chase in the chair. Mr. Johnson appeared by counsel, and, on asking forty days in which to prepare an answer to the charges, was allotted ten. The preliminaries having been settled, the trial actually began on the thirtieth of March, with an opening address for the prosecution by Mr. Butler.[1]

[1] The "managers" appointed by the House to conduct its case

III

As to the issues involved in the trial, all that the limits of this paper permit is a consideration of the most fundamental questions of constitutional law presented. The eleven articles of impeachment exhibited to the Senate charged the President with high crimes and misdemeanors in office, in connection with five different matters: (1) The order removing Stanton; (2) the order appointing Thomas; (3) a conversation with Major-General Emory, in which Mr. Johnson declared unconstitutional the law requiring all orders to be issued through the General of the Army; (4) three public speeches of the President, in which Congress was criticised in very harsh and intemperate language; and (5) his opposition to the execution of the reconstruction measures of Congress.[1]

By the first article, the order removing Stanton was declared to be an intentional violation of the Tenure-of-Office Act, and also of the constitution. Articles four to eight represented the removal as

were Messrs. Bingham, Boutwell, Wilson of Iowa, Butler, Williams, Logan and Stevens. Of these, Bingham and Wilson had opposed the first attempt to impeach, but the others were all radicals of the most extreme type. For the defence of the President appeared Mr. Stanbery (who resigned the office of attorney-general to take part in the trial), ex-Judge Benjamin R. Curtis, and Messrs. Evarts, Nelson and Groesbeck.

[1] For the articles, see Trial of the President (supplement to the Cong. Globe), p. 1.

the result of a conspiracy, on the part of the President and General Thomas, to prevent Stanton from holding his lawful office, to prevent the execution of certain laws, to seize the property of the United States in the War Department, and for other illegal purposes. The conspiracy charges were based on the law of July 31, 1861, which had been enacted to make criminal the actions of the rebels.[1] Article two declared the President guilty of intentional violation of the constitution and of the Tenure-of-Office Act, in issuing the letter of authority to Thomas, without the consent of the Senate, though in session, and when there was no vacancy in the office of secretary of war. The third article represented the same act simply as being without authority of law. Article nine charged the President with a high misdemeanor in seeking to induce General Emory to violate the law in reference to the issuing of orders in the

---

[1] The act was as follows: " If two or more persons within any State or Territory of the United States shall conspire together to overthrow, or to put down or to destroy by force, the government of the United States, or to levy war against the United States, or to oppose by force the authority of the government of the United States; or by force to prevent, hinder or delay the execution of any law of the United States; or by force to seize, take or possess any property of the United States against the will or contrary to the authority of the United States; or by force or intimidation or threat, to prevent any person from accepting or holding any office or trust or place of confidence under the United States; each and every person so offending shall be guilty of a high crime, *etc.*" — 12 Statutes at Large, p. 284.

army.   The tenth article was only adopted by the House after the most strenuous efforts of General Butler to secure such action.   It quoted from the published reports of divers speeches delivered by Mr. Johnson during the campaign of 1866,[1] and charged him with having sought "to destroy the regard and respect of all the good people of the United States for the Congress and legislative power thereof," and to excite the odium and resentment of the same good people against Congress and the laws by it duly and constitutionally enacted.   The eleventh article was rather difficult to analyze, but Chief Justice Chase decided the gravamen of the article to be that the President attempted to defeat the execution of the Tenure-of-Office Act; but his attitude toward Congress and its reconstruction policy was introduced as means contrived in furtherance of this attempt.[2] Skilful hands in the House had drawn up this article to accommodate the conscientious scruples or inconvenient records of certain senators in reference to the scope of the President's power of removal.   By involving the general reconstruction issue this object was attained.

Of the conspiracy charges little need be said.

[1] The three speeches from which extracts were made in the specifications under article ten were delivered respectively at Washington, Cleveland and St. Louis, on August 18, September 3 and September 8, 1866.   For the full reports of the speeches, see McPherson, Reconstruction, pp. 127, 134 and 136.

[2] Trial of the President, p. 409.

The evidence introduced to support them was ludicrously insufficient.   No vote was ever reached on the articles embodying them, but the written opinions of the senators indicate clearly that none but the most violent radicals would have regarded the charges as proved.   The same may be said of the Emory article.   It appeared from the testimony that the President's expression of opinion to the general on the law in question was of the most casual nature, and wholly devoid of any indication of a design to corrupt the officer.[1]   As to the speeches of Mr. Johnson, they had constituted one of the grounds for the previous attempt to impeach.   One of the managers now acting for the House, Mr. Wilson, of Iowa, had written an elaborate report from the judiciary committee, denying that the President's speech-making constituted an impeachable offence.   The report had been sustained by the House's action, and it now required all the assurance which General Butler could boast to ask for conviction on the article thus condemned.   The defense paid slight attention to this part of the case, and in argument relied almost entirely on the authorities which Manager Wilson had so kindly provided.   Such of the moderate Republican senators as deigned to notice the tenth article in their written opinions, did so only to deny its constitutionality.

[1] See testimony of General Emory and of Secretary Welles and his son, Trial, pp. 78, 221, 235.

The questions, therefore, to which our attention will be confined are such as arose in connection with the removal of Stanton and the appointment of Thomas, and the relation of these acts to the constitution and the laws. What these questions were will appear from the President's formal reply to the articles presented by the House. To the first article the response [1] was substantially as follows: Stanton was appointed by Lincoln, and commissioned, under the act of 1789 establishing the War Department, to hold his office during the pleasure of the President. For the conduct of this department the President, as chief executive, is, under the constitution, responsible. A sense of this responsibility contributed to the conviction in the mind of the President, in August, 1867, that Stanton should no longer continue in the office. An additional ground for this conviction was the fact that the relations between Stanton and the President no longer permitted the latter to resort to the secretary for advice, as was his constitutional right. He had accordingly suspended Stanton from office, not under the Tenure-of-Office Act, till the next meeting of the Senate (and now is revealed the true bearing of the President's silence, before mentioned, in respect to his authority for the suspension), but indefinitely, and at the pleasure of the President, under the belief that the power of removal confided to the executive by the con-

[1] Trial, p. 12.

stitution included the power of indefinite suspension. The President further maintained that the power of removal was a constitutional right which no legislation could take from him. Such being the case, the Tenure-of-Office Act was void. But even while he entertained this belief, and was further satisfied that the first section of the act did not apply to Stanton, the President had felt so strongly the importance of getting rid of the secretary that he had sought, by reporting the suspension to the Senate in apparent conformity with the obnoxious act, to accomplish that high purpose without raising the conflict on the constitutional question. Having failed in securing his object, nothing remained for him but to take such steps as he should deem necessary and proper for bringing to judicial decision the question of Stanton's right to resume his office. With this end, and this end only, in view, the President had issued the order of removal to Stanton, and the letter of authority designating General Thomas as secretary *ad interim*. As to this designation of a temporary officer, the President denied that it was an appointment such as required the consent of the Senate, but claimed that it was in accordance with long practice, based on a law of 1795.

From these pleadings it appeared that the judgment of the Senate must involve some answer to the following questions:

1. Is the power of removal in our system in the

President alone, or in the President and Senate conjointly?

2. Does the power of removal include the power of indefinite suspension of an officer?

3. Can a vacant office be filled indefinitely by an *ad interim* appointee, installed without reference to the Senate?

4. Most important of all, is it lawful in our system for the President to violate an act of Congress which he considers unconstitutional, in order to secure a judicial decision as to its validity?

But before entering upon an examination of these points it is necessary to notice the Senate's judgment on the preliminary questions previously touched upon: What are impeachable offences under the constitution; and what is the character and capacity of the upper branch of the legislature when sitting as a court of impeachment? As to the first question, the different theories held have already been stated. The managers in the pending trial were obliged, on account of the article which Butler had forced in, to maintain the doctrine that "high crimes and misdemeanors" were not limited to indictable offences; for the public addresses of the President were not of a criminal character under any law, either common or statute. An impeachable high crime or misdemeanor was held by the prosecution to be "one in its nature or consequences subversive of some fundamental principle of government, or highly prejudicial to the public interest." Besides the violation of positive law, it might consist in "the abuse of discretionary powers from improper motives, or for any improper purpose."[1] That this was the doctrine of the English law could scarcely be doubted.[2] The few American precedents up to this time pointed unmistakably to the same conclusion. There had been five cases of impeachment by the House of Representatives. Of these one had been against a senator,[3] and the Senate had decided that the accused did not fall within the designation "civil officers of the United States." All the rest had involved judges, and in every instance the articles exhibited by the House had charged some offence not a technical violation of law. Two of the impeached persons were convicted.[4] Pickering, in 1802, was found guilty, among other things, of drunkenness and profanity on the bench of his court. Humphreys, in 1861, was removed from office on conviction of advocating secession in a public speech, and of other acts favoring rebellion, when those acts were not criminal under any law of the United States. This latter case was, for obvious reasons, of little value, and especially as no defence was made. But the

---

[1] Trial, p. 29.

[2] See brief of authorities, by Lawrence, of Ohio, Trial, p. 41.

[3] Blount, of Tenn., 1797.

[4] Chase, Associate Justice of the Supreme Court, was acquitted, 1805; Peck, a district judge, 1830.

fact remained that the House had on four occasions construed its power of impeachment to extend to offences not indictable, and in one case had secured the Senate's ratification of its construction by a conviction.

But it was not alone in precedent that the prosecution had a strong case. Substantial grounds were not wanting on which to base the claim that a misdemeanor in office was not distinct from misbehavior in office. On any narrower interpretation of the term misdemeanor, the constitution affords no method by which an insane judge may during his lifetime be divested of his official functions. The fact that the penalty in case of impeachment is limited to disqualification for holding office was declared to indicate a purpose rather to protect the people from bad officials than to establish a jurisdiction for the punishment of crimes. It was in the development of this view that General Butler brought forward the further proposition of his school, namely, that the Senate, when acting on impeachment cases, was not a court, nor its procedure a trial. Such being the case, the ordinary restrictions of judicial process, it was argued, have no application. The guaranties accorded to the accused in jury trials need not be granted here. There is no right of challenge to any member of the Senate for any cause whatever, and no appeal to any law save the constitution. In short, the body sitting to determine the accusation against the President was held to be, not a court, but the Senate of the United States, "convened as a constitutional tribunal to inquire into and determine whether Andrew Johnson, because of malversation in office, is longer fit to retain the office of President of the United States, or hereafter to hold any office of honor or profit."[1] A very important deduction from this proposition was that the ordinary rules of evidence need not be observed, and that each senator in giving judgment was free to rest his opinion upon any personal information he possessed that bore on the general question of fitness, without being at all confined to the merits of the case made on the particular articles. Each senator must be a law unto himself, and must give his verdict on his own views of what the country's welfare demanded.

As against this doctrine, the defenders of the President pointed out that to adopt these extreme conclusions would obviously destroy every vestige of judicial character in the Senate's action. A presentation of formal articles of impeachment by the House would be unnecessary, and the form of a trial a work of supererogation. The constitution, it was argued, contemplates the substance as well as the form of judicial action by the Senate. That body is empowered to "try" impeachments. It assumes a peculiar character through the oath required by the senators when sitting for that

[1] Trial of the President, p. 30.

purpose. Its concurrence in the charges is a "conviction," and is followed by a "judgment."[1] This adherence to the technical terminology of the law is significant. The precedents, moreover, it was contended, had already, before Mr. Johnson's trial, established the reality of the Senate's judicial character. This conclusion was sanctioned now by a test vote forced by the managers early in the proceedings. A question arose as to whether the chief justice should decide in the first instance on the admissibility of evidence, or refer the matter immediately to the Senate. It had been argued that the Senate's capacity as a court had been fixed by the constitutional mandate calling the chief justice to preside in the most important case that could come before it. The managers maintained that the chief justice acted, not as a presiding judge and an integral part of the trying body, but only as the mouthpiece of the Senate. He could decide nothing himself. He was not the chief of a court in *banc*, but the presiding officer of the Senate for a particular purpose. Under the constitution the Senate of the United States was given the sole power to try all impeachments. No one not a senator, therefore, could take any part in the trial save as the ministerial agent of the Senate.

After full discussion the question was decided by an amendment to the rules which gave the chief justice power to decide questions of law, his

---

[1] Constitution, art. i., sec. 3.

ruling to stand as the judgment of the Senate unless a vote should be demanded by some senator. The amendment was adopted by a vote of 31 to 19.[1] On the same day the chief justice had occasion to give the casting vote in case of a tie. Senator Sumner thereupon offered a resolution declaring that such vote was without authority under the constitution of the United States. The resolution was lost, 21 to 27.[2] These votes seem conclusive of the Senate's opinion that on this occasion, at least, it was sitting in the capacity of a court.

On the question as to what are impeachable offences, the whole history of Mr. Johnson's case supports the view that, contrary to the precedents, a violation of some positive law must be proved. The House refused once to impeach on the speeches. Its later adoption of the article based on them was prompted by an apparent defiance hurled at Congress by the President, and even then was determined largely by the plea that the inclusion of this article could do no harm even if it did no good.[3] And finally, no vote was ever demanded from the Senate on this article, while the tenor of the opinions filed by senators renders it doubtful that even a simple majority would have voted to convict, much less the two-thirds required.

[1] Trial, p. 63.
[2] *Ibid.*
[3] See Globe, 2d sess., 40th Cong., p. 1642.

IV

Taking up now the questions presented in immediate connection with the pleadings, the first is that as to the power of removal. Summarily, the case which the prosecution sought to establish was this: 1. The removal of the secretary of war without the advice and consent of the Senate was a violation of the Tenure-of-Office Act. 2. Whether or not this was true, the removal while the Senate was in session, and otherwise than by the appointment of a successor, was a violation of the constitution. 3. These violations of law and constitution were intentional and were designed as an open defiance of Congress. 4. Even if the President's motive had been merely to get a judicial construction of a doubtful constitutional point, as he claimed, that fact would have no bearing on the determination of his guilt; for his duty is to execute without discretion the legally enacted will of the legislature.

In what organ of the government the constitution vested the power to remove an officer from his position, is an old and familiar question. Its practical discussion began in the halls of the First Congress. In providing for the organization of the executive departments in 1789 the whole subject of removal from office was fully debated. The cardinal point of the discussion was the nature of the power — whether it was absolute and an independent attribute of the executive office, or whether it should be regarded as only to be exercised through the clearly defined process of appointment. The former opinion prevailed, though by a very slender majority.[1] A construction was thus put upon the constitution by legislative action, and that construction was accepted by all. Though the debates upon the adoption of the constitution rather favored the doctrine which Congress rejected,[2] yet up to 1867 no successful practical objection had been made to the exercise of the power early conceded to the President.

The managers endeavored to break the force of these facts by developing the theory of a distinction between removals during the session of the Senate and removals during recess. They admitted that the act of 1789 warranted the President in dismissing an unworthy officer peremptorily when the impossibility of consulting the Senate prevented resort to the ordinary method. The desirability of a speedy means by which the service could be purged of incompetent or corrupt officials had been the chief argument for Congress' action in 1789. But this reason had no application when the advisory body was ready to act on an hour's notice in supplanting the objectionable person. It was confidently claimed that an examination of the

[1] The bill in which the issue was involved passed the Senate only by the casting vote of the Vice-President.

[2] See *Federalist*, No. 77.

records would disclose a uniform recognition of this distinction in the practice of the departments. A single perfectly defined precedent, however, nullified the claim. It was revealed that on the 13th of May, 1800, Timothy Pickering, Secretary of State, was summarily removed by President Adams, after having declined to comply with a request to resign.[1] It is true the nomination of his successor was sent in on the same day, but the acts appear on the record as entirely separate and unconnected. The case bears a striking analogy to that of Stanton and it was a strong support for the defence. Above all, however, stood the fact that in all the discussion of the theoretical question no distinction had ever been drawn on the basis of the Senate's readiness to act. The power of removal had always been treated as unsusceptible of qualification in that respect, and the only question had been, should it be exercised by the President alone, or by the President and Senate together.

Prior to the passage of Tenure-of-Office Act, the practice of removal during recess at the will of the executive had become not only a notorious fact, but a most conspicuous abuse. By the constitution, the President was empowered to fill vacancies "happening" during the recess of the Senate by granting commissions running to the end of the next session. As a matter of practice, the temporary

[1] Trial, pp. 117-119.

appointee was regularly nominated and confirmed when the Senate met, and no questions were asked about how the vacancy "happened." [1]   By the act of 1867 Congress wholly reversed the conclusion reached in 1789, and borne out in the later practice. The power of removal, as an independent right, was annihilated. Every officer appointed by the advice and consent of the Senate was declared entitled to hold the office till the Senate had agreed to his removal by advising and consenting to the appointment of his successor. This, of course, withdrew removal from the category of causes through which a vacancy could "happen" during the recess of the Senate. For the sake of discipline, however, the President was authorized, in case of misconduct, crime, incapacity or legal disqualification, to suspend an officer, and designate some one to perform his duties till the Senate should act on the case. A full report on the subject must be made to the Senate within twenty days of its next meeting. If that body agreed that the cause for suspension was sufficient, the officer might be removed; if it did not concur, the officer should forthwith resume the functions of his office.[2] It was by virtue of these provisions that Stanton was now held to be regularly in authority as secretary of war.

[1] A futile attempt was made to reform this practice as early as 1826. Benton, Thirty-Years' View, ch. xxix.

[2] Tenure-of-Office Act, sec. 2.

Assuming for the present that Stanton was not excepted from the operation of this law by a proviso to be noticed later, Johnson's attitude with reference to the act was certainly one of defiance. But the defiance was hurled from the higher ground of a constitutional mandate. The President claimed that his power to remove at pleasure was derived from the constitution, and was, therefore, as far beyond the range of legislative restriction as, for example, the right to grant pardons. For, wherever the organic law had placed the power of removal, it was certainly not in Congress. The act of 1789 did not confer the right on the President; for Congress never had the right to confer. That act had by its terms merely recognized that the power of removal had been vested in the executive by the same authority which had vested other powers in Congress — namely, the constitution.[1] This view had been adopted by commentators and by all departments of the government, and had served as a working principle of our polity for seventy-eight years. Such concurrence of all authorities of weight in our system had clothed an implied function of the executive with all the sanctity of an expressly granted power. The Tenure-of-Office Act was therefore void, and its execution could not be a duty of the President.

Against this argument the managers maintained

---

[1] Annals of Congress, 1st Cong., pp. 600–608. See especially Benson's remarks.

that the Congressional construction of 1867 was as good as that of 1789. The constitution was unchanged in respect to the power of removal. Wherever the right was seventy-eight years ago, it still continued to be. If the legislature's view of its location was conclusive upon the other departments then, so must the later opinion be now. The earlier position had been taken mainly with reference to the exalted character of the first President, and the confidence everywhere reposed in him. Experience had proved that the principle thus apparently sanctioned was hostile to the true interests of the nation. In the hands of bad men, the power of removal had been used to exalt unduly the executive at the expense of the other departments. It was the duty of the people's immediate representatives in Congress to correct a pardonable error of the fathers, and to preserve the system from degenerating into a despotism. In pursuance of this duty, and under the authority conferred by the constitution to make all laws necessary and proper for carrying into execution the powers vested in the government and its officers, Congress had passed the Tenure-of-Office Act. Further, it was argued, by enacting the law, Congress had expressed its opinion on the question of constitutionality. By a two-thirds majority in each house overriding a veto supported by all the arguments at the President's command, a conclusive emphasis had been put upon that opinion.

If any doubt still remained as to the constitutionality of the act, it surely was not for the President
to resolve it.   By neither constitution, nor law,
nor practice had the executive been endowed with
authority to declare a law void on any ground.
His duty was faithfully to execute the laws.
What must be considered laws?   A bill passed by
both houses and signed by the President is a law.
Or when the President has sent back a bill with
objections, and both houses have passed it again,
and by two-thirds in each case, the constitution
declares that "it shall become a law."   Such a
law must be faithfully executed, or the President
fails in his duty.   On no pretence can he refuse
compliance with the constitutionally expressed will
of the legislature.

At this point was focussed the whole issue between the two political departments.   Here Congress concentrated its heaviest fire, and sought to
crush once for all the independence of the executive.   If Andrew Johnson had been convicted on
a direct presentation of the question here raised,
the co-ordination of the departments in the American system would have been a thing of the past;
and, on the other hand, if an acquittal had been
secured on the same issue, the natural vantage-
ground occupied by the legislature under the constitution would have been thenceforth held by the
executive.   Divested of all qualifications, the bare
question was: Could the President, for any pur-

pose, decline to execute or deliberately violate a law duly enacted under the forms prescribed by the constitution? If he could, *his* will, and not that of the legislature, would be the law; if he could not, he would be only the ministerial agent of Congress, and not the chief of a co-ordinate department.[1]

If it be held that the President has the unqualified right to violate an act of Congress at his will, the absurdity is obvious, as was practically conceded by the defence. If, on the other hand, he be denied the right to do it under any circumstances, what, they asked, is to be considered his duty in case, for example, Congress forbids him to negotiate a treaty, or to grant a pardon, or to act as commander-in-chief of the army? These powers are conferred upon the President in unmistakable terms by the constitution. For their exercise he is responsible not to Congress, but to the makers of the constitution, that is, the people. An act of Congress that deprives him of these rights, he certainly is not bound to obey. Again, there are powers which are clearly placed in other hands by the constitution. Laws for the carrying out of such powers he is bound to execute without ques-

---

[1] Bingham, especially, in closing the argument for the prosecution, labored to make the verdict depend on the bare question whether the President could interpret judicially the acts of Congress. His appeal to Senatorial *esprit de corps* was very thinly disguised. Trial, p. 385.

tion; any violation of rights by such laws can only be remedied by repeal of the laws or by resort by the aggrieved parties to the protection of judicial interpretation. But suppose Congress assumes the exercise of a doubtful power, — a power which certain precedent and respectable authority concur in attributing to the executive? Such assumption is considered to violate a constitutional right of the President. He is not warranted in simply resisting the law, decreeing it to be unconstitutional; for that would be arrogating to himself the functions of the judiciary. But there is no good reason why he should not take steps toward securing an opinion on the act from the third department of the government. The Supreme Court, however, can give no decision, save on a special case brought before it. Such case could never be made up by the President, save by a technical violation of the doubtful law. For the purpose, then, of defending his right through the courts of law, and for this purpose alone, the preservation of the constitution warrants the executive in transgressing duly enacted legislation. "But," replied the managers, "the President, like any private citizen, if he violates law, for whatever purpose, does it at his peril. The peril in his case is impeachment. Hence Mr. Johnson is rightly presented." This the defence could not deny. If the violation of the law were a high crime or misdemeanor, the House might bring the offender

before the Senate for trial.   But the gravamen
of the charge in that case would have to be not
the act only, but the motive of the President.   If
it were proved that his intention was not merely
to secure a judicial decision on his alleged right,
but to inaugurate revolutionary resistance to Congress, then conviction must follow.   This view,
however, the managers rejected altogether, and
demanded that Mr. Johnson's motive, though without doubt an impeachably bad one, must not at all
be considered.   They called upon the Senate to
remove the officer who had deliberately violated
a solemn law.   Nor did they heed the suggestion
that if this alleged solemn law was in conflict with
the constitution, it was no law at all.[1]

The vital principle of our constitution involved
in this question could not be brought to a direct
issue in the present case on account of a special
doubt that arose as to whether the leading provision of the Tenure-of-Office Act applied to Secretary Stanton.   At least two of the Republican
senators who voted for conviction on the other
articles, expressed their inability to resolve this
doubt in such a way as to sustain the charge that
the removal of the secretary had violated that
law.[2]   The first section of the act, after declaring
that every civil officer appointed with the consent

[1] *Cf.* Bingham's argument, Trial, p. 387.
[2] Sherman and Howe; see their opinions in Trial, pp. 449 and
496.

of the Senate should be entitled to hold his office until a successor should have been in like manner appointed, contained this proviso:

Provided, That the secretaries of state, of the treasury, of war, of the navy, and of the interior, the postmaster-general, and the attorney-general shall hold their offices respectively for and during the term of the President by whom they may have been appointed, and for one month thereafter, subject to removal by and with the advice and consent of the Senate.

It was part of the bill's history that the subject of the cabinet officers had been a point of contention between the Senate and the House. By decisive votes the former had insisted on excepting these officials entirely from the operation of the law. The House, on the other hand, had desired to avoid all concession to the cabinet idea, and to make no distinction between the President's advisers and other civil officers. A conference committee had reported the section as it stood, with the disputed topic thrown into the proviso by way of compromise. The question had been raised at the time whether the proviso fixed Johnson's secretaries in their positions irrespective of his wish, and Sherman, a Senate conferee, had distinctly denied that such was the case.[1] It was Mr. Johnson's belief, moreover, that when considering the bill in cabinet meeting, he had been supported by all his

---

[1] Globe, 2d sess., 39th Cong., p. 1516.

advisers, including Stanton himself, in the opinion that the law did not affect their tenure.[1] These facts, however, could not be conclusive of the construction of the law, and the question had to be argued from the terms of the statute.

It was declared that the secretary of war should hold his office for and during the term of the President by whom he was appointed. Mr. Stanton's commission bore the date January 11, 1862, and was signed by President Lincoln. In common with Messrs. Seward, McCullough and Welles, he had continued without specific reappointment either by Lincoln, after his second inauguration, or by Johnson. The question presented, then, was whether they were still serving in the term of President Lincoln. A vast amount of metaphysical subtlety was expended on the solution of this problem so far as it involved the definition of the word "term." It was pretty generally agreed, in the first place, that a Presidential term ended and a new one began on the fourth day of March, in every fourth year after 1789. The Vice-President is chosen for the same term as the President. Was Johnson then serving in his own term or in that of Lincoln ? As far as the mere time was concerned, apparently in both. But the crucial query was as to whether the words "term of the President by whom appointed" referred to the time for which a man was chosen President, or

[1] Johnson's message to the Senate, Dec. 12, 1867; Trial, p. 20.

the time during which he actually filled the office. In other words, whether the essence of the expression which fixed the cabinet's term, was in the office of President, or in the man who filled it? If the former, Stanton was entitled to hold on till April 5, 1869; if the latter, he had no claim to his office.[1]

The best method of determining the disputed point was to look at the intendment of the proviso. The managers held that it was designed merely to enable each President, on assuming office, to get rid of his predecessor's cabinet. If a President was re-elected, as Lincoln had been, the tenure of his cabinet officers was not interrupted. "Term of the President," they argued, meant the whole time during which the same individual was assigned to the office. Stanton, therefore, having been appointed by Lincoln, was entitled to his office for the whole time for which Lincoln was chosen, and one month more. Johnson had no term as President. He merely exercised the duties of President in the term for which he was chosen Vice-President. As against this argument of the managers the defence held that the intent of the act was to give each President a chance to choose once his constitutional advisers. Johnson was

---

[1] For a bit of verbal analysis that would do credit to a mediæval dialectician, see Edmunds' opinion, Trial, p. 426. The learned senator deduces his conclusions chiefly from a construction put upon the word "of."

President. It was now too late to hold that he was only acting-President; Tyler's course had settled that point. Such being the case, Stanton's term had expired in May, 1865; and the office of secretary of war never having been filled by Johnson, he had the right under the plain meaning of the law to get rid of his predecessor's appointee and secure one to his liking.

This proviso was in fact one of those cases so common in the history of our legislation, where, upon vital disagreement between the houses, a conference committee has finally reported a compromise that can be construed to satisfy either of the conflicting interests. It is sufficient to observe here that the doubts raised about this clause prevented a direct issue on the much more important constitutional question. Even those who held Johnson guilty in other respects, could scarcely vote to remove him from office for the mere adoption of a possible interpretation of so uncertain an expression as that of the proviso.

After the charge of unlawful removal, and the accusations incidental thereto, the next high misdemeanor alleged against the President was the authorization given to Thomas to act as secretary of war *ad interim*. This was assailed as a violation of the constitution and of the laws and also as done without authority of law.

The practice of temporary appointments to offices made vacant by unexpected contingencies

was a long-established one, and had been made the
subject of regulation by law on three different occasions prior to the passage of the Tenure-of-Office
Act.   It is not important to follow the discussions
on the legal questions involved in the interpretation of these laws.[1]   The only constitutional question that arose was, whether the executive had
power to evade the advisory right of the Senate
by repeated *ad interim* appointments.   Mr. Johnson did not claim that power.   His designation of
Thomas was, indeed, without limitation as to time;
but the nomination of Thomas Ewing, Sr., of Ohio,
as secretary of war, had been sent in to the Senate on the next day after Stanton's removal.   The
intention to evade the constitutional requirement

[1] The whole case from the President's standpoint, both as to the
law and the practice, is summed up in a message of Buchanan to
the Senate, of January 15, 1861.   It was in reply to a request for
information in regard to the appointment of an *ad interim* secretary of war in place of Floyd, resigned.   The message was accompanied by a list of appointments showing the practice in the matter.
This whole document was put in evidence by counsel for Mr. Johnson.   Trial, p. 191.   Subsequently to the action of Mr. Buchanan
a new law had been enacted in reference to the matter, and the
main point in discussion was whether this later act repealed the
previous legislation.   See 12 Statutes at Large, p. 656.   It was
here enacted that in case of death, resignation, absence from the
seat of government, or sickness, of certain officers, including heads
of departments, the President might authorize any other corresponding officer of either of the departments to perform the duties
of the office, but for not more than six months.   The defence
held that this did not apply to vacancies caused by removal.   See
also 1 Statutes at Large, p. 415.

was thus made very doubtful, to say the least. A point strongly pressed by the managers was that the President ought not to be permitted to make *ad interim* appointments while the Senate was in session, to fill vacancies created by his own action. The records reveal few precedents of this sort, and it is undeniably a convenient path to usurpation. The laws regulating *ad interim* appointments say nothing as to whether or not the Senate may be in session at the time the vacancy occurs; but in specifying the causes by which temporary vacancies are produced, reference is made only to death, resignation, absence from the seat of government, or sickness — that is, to contingencies not under the control of the President; and by act of 1863, the *ad interim* appointment is limited to a period of six months. It is obvious that these limitations are well founded, and that the spirit of the legislation, as well as of the constitution, is opposed to Mr. Johnson's claim that the power of removal included the power of indefinite suspension.

V

The trial proper was terminated, with Manager Bingham's argument, on the 6th of May. It had become evident by that time that the legal case of the prosecution had not the strength it was at first supposed to have. Serious indications of disaffection had appeared in the Republican ranks. The radical majority determined to pass over the doubtful charges and get a vote first on those which were most likely to be successful. Careful consideration convinced them that the last article in order, the eleventh, promised a result the most satisfactory to the prosecution. As has been stated above, the gravamen of the charge in this article was an attempt to defeat the execution of the Tenure-of-Office Act. But the essence of the attempt was alleged to consist in either the removal of Stanton or the appointment of Thomas, or in both together. The article, moreover, was so framed as to allege the President's opposition to military reconstruction as incidental to the attempt charged. Such an article might reasonably be expected to secure the greatest vote for conviction. It was therefore brought up for action first. Amid the most intense excitement the vote was taken May 16th. The result was: guilty, 35; not guilty, 19. Seven regular Republicans[1] stood with the twelve opposition senators for acquittal. The opinions filed by these seven leave no room for doubt that the danger which threatened the balance of the constitutional system was the motive which most largely influenced their verdict.

Once set the example [said Trumbull] of impeaching a President for what, when the excitement of the hour shall

---

[1] These Republicans were Fessenden, Fowler, Grimes, Henderson, Ross, Trumbull and Van Winkle.

have subsided, will be regarded as insufficient causes . . . and no future President will be safe who happens to differ with a majority of the House and two thirds of the Senate on any measure deemed by them important, particularly if of a political character. Blinded by partisan zeal, with such an example before them, they will not scruple to remove out of the way any obstacle to the accomplishment of their purposes, and what then becomes of the checks and balances of the constitution, so carefully devised, and so vital to its perpetuity?[1]

The radicals were greatly chagrined at this verdict, especially as they had come within a single vote of success in their purpose. A recess of ten days was taken, during which vigorous but not very hopeful efforts were made to overcome the scruples of the Republican dissidents. The second and third articles, concerning the appointment of Thomas, were the only ones left that gave the slightest hope of success. The legal case on these, especially the latter, was considered to be very strong. On the 26th of May the vote was taken, but with the same result as before. It was clear that the plan to oust the President had failed.

After the announcement of this vote, the Senate, sitting as a court of impeachment for the trial of Andrew Johnson, adjourned *sine die*. On the same day, Mr. Stanton addressed to the President a note in these terms:

SIR: — The resolution of the Senate of the United States, of the 21st of February last, declaring that the President " has

[1] Trial, p. 420.

no power to remove the secretary of war and designate any other officer to perform the duties of that office *ad interim*," having this day failed to be supported by two thirds of the senators present and voting on the articles of impeachment preferred against you by the House of Representatives, I have relinquished charge of the War Department, and have left the same, and the books, archives, papers and property, heretofore in my custody as secretary of war, in care of Brevet Major-General Townsend, the senior assistant adjutant-general, subject to your direction.

                    (Signed)   EDWIN M. STANTON,
                                        Secretary of War.

The President having meanwhile nominated General Schofield as secretary of war, "in place of Edwin M. Stanton, removed," the Senate, on May 29th, passed a resolution confirming the appointment, but preceded by a preamble declaring that Stanton had not been legally removed from his office, but had "relinquished his place as secretary of war for causes stated in his note to the President." With this final shot, the crisis of the conflict between Johnson and the radical Congress ended. The radicals retired, and the President was left in possession of the field.

As a mere matter of partisan politics, it is now generally conceded that the impeachment was a mistake. In the view of constitutional history, the impeachment must be considered as marking the utmost limit of the sharp reaction which followed the sudden and enormous concentration of power in the executive department during the stress of arms. Since 1868 the progress toward the normal equilibrium of forces has been constant. With the accession of President Grant, in 1869, the most offensive clauses of the Tenure-of-Office Act were repealed. Twenty years later, the whole act, having become practically obsolete, was struck from the statute-book almost without opposition. The single vote by which Andrew Johnson escaped conviction marks the narrow margin [1] by which the Presidential element in our system escaped destruction. It is highly improbable that circumstances so favorable to the removal of a President on political grounds will again arise. For better or for worse, the co-ordinate position of the executive has become a permanent feature of the constitution.

[1] The margin was not in fact quite so narrow as it appeared. Two senators who actually voted " guilty " had pledged themselves to vote " not guilty " in case such vote should be indispensable to acquittal.

ARE THE STATES EQUAL UNDER THE CONSTITUTION?

In respect to the question of ultimate political supremacy under the constitution of the United States, the result of the Civil War gave an answer that was decisive. No argument based in any particular upon the principle of state-sovereignty can ever again be tolerated in the arena of constitutional debate. Our fundamental law must always henceforth be viewed as the expression of a nation's will. There is abundant room for difference of opinion as to the extent of the authority that is entrusted to the government by the people; there is food for endless controversy in the distribution of powers among the many governmental organizations, and among the various departments of each; but the right of any particular community to maintain its own idea on either of these points against the contrary assertion of the organ of the whole people will never again call for recognition. The conviction in the South that the state had absolute rights as against the nation was well known to be the basis of the secession movement and the source of the country's woes. Public opinion in the victorious section demanded as the first fruit of its triumph the annihilation of every principle upon which the pernicious dogma could possibly find support. Hence the sweeping invasion by national legislation of the region hitherto deemed sacred to state rights. Hence the culminating doctrine that resistance to the will of the nation instantly divests the state of all rights whatever.

In the circumstances of the time it was a very easy matter to legislate away what had been claimed to be rights of the states. To provide for the permanence of the legislation required care. The last three amendments to the constitution, especially the fourteenth, make a number of extremely important powers irrecoverable. Besides these, the precedents of the mere legislation oppose a substantial barrier to any future demonstration against the central stronghold. Among the less prominent features of this barrier was the series of acts which has suggested the subject of this paper. Between the outbreak of the war and the close of the reconstruction two new states were admitted to the Union, and eleven of the old states were restored to the constitutional relations which were broken off by secession. In both the acts admitting the new states and those restoring the old, the operation of the laws was made contingent upon the acceptance by the states of certain fundamental conditions. The mere fact of conditions in an act of admission was no novelty ; the content, however, of those under consideration was in a large measure unprecedented, and was wholly significant of the times. In the discussion of the matter, the ancient dogma that all the states of the Union are constitutionally endowed with precisely equal powers was subjected to a careful examination in the light of the modern conceptions of our system. Under the influence of the state-sovereignty theory, the principle had been generally considered axiomatic. But now, like so many other monuments of the *ante-bellum* system, it was boldly attacked and was threatened with utter demolition.

It is the purpose of this paper to determine not so much whether the states *ought* to be equal in powers, but whether, as a matter of fact, they *are* equal, under the authoritative construction up to date of the constitution and the laws. The method adopted will be, first, to examine historically the process of admitting states to the Union, and, second, to discuss the bearing of the process upon the relations of the states to the general government.

I

The germ of the doctrine of equal states and the model for all the pertinent provisions of *antebellum* legislation in admitting new members to the Union are found in the various acts by which the United States, under the Articles of Confederation, acquired dominion and established government in the great region between the Alleghanies and the Mississippi. In 1784 Virginia executed the deed of cession by which all her claim to lands northwest of the Ohio River was transferred to the United States.[1] The cession, however, was conditional. It was stipulated that the ceded region should be laid out and formed into states, and that the states so formed should be distinct republican states, and should be "admitted as members of the Federal Union, having the same rights of sovereignty, freedom and independence as the other states." Other stipulations also were inserted, looking to the security of certain land-grants previously made by Virginia, and all were formally accepted by the Congress. The latter body had indeed willingly offered the pledge to form the territory into equal states as an inducement to the states to make the much desired cessions.[2] It thus appears that the principle of equality between the original and the newer states finds its first expression as an indispensable prerequisite to an enormous increase of the central government's dignity and power.

Shortly after the cession of the territory northwest of the Ohio, the Congress provided by resolution for its government. This act of 1784 was

---

[1] Poore, Federal and State Constitutions, I, 427–8.
[2] Story, Commentaries, sec. 1316.

the immediate predecessor of the more famous
ordinance passed three years later.   Its provisions are of interest as embodying certain forms
of compact which have appeared in almost every
act of admission up to the present day.   After
a description of the process by which the new
states to be formed in the territory should become full-fledged members of the Union, a series
of clauses was recited which were to stand as a
compact between the United States and each of
the new states, unalterable except by common
consent.   These clauses provided that the states
should forever remain a part of the Confederacy,
that they should in no case interfere with the disposal of the soil by Congress, that they should
impose no tax upon lands owned by the United
States, that their governments should be republican, and that the lands of non-resident proprietors
should not be taxed higher than those of residents before the state's delegates should be admitted to vote in Congress.[1]   When this law was
superseded by the Ordinance of 1787, the same
provisions were included in the "articles of compact between the original states and the people
and states in the said territory."   They constituted, however, only a small proportion of the
terms in the new instrument.   Among the additional clauses of interest to our investigation were
these : no person shall be molested on account of

[1] Curtis, History of the Constitution, vol. i, p. 297.

his mode of worship or religious sentiments; navigable rivers must remain free public highways; whenever any of the states to be formed shall have 60,000 inhabitants, "such state shall be admitted by its delegates into the Congress of the United States on an equal footing with the original states in all respects whatever";[1] and finally, the celebrated anti-slavery clause which had been voted down in 1784.[2]

The Ordinance of 1787 contains substantially every provision that is to be found, by way of compact or fundamental condition, in any act of admission prior to the Civil War. On it were based the forms of cession and government by which the lands west of Georgia and North Carolina became territories of the United States. There was room for serious doubt as to the power of the old Congress to guarantee the admission of new states on equal terms with the old. Madison regarded the promise in the Ordinance of 1787 as wholly unauthorized by the Articles of Confederation.[3] But a new condition of affairs was brought about by the adoption of the constitution of 1787, and the re-enactment of the territorial ordinance by the new Congress in 1789. There was no

---

[1] Poore, Constitutions, I, 432.

[2] "There shall be neither slavery nor involuntary servitude in the said territory, otherwise than in the punishment of crimes, whereof the party shall have been duly convicted."

[3] *Federalist*, No. 38, end.

doubt whatever of the power of Congress under the constitution to admit states on an equal footing with the original thirteen. The uncertainty now was as to whether the new-comers could enter on any other terms. The debates in the convention revealed considerable soreness among many politicians of the Northern and Eastern states at the prospect of the overwhelming weight of the South and West when the new states should be well settled. Manifestations of this feeling were frequent during the long struggle over the adjustment of representation.[1] Gouverneur Morris was the most outspoken in hostility to the equality of the new members of the Union. Having failed in an effort to discriminate against them in the matter of representation, he was more successful when the clause in reference to the admission of new states came up for discussion. As reported from the committee of detail, this clause provided that such states should be admitted by a two-thirds vote of Congress. Only in reference to those arising within the boundaries of any of the old states was it declared that they should be admitted on the same terms with the original thirteen. All others were, by implication, subject to the discretion of the legislature. Morris, however, objected to limiting this discretion in any way, and on his motion the distinction was stricken out and the clause was remodelled

[1] Bancroft, History of the Constitution, II, pp. 84, 85, *et passim.*

in its present form: "New states may be admitted by Congress into this Union."[1] So far as the intention of this clause is concerned, therefore, there seems to be no reason to assert that the constitution forbids inequality. Let us now review the practice and precedents in the further growth of the nation.

Vermont was the first new state to enter the Union. Her admission had been contemplated by the framers of the constitution, and the final form of the clause in reference to new states within the jurisdiction of the old had been determined with a view to her quarrel with New York.[2] Congress' act of admission consisted of a simple statement that Vermont should be a member of the Union. The same simplicity characterized the entrance of Kentucky. This state originally formed the western half of Virginia. Virginia agreed to the separation of the territory on certain conditions, which were to be accepted by the latter and by the United States. The act of admission simply recognized the new state. Tennessee was the next to enter the Union. The act of cession by North Carolina contained about the same stipulations as the instrument by which the Northwest Territory was granted by Virginia. The act of admission presented for the first time in a Congressional enactment the formula: "On

---

[1] Elliot's Debates (Lippincott, 1876), V, p. 493.
[2] Curtis, Hist. of the Const., vol. ii, p. 353.

an equal footing with the original states in all respects whatever." [1]   This clause occurs in either the enabling act or the act of admission of every state subsequently admitted.

The first state formed from the Northwest Territory was Ohio, in 1802.   She was also the first to pass from the territorial form under the direction of an enabling act.   This act has been the model for all succeeding legislation of the kind, and in it may be found provisions that have since furnished a basis for the claim of Congress' right to exact conditions of an applicant for admission. By it the inhabitants of the territory included in certain designated boundaries were authorized to form a constitution which must be republican and not repugnant to the Ordinance of 1787.   These two requirements were designed to fulfil the duty of the United States, first to the constitution, in guaranteeing a republican form of government, and second, to Virginia, in carrying out the terms of the act of cession, as embodied in the Ordinance of 1787.   The enabling act then offered to the state's convention, for its free acceptance or rejection, three propositions : first, to grant to the state certain lands for the support of schools ; second, to grant to the state the salt-springs and sufficient adjacent land to work them ; and third, to apply to the building of roads and canals for the benefit of the state five per cent of the pro-

[1] Poore, Constitutions, II, 1677.

ceeds of public lands sold within the state. These propositions, if accepted, were to be binding upon the United States, provided that the acceptance should be accompanied by an ordinance, irrevocable without the consent of the United States, declaring that lands sold by Congress should be exempt from taxation for a period of five years after the sale. The convention accepted the propositions and the required ordinance was duly enacted.

In 1812, Louisiana became a state. The enabling act in this case laid down a large number of requirements to which the constitution of the new state must conform. These were based mainly on the Ordinance of 1787, and were obviously designed to counteract any foreign influences that might have taken root while the territory was under European dominion. No terms were *offered* to Louisiana as to Ohio. But an irrevocable ordinance was *demanded*, which should bind the state to substantially the same stipulations that were contained in the Ordinance of 1787 in respect to unappropriated lands and navigable waters, as well as to the five-year exemption from taxation of public lands sold by the United States. There is no equivalent whatever offered in return for these demands, and the peremptory character of Congress' dealing with the state is revealed still more distinctly in the act of admission. For some reason, the irrevocable ordinance which the Louisiana con-

vention adopted omitted the declaration that the
Mississippi and other navigable rivers should be free
from tax or toll. Congress, therefore, made that
declaration a proviso of the state's admission, and
clinched it with these words: "The above condition, and also all other the terms and conditions
contained in the third section of [the enabling act]
shall be considered, deemed and taken fundamental
conditions and terms upon which the said state is
incorporated in the Union."[1] Such language might
be thought fatal to the claim of equality among the
states, were it not that, in the same section, the act
declares Louisiana admitted "on an equal footing
with the original states in all respects whatever."
The legislator could have joined these two provisions only on the understanding that all the original states labored under the same restrictions that
were imposed upon Louisiana.

No new principle appeared in the admission of
the next five states. The familiar irrevocable ordinance was a feature of each case, except that of
Maine. Indiana, Illinois and Alabama received an
equivalent for their concessions, like Ohio; Mississippi followed Louisiana in granting the ordinance absolutely. Maine came in with the consent
of Massachusetts, and with no provision further
than that of equality with the original states.

The admission of Missouri suggests immediately the ominous struggle over slavery restriction.

[1] Poore, Constitutions, p. 710.

Tallmadge's famous motion[1] was to impose as an absolute condition upon Missouri's existence the identical proposition which had, in the states formed in the Northwest Territory, assumed the form of a compact. Without stopping at this point to examine the line of argument adopted by the friends of slavery, it is sufficient to remark that the strenuous denial of any power in Congress to withhold from a new state a right possessed by the original members of the Union was the position which proved most troublesome to the restrictionists. Only the boldest spirits ventured to combat the proposition that the nature of the Union demanded perfect equality among its members. The great struggle occurred over the enabling act. Outside of the clause which embodied the celebrated compromise, this act was substantially the same as its immediate predecessors. The resolution admitting the state, however, presented another case of absolute condition. It declared that

Missouri shall be admitted into this Union on an equal footing with the original states in all respects whatever, upon the fundamental condition, that the fourth clause of the 26th section of the third article of the constitution submitted on the

[1] To amend the bill for admission by adding this clause: "*Provided*, That the further introduction of slavery or involuntary servitude be prohibited, except for the punishment of crimes, whereof the party shall have been duly convicted; and that all children born within the said state, after the admission thereof to the Union, shall be free at the age of twenty-five years."

part of said state to Congress, shall never be construed to authorize the passage of any law

that shall conflict, in short, with the inter-state rights of citizens as provided for by the constitution of the United States.[1] And the assent of the legislature of the state to this condition was demanded and was duly given.

Arkansas organized a state government without waiting for an enabling act. Congress admitted her, upon the express condition that the people of the state should not interfere with the primary disposal of the public lands, nor tax them while United States property. This proceeding, however, was evidently unsatisfactory; for a supplementary act was passed in which these same conditions were made, with others, the equivalents for the customary land grants for education and other public purposes, and were put in the form of an irrevocable ordinance.[2] The difficulty between Ohio and Michigan about their dividing boundary[3] accounts for the express condition in the act admitting the latter that her boundaries shall be as described in the act. Iowa was admitted on the fundamental condition that the assent of the township electors should be given to the act of admission. From this time (1846) to the admission of Nevada, in 1864,

[1] 3 Statutes at Large, 645.

[2] Poore, Constitutions, I, 118.

[3] Michigan, by Judge Cooley, in American Commonwealths series, p. 214 *et seq.*

the legislation of Congress reveals no novelty pertinent to our subject. Every clause of both enabling acts and acts of admission is a copy of some one of those that have been noticed.

Nevada entered the Union to the accompaniment of Grant's guns on the Potomac and Sherman's on the Chattahoochee. It would be strange if no mark of those fateful times appeared impressed upon her. In the enabling act, we discover that her constitution was required to harmonize not only with the constitution of the United States, but also with the principles of the Declaration of Independence. Further, the convention was required to provide by ordinance, irrevocable without the consent of the United States and the people of the state : first, that there should be neither slavery nor involuntary servitude in the state ; second, that there should be perfect toleration of religious sentiment; and only third, that the public lands should be secured to the United States. These first two provisions were not absolutely unprecedented. Both were contained in the Ordinance of 1787, and had, therefore, become part of the fundamental law of five states. But the special mention of them in an enabling act was significant.

It was left for Nebraska, in 1867, to become a state under an entirely novel restriction. The act of admission was to take effect upon the fundamental condition that within the State of Nebraska there shall be no denial of the elective franchise or of any other right to any person because of race or color, excepting Indians not taxed, and upon the further fundamental condition that the legislature of said state, by a solemn public act, shall declare the assent of said state to said fundamental condition.

Colorado (1876) had the provision for religious tolerance thrown into the irrevocable ordinance by which national control of the public lands was established. The grants of lands for schools, public buildings, *etc.*, were in her case, as in that of Nevada and Nebraska, made absolute benefactions. The two Dakotas, Montana and Washington (1889) and Utah (1895) came in on much the same terms.[1] In their case, however, the irrevocable ordinance that was required of each included two new provisions: first, that public debts contracted under the territorial form should be assumed by the state; and second, that a public school system should be established, open to all children of the state and free from sectarian control. And in the act relating to Utah the peculiar circumstances of her history were suggested by the proviso, attached to the requirement of religious toleration, that "polygamous, or plural, marriages are forever prohibited." Like the institution which made it necessary, this provision is unique in our history. Idaho and Wyo-

---

[1] 25 Statutes at Large, 676; 28 *Ibid.*, 107.

ming (1890) escaped all conditions, whether in form or in substance.[1]

This completes the review of the legislation upon the addition of new states. It remains now to consider the case of the so-called rebel states, which were declared by Congress to have forfeited, by the attempted secession, all rights guaranteed by the constitution to members of the Union. By act of March 2, 1867, Congress announced the circumstances under which the forfeited rights would be restored. Later acts provided for carrying out the proposed plan of reconstruction. Tennessee had previously been admitted, upon conforming voluntarily to the general lines of Congress' desire. Of the other ten, all but three were finally admitted to representation in Congress, as states of the Union, upon the fundamental condition that their constitutions should never be so amended as to deprive any citizen or class of citizens of the right to vote, except as a punishment for crime. Virginia, Mississippi and Texas were delayed in fulfilling the requirements of Congress; as a consequence the ardor of the advocates of conditions rose in the meantime to such an extent that two additional limitations on the equality of those states were imposed; the first forbade any law excluding negroes from the right to hold office; the second forbade any amendment of the state constitution

[1] 26 Statutes at Large, 215, 222.

that should deprive negroes of equal school privileges with the whites.[1]

From this survey of the practice since the United States became an independent nation, one fact stands out very distinctly, and that is, that Congress, whether authorized by the constitution or not, has, in the exercise of its power to admit new states, imposed conditions on the applicants, and that too, both in substance and in express terms. It is equally undeniable that, if these conditions are valid, and if by virtue of them rights are withheld that are enjoyed by the original states, the ancient dogma that this is a union of equal states is without foundation in constitutional law. The first question then that must command our attention is this: Are the laws of Congress imposing conditions upon new states, in accordance with the constitution of the United States?

II

The conditions that we have found in our examination may be grouped in respect to their form in three classes as follows: first, compacts, which, by unconstrained agreement, limit not only the states but also the United States in specified particulars; second, conditions upon admission which are absolute in form, but which are explicitly

[1] McPherson, History of the Reconstruction, p. 573 *et seq.* *Cf. ante,* p. 235 *et seq.*

conditions precedent, and hence exhaust their force at the moment the admission is perfected — as for example, that which required the antecedent consent of the township electors in Iowa; and third, absolute conditions whose force is obviously intended to be permanent, and forever to restrict the power of the state. The best example of this last class is the prohibition of the reconstructed states ever to amend their constitutions in certain respects.

The subjects in respect to which Congress has enacted permanent limitations may be grouped under seven heads: first, public lands; second, navigable waters; third, inter-state rights of United States citizens; fourth, the principles of civil and religious liberty; fifth, public debts of the states; sixth, the public school system; and seventh, equality in political and civil rights.

Let us now ascertain upon what grants of power in the constitution the right of Congress rests to legislate in each of these forms and upon each of these subjects. And first, is Congress authorized to make a compact with a state of the Union, either existing or in embryo? The theory of our system is that the central government is one of strictly limited powers. For the definition of such powers as it has, only the constitution is to be consulted. By that instrument Congress is established as a law-making body. Especial care is taken to prevent the effectiveness of any action

of the two houses under any other form than that
specifically laid down in the constitution. Every
order, resolution and vote must be in fact a law.[1]
In the same way, a compact to which Congress is
a party can have no extraordinary force on account
of its special form. It is nothing more or less
than a law. The agreement by the state to its
terms adds nothing to its efficacy. Its validity
can be tested only by the constitution. If Congress is authorized to enact that a certain regulation shall take effect upon the performance of some
act by a certain community, it is authorized to enforce the regulation without regard to such act.
A compact must be regarded then, so far as Congress is concerned, simply as a law. The question
as to Congress' right to enter into a compact with
a state becomes merely a question as to the constitutional power of the national legislature to
enact a law involving the same principles. Our
examination of the validity of the compacts which
are supposed to create inequalities among the
states must therefore deal with the substance
rather than the form. We must ascertain under
what grant of power in the constitution the various
terms of the acts were enacted.

Conditions precedent to admission must be
treated on the same principle. The constitution
itself, however, renders discussion of these practically of no importance to our subject. Any act

[1] Constitution, art. i, sec. 7.

of Congress which affects United States territory only before its assumption of the state form may be justified under the plenary power granted by article four, section three.[1] The violent and protracted controversy as to the construction of this clause in connection with the slavery question may be considered to have been settled by the Civil War. In spite of the contrary opinion in the Dred Scott Case, the power of Congress to make rules and regulations concerning the territories will be generally conceded now to be unlimited save by the express prohibitions of the constitution. Conditions, therefore, which prescribe certain acts by either the people or the government of a territory as preliminary to admission as a state, are wholly within the power of the national legislature.

An entirely different principle is involved in the matter of conditions subsequent, *i.e.*, restrictions imposed while the territorial form prevailed, but intended to be of binding force after the assumption of the state dignity. The solution of the problem here is very similar to that in the case of compacts. The condition is only a law of Congress and has no greater force than any other law. The validity of the law depends on the constitutional authority for it ; or, in short, upon the substance rather than the form. It is held by some, however, that by

---

[1] "The Congress shall have power to dispose of, and make all needful rules and regulations respecting, the territory or other property belonging to the United States."

the wording of the constitution, Congress is given unlimited control over the substance of the admitting act. " New states may be admitted by Congress into this Union," is the form the clause takes. It has been shown above that the probable intention of Gouverneur Morris in thus phrasing it was to leave room for an implication of power in Congress to impose conditions upon new states. The probability of such a purpose becomes certainty in the light of a letter written by Morris in 1803. "I always thought," he says, "when we should acquire Canada [*sic*] and Louisiana, it would be proper to govern them as provinces and allow them no voice in our counsels. In wording the third section of the fourth article, I went so far as circumstances would permit to establish the exclusion." He significantly continues : " Candor obliges me to add my belief that had it been more pointedly expressed, a strong opposition would have been made."[1] At the time of Louisiana's admission as a state, in 1811–12, the Federalists made a violent resistance to the equality clause, and Josiah Quincy went so far as to assert his solemn conviction that the admission of new states from acquired territory on equal terms with the old, was sufficient ground for a dissolution of the Union. The principle, however, was established, and continued in practice down to the Civil War,

[1] Quoted by Judge Campbell in the Dred Scott Case; 19 Howard, 507.

of not making the implication for which Morris so craftily left room.

With the tide of loose construction that set in with 1861, the usage in this matter shared the fate of so many others. While the doctrine of unlimited Congressional discretion as to conditions upon a state's admission cannot be said to be definitely established, yet it is beyond doubt that such an idea finds support in a very respectable body of constitutional lawyers. The argument of the supporters of this theory is that Congress is the agent of the nation in creating political corporations called states. Through the constitution, the nation has given Congress a discretion as to the powers it may confer on such corporations, limited only by the positive prohibitions of the fundamental law. There is nothing in the constitution requiring that the states shall be equal. The character of each corporation is impressed upon it by the special act by which it is admitted. No court can go behind the provisions of such an act to apply any extra-constitutional theory that all states have equal rights. In respect to such powers and duties as are positively ascribed to the states by the constitution, there is, of course, equality. Every state is entitled to an equal representation in the Senate, and to a proportionate number of members in the House of Representatives. Every state, whether new or old, is equally entitled to the guarantee of a republican form of government. But beyond such clearly defined rights, Congress may determine as it pleases the degree of restriction which it deems best for any particular community.[1]

In opposition to this view, the older theory maintains that the equality of rights in the states is distinctly embodied in the constitution. Even if the above stated construction of the clause about the admission of states were good, it must be modified by the amendments which have been added to the original instrument. Article ten of these amendments declares that "the powers not delegated to the United States by the constitution, nor prohibited by it to the states, are reserved to the states respectively, or to the people." This does not say "to the old states," or "to some of the states," but "to the states"; and it would be palpably erroneous to construe this expression to refer to less than every state in the Union. But if this is the case, any state can claim every right that is not delegated to the United States or prohibited to the states. In short, the instant a community becomes entitled to the name of state, it has every power that is exercised by any other community bearing that name. A court, in deciding upon a state's right to exercise a given power, must look not to the act of admission, but to the

---

[1] See debates on the admission of Nebraska, Cong. Globe, 2d sess., 39th Congress. The subject was most exhaustively debated, also, in connection with the bills restoring the rebel states to representation, in 1868–70.

constitution under which this act of admission was passed. If the power in question is not delegated to the United States by the constitution nor prohibited by it to the states, it rightfully belongs to the state, anything in the act of Congress to the contrary notwithstanding. But without reference to this amendment, the clause respecting admission, it is maintained, will not bear the construction sought to be put upon it. This clause does not authorize Congress to *create* states, but to *admit* them. The creation of the state is antecedent to the admission, and springs from the will of the people inhabiting the territory. The enabling act merely puts the stamp of the nation's approval upon the expression of this will. This may be, and in many cases has been, dispensed with. The genius of our institutions does not recognize the possibility of forever withholding from a community desiring it, the privilege of local self-government under the constitution.

It must be confessed that, with all the strength of this theory, the derivation of the right to the state form from the genius of our institutions, or, as some have it, from the nature of things, is a little unsatisfactory. The foundation is a trifle too shadowy for the very substantial structure that rests upon it.

No case has ever been decided by the Supreme Court in such form as to settle definitely which of these two conflicting theories is correct. As might be supposed, a very strong leaning towards the latter is discernible in several opinions rendered in the two decades immediately preceding the war. It was found possible, however, in every case, to decide the issue under some clause of the constitution other than that referring to the admission of states. The substance rather than the form of the admitting acts was considered. But whichever of these theories may ultimately prevail, the answer to the question we have set before us — *viz.*, whether at the present time there is any inequality among the states — must be sought in the content of the supposed restrictions that thus far have been enacted. Compacts have been made with new states, by which those states resigned certain powers; fundamental conditions have been imposed, prohibiting the exercise of certain powers. Whether or not Congress was authorized to make the limitations, let us consider to what extent such limitations discriminate against the newer states.

III

We have already classified the restrictions that have been enacted and have found the first prominent subject to be the public lands of the United States. Either in the form of a compact or by way of fundamental condition, all but five of the states admitted since the formation of the constitution are to-day forbidden to tax lands which are the property of the United States; and in most cases the exemption covers the lands for from three to five years after their sale. The power of taxation has always been held to be an incident of sovereignty. Does this limitation upon the state's taxing power, then, interfere with the sovereignty which belongs to the state in respect to matters not delegated to the United States by the constitution?

As to the property of the United States, it has been settled that wherever it is situated it is above the state's demand for tribute. In practice, the national government regularly secures a cession of jurisdiction by the state within whose limits land is secured for a mint, post-office or other necessary institution. This custom has tended to obviate all controversy on this precise point. The general question of a state's right to tax property of the United States was discussed quite fully by the Supreme Court in McCullough *vs.* Maryland. Here the state's lawyers contended that by the constitution the taxing power of the state was unlimited save as to imports and exports.[1] This view was explicitly rejected by the court; but a positive opinion was not required upon more than the single matter of the United States Bank. This, it was decided, the states could not tax; for

[1] 4 Wheaton, p. 328 *et passim. Cf.* constitution, art. i, sec. 10, cl. 2.

the bank was a constitutional means for carrying into execution the powers vested in the general government. Whether land was such a constitutional means, was until recently an unsettled question. Justice McLean is responsible for the assertion that the government has paid taxes to the old states on its lands.[1] Not till 1886 was the problem authoritatively solved by the Supreme Court. In Van Brocklin *vs.* Tennessee,[2] Justice Gray, in an opinion extraordinarily clear and exhaustive, concludes that neither the people nor the legislature of Tennessee had power, by constitution or statute, to tax land so long as the title remained in the United States. The basis of the opinion was the principle of McCullough *vs.* Maryland, and the further conclusion that

the United States do not and cannot hold property, as a monarch may, for private or personal purposes. All the property and revenues of the United States must be held and applied, as all taxes, duties, imposts and excises must be laid and collected, "to pay the debts and provide for the common defense and general welfare of the United States."

This decision leaves no room for any claim that the conditions prohibiting new states to tax government lands deprives them of any right enjoyed by the old members of the Union.

The exemption of the first purchaser of public

[1] U. S. *vs.* R. R. Bridge Co., 6 McLean, 531.
[2] 117 U. S. 151.

land from the taxing power of the state for a time falls within a different category from the matter just discussed. In by far the greater number of instances, this exemption has been one of the considerations in a compact between the United States and the new state at its admission, by which, in return for the promise of exemption, various tracts of land are donated to the state. The transaction differs in no respect from an ordinary fiscal contract. The state foregoes the proceeds of the tax on certain property and receives value in the shape of certain other property. No political right is resigned by the state, and the United States is vested with no new political power. But it may be said that the state, as a sovereign power in respect to real estate within her boundaries, may repudiate the bargain at will. How could a purchaser obtain redress, if a tax were imposed before the expiration of the specified time? Would the United States courts undertake to restrain a state from taxing its own citizens? There seems to be good reason to believe that they would. In the early case of Green *vs.* Biddle,[1] the Supreme Court decided that a compact by which Kentucky agreed to apply the law of Virginia to certain land cases could not be violated by the former without bringing her in conflict with the constitutional provision in reference to impairing the obligation of contracts. There is no reason why a compact with

[1] 8 Wheaton, 1.

the United States should not be subject to the same rule. But the compact in this case could not, of course, be binding on the state if the other party had exceeded its powers in making the agreement. The United States can only contract within its constitutional powers. Its power in this case, however, may very fairly be derived from the authority to dispose of the territory of the nation.[1] This same authority could also be made to cover those cases in which the five-year exemption is enacted not as a contract but as a mere condition. Here there would be more room for debate, but in view of the very liberal margin of discretion which the court has recognized to Congress in the choice of means for executing its powers, it is not at all likely that this extra inducement to purchasers would be adjudged beyond the line.

In addition to this limitation of the taxing power of the new states, we find in most acts of admission the provision that the respective states shall disclaim title to the public lands, or shall not interfere with the primary disposal thereof. That such a provision is no real restriction does not require demonstration. The land is the property of the United States, and cannot be made more so by any law of Congress. These formulas were inserted in the early acts out of abundant caution, and they are at the present day mere survivals.

[1] *Cf. dicta* in Pollard's Lessee *vs.* Hagan, 3 Howard, p. 224.

A special case that falls under this same head is that of Michigan's southern boundary. Michigan claimed that she had, by the Ordinance of 1787, an indefeasible right to enter as a state with the boundaries described therein. These boundaries would have included a strip of territory that had been assigned to Ohio. Congress settled the hot controversy which raged on the point by admitting the new state on condition that she accepted a boundary that included less than she demanded. The question involved here seems to be rather the construction of the Ordinance of 1787 than the ultimate control over the lands, and the so-called condition is only a regulation by which conflicting constructions are compromised.[1]

To sum up our conclusions in reference to the clauses of the admission acts affecting public lands, it appears that no power has been exercised therein which could not be applied with the same effect to the older states, — in short, that no inequality of rights among the states exists by virtue of such clauses.

The second subject which has been covered by fundamental conditions is the navigable waters of the new states. The right of Congress to make the rule that they shall be free from toll is no longer a debatable question. By the constitution Congress is authorized to regulate commerce among the several states. In the case of Pollard's Lessee

[1] Cooley, Constitutional Limitations, 4th ed., p. 34.

vs. Hagan,[1] the Supreme Court was called upon to construe the article of compact by which Alabama resigned the right to impose any burden on the navigation of her rivers. "This supposed compact," the decision runs, "is nothing more than a regulation of commerce, to that extent, among the several states."[2] This same principle was reaffirmed and enlarged upon in Withers *vs.* Buckley *et al.*,[3] some years later; and finally in Gilman *vs.* Philadelphia,[4] decided in 1865, the court clinched its former judgments by the broad assertion that "the power to regulate commerce comprehends the control for that purpose and to the extent necessary, of all the navigable waters of the United States which are accessible from a state other than those in which they lie." In view of this record, it is idle to seek for inequality among the states in this particular. Congress controls the Hudson and the Susquehanna to precisely the same extent that it does the Missouri and the Arkansas.

The third class of conditions — those relating to the inter-state rights of citizens — includes, first, the common clause that lands of non-resident citizens of the United States shall not be taxed higher than those of residents of the state ; and second, the condition under which Missouri was admitted, *viz.*, that no law should be passed by the state by which any citizen of any other state should be

---

[1] 3 Howard, 212.
[2] *Ibid.*, p. 230.
[3] 20 Howard, 93.
[4] 3 Wallace, 724.

excluded from the enjoyment of any privileges and immunities to which such citizen was entitled under the constitution of the United States.[1] As to this latter matter, no discussion is necessary to show that there is no restriction placed upon Missouri that does not rest upon every other state. Missouri is forbidden to infringe, under color of her constitution, a clear provision of the federal constitution. But the prohibition would be just as imperative in law without the act of Congress as with it; and Massachusetts has no more power to deprive a citizen of another state of his constitutional privileges and immunities than has Missouri.

The same principle applies to one phase of the taxation of non-residents. Taxes are a burden upon citizens, and exemption from taxation is therefore an immunity. Equal exemption of residents and non-residents is accordingly secured by the constitution, so far as concerns citizens of the several states. This has been so determined by the Supreme Court in the case of Ward *vs.* Maryland.[2] But the clause concerning the inter-state rights of citizens does not protect against discrimination such citizens of the United States as reside in the territories or in the District of Columbia. Can the land of such persons, then, be taxed by any state

---

[1] "The citizens of each state shall be entitled to all privileges and immunities of citizens in the several states." — Const., art. iv, sec. 2.

[2] 12 Wallace, 418.

higher than the land of resident citizens of the state? If it can, the original states enjoy a right which is denied to almost every other member of the Union. The question, it must be confessed, is never likely to become of any practical importance. If it ever does come up for consideration, the Fourteenth Amendment will unquestionably be relied upon to settle it. It is there declared that "no state shall make or enforce any law which shall abridge the privileges or immunities of citizens of the United States." Whether an equal rate of taxation with the other citizens of a state in which his land is situated is a privilege or immunity of a citizen of the United States, is what must be decided. In view of the narrow construction of the Fourteenth Amendment adopted by the Supreme Court in the Slaughter House and succeeding cases, it is not likely that any power over state taxation would be assumed under the prohibition of the amendment; and it seems certain that in no other part of the constitution is authority for the substance of the restriction under consideration to be found. If then, Congressional conditions upon the admission of states are ever binding, there does exist in reference to the power of taxation, an inequality among the states.

The fourth class of restrictions is that which embraces various provisions designed to secure the fundamental principles of civil and religious liberty in the states. First, as to slavery. By the Ordinance of 1787 slavery was prohibited in all the states to be formed from the Northwest Territory. This ordinance was enacted as a law of Congress in August, 1789. Was its prohibition of slavery a valid restriction on the right of a state to determine for itself its domestic institutions? The violent and prolonged controversy on this point is familiar to every reader of our political history. As none of the states under the ordinance ever wished to establish slavery, the question never became a practical one. The Supreme Court held, in two cases,[1] that the ordinance had no more authority than any other law of Congress, and that its principles were only effective so far as discoverable in the constitution of the United States or in the constitutions and laws of the states respectively.[2] This view throws the question back again upon the constitution. No power to abolish slavery within a state was granted to Congress. Unless, then, the general power to impose restrictions on new states belongs to the national legislature, Ohio and the adjoining states, in spite of the slavery prohibition in the ordinance, enjoyed equal power over the

[1] Permoli *vs.* Municipality, 3 Howard, 589. Strader *et al. vs.* Graham, 10 Howard, 94.

[2] For a different opinion, see Spooner *vs.* McConnell, 1 McLean, 344. Judge Cooley thinks that the weight of judicial authority favors the validity of the ordinance even in respect to such of its principles as are not re-enacted in the state laws. Constitutional Limitations, 4th ed., p. 34, note.

subject with the remaining members of the Union.
In admitting Nevada, in 1864, Congress made the
prohibition of slavery an article of fundamental
compact with the state, and she was thus thrown
into the same category with those formed from
the Northwest Territory. All question as to the
equality of the states in this respect, however, was
removed by the ratification of the Thirteenth
Amendment in 1865. If before that time the six
states were inferior to the majority in their abstract power, to-day these latter are reduced to
the lower level.

It is only when we take up a further consideration of civil and religious liberty that we come to
a still enduring uncertainty. The states formed
from the Northwest Territory, as well as several
others, are to-day bound by the terms of their
admission forever to maintain in their constitutions what are recognized as the fundamental
guarantees of civil liberty. The second article
of compact in the Ordinance of 1787 secures to
the inhabitants of the territory the benefit of the
writ of *habeas corpus* and of trial by jury, judicial
proceedings according to the course of the common
law, exemption from excessive fines and cruel or
unusual punishments, and due process of law in
the deprivation of life, liberty or property. Moreover, compensation is required for property or
services taken by the state without consent, and
any law impairing the obligation of contracts is
declared void.

Only the last of these restrictions was placed upon all the states by the original constitution. The rest are contained substantially in the constitution of every state, and until after the Civil War the rights which they protected were considered secure enough without the guarantee of the national government. In the Fourteenth Amendment, however, three clauses were inserted, with a purpose to guard against any invasion of the fundamental civil rights by the states.

No state shall make or enforce any law which shall abridge the privileges or immunities of citizens of the United States; nor shall any state deprive any person of life, liberty or property, without due process of law; nor deny to any person within its jurisdiction the equal protection of the laws.

To what extent, then, do these clauses give the federal courts a corrective jurisdiction over state legislation and procedure? Do they afford a constitutional foundation for the power assumed by Congress in laying upon the states the restrictions under consideration?

It was held at first by many lawyers that the phrase "privileges and immunities of citizens of the United States" would include all the ordinary ingredients of civil liberty. This was denied by the Supreme Court in the Slaughter House Cases, and it was there decided that the fundamental civil rights were still, as before, primarily under the care of the states.[1] A limitation is put upon

[1] 16 Wallace, 77.

the latter, however, by the prohibition to deprive
of life, liberty or property without due process of
law, or to refuse to any one the equal protection
of the laws. "Due process of law" has been authoritatively defined to mean the process and procedure of the common law.[1] The courts have
always manifested a disposition to construe the
expression with the greatest liberality in favor of
the individual.[2] Under such circumstances there
can be no doubt that every state can now be held
within the bounds that were established only for
particular states by the Ordinance of 1787 and the
various admission acts. The privilege of bail, exemption from immoderate fines and cruel punishments, and compensation for expropriated property
are elements of the due process which must,
under the constitution, be observed in every state.
Whether the privilege of the writ of *habeas corpus*
is required by the clause under discussion may not
be perfectly clear, but probability is strongly on
the side of an affirmative answer. Judge Cooley
considers that "due process" does not refer to
rules of procedure only, but to "those principles
of civil liberty and constitutional protection which
have become established in our system of laws."[3]
There can scarcely be a doubt that the principle

---

[1] Murray's Lessee *vs.* Hoboken Land Imp. Co., 18 Howard, 272.
[2] Davidson *vs.* New Orleans, 96 U. S. 97; R. R. Tax Cases,
13 Federal Reporter, 763.
[3] Constitutional Limitations, 4th ed., p. 441.

of protection by the *habeas corpus* has become so established.

A single clause of the second article of the great ordinance has been left unconsidered. It is prescribed that the people shall always be entitled to proportionate representation in the legislature. It is obvious, without further comment, that this privilege is covered by the guarantee of a republican form of government in the constitution.

In the sphere of civil rights, properly so called, there is thus no distinction among the states in respect to their authority. Let us examine the matter of religious liberty. The first article of the Ordinance of 1787 is in these words: "No person demeaning himself in a peaceable and orderly manner shall ever be molested on account of his mode of worship or religious sentiments in the said territory." This restriction, as part of the ordinance, was imposed upon a number of the states admitted early in the century, but disappeared from view for a long time till it once more came to the surface in the admission of Nevada. It purports to put the freedom of worship and of religious belief in certain states under the protection of the national government. There has never been a pretence made that authority over this subject is conferred upon the national government by the constitution. The United States is prohibited by the First Amendment from interfering with the free exercise of religion. The same clause forbids any

abridgment of the right peaceably to assemble and
to petition for redress of grievances. An opinion
on the latter prohibition was rendered by the
Supreme Court in the case of United States *vs.*
Cruikshank.[1] It was argued by counsel that the
prohibition implied that the right to assemble was
a privilege of United States citizenship, and that
it was therefore under the protection of Congress,
by the Fourteenth Amendment. The court flatly
rejected the plea. The claim to control by the
United States over freedom of worship rests upon
precisely the same ground. It follows, therefore,
that the absolute power of Congress to impose restrictions upon states at their admission is the only
foundation for the condition under discussion, and
that if this power exists, the states which have
entered with this limitation are to that extent inferior in rights to the others. As long, however,
as the spirit of tolerance remains as it is among
the people, this fact can have no more than a
speculative interest.

In the act providing for the admission of Utah,
the usual clause in reference to toleration is accompanied by a proviso forever prohibiting polygamy.
This proviso may be construed either as a declaration that polygamy is not to be considered a "mode
of worship" such as to fall under the toleration
secured by the clause, or as an independent restriction upon the state. In the former case Utah falls

[1] 92 U. S. 542.

into the same category with the states just considered ; in the latter she must be regarded as subject
to a restriction not resting upon any other state.
In neither case is there any constitutional basis for
control of the matter by the national government
other than the assumed power to impose restrictions upon states.

The fifth class of restrictions includes the requirements that five of the states last admitted
shall assume the territorial public debts.   This is
probably to be regarded as merely a transitional
requirement, whose force is exhausted when the
admission is complete.   It would be possible to
contend that, inasmuch as the ordinance assuming
the debts is "irrevocable without the consent of
the United States," the national government would
be bound to interpose in case the state failed to
discharge its obligation in respect to this particular
part of its debt.   Such a contention, however,
would have to be based on the claim that the constitution authorized the United States to see that
a state paid its debts — a claim which the familiar
history of our state debts would prohibit any
rational man from bringing forward.

The sixth class of restrictions is found in the
provision requiring a non-sectarian public school
system.   There is no direct ground whatever in
the constitution for any control by the national
government over education in the states.   The
provision under consideration, if valid, must rest

upon the power to limit states at their admission. It would be possible to claim that the requirement of a public school system of the character stated should be considered an equivalent for the grants of land for school purposes embodied by Congress in the laws admitting the states. Historically there would be some basis for this claim; in the early admitting acts the grants were made in the form of contracts involving some return by the states. These early equivalents, however, were in the form of tax-exemptions — involving actual pecuniary considerations. The cession of jurisdiction over an institution of the greatest political and social importance could hardly be said to stand upon the same basis. Moreover, the Supreme Court has held, in a somewhat analogous matter, that the observance by the states of a condition attached to the grant of lands "rests upon the good faith of the states."[1]

The last class of restrictions includes only the new condition demanded of Nebraska. The rebel states, it is true, were obliged to admit the negroes to the polls and to recognize them as equal in civil rights, as a condition of restoration after the war; but the action of Congress in this instance was acknowledged on all sides to be an extraordinary proceeding, based upon the war powers of the national government. Nebraska, however, on no special ground of necessity, was distinctly pro-

[1] Mills County *vs.* R. R. Co., 107 U. S. 557.

hibited to deny the right to vote or any other right to any citizen on account of race or color. At this time, many of the Northern states still retained the word white in the suffrage clauses of their constitutions, and in the border states, at least, the blacks were under important limitations as to civil rights. No authority of any weight whatever questioned the right of the states to determine the qualifications of electors for themselves, or admitted any power in Congress to interfere with the rule adopted. If the law of Nebraska's admission, therefore, was valid,[1] that state passed the first years of its existence on a plane of distinct inferiority to the other states. The Fourteenth and Fifteenth Amendments, however, removed the irregularity. By them, the limitations which had been imposed upon Nebraska by law were made effective upon all the states by the constitution.

This completes the review of restrictions imposed upon states at their original admission into the Union. A special case now requiring notice is that of the rebellious states which were reconstructed by Congress. Practically these states were reduced to the condition of provinces, and then erected *de novo* into autonomous commonwealths. From a legal point of view, however, the Supreme Court refused to admit that the conti-

[1] The reasons assigned for the votes on the passage of the restricting clause in the Senate are interesting. See Globe, 2d sess. 39th Cong., p. 360; also p. 450.

nuity of the state life had ever been broken.[1] The
course of Congress throughout reconstruction was
declared to have been a legitimate exercise of the
power to guarantee a republican form of government. Upon this authority in the constitution,
therefore, the justification of the conditions of
restoration must rest. The first Reconstruction
Act[2] required that in each rebel state a constitution should be framed by representatives chosen by
impartial suffrage, and that this constitution should
insure the franchise to the blacks. The ratification of the Fourteenth Amendment (and in case
of Virginia, Mississippi and Texas, of the Fifteenth) was also demanded. These were conditions
precedent to the resumption of state rights ; their
force was of course exhausted at the moment of
such resumption. But the acts of Congress restoring normal relations contained the most stringent
form of condition subsequent to be found in our
history. It was declared a fundamental condition
of each state's representation in Congress, that the
state constitution should never be so amended as to
deprive of the right to vote any citizen or class of
citizens entitled to vote by the constitution in question. This limitation of the right to fix the qualifications of voters produced a most vital inequality
between the reconstructed and the loyal states.

---

[1] Texas *vs*. White, 7 Wallace, 700.   *Cf.* Shortridge *vs*. Macon,
Chase's Decisions, 136; Gunn *vs*. Barry, 15 Wallace, 623.

[2] Act of March 2, 1867.

The inequality was greatly reduced, however, by the Fifteenth Amendment. The chief purpose of the restriction in the restoring acts was to prevent the reconstructed states from taking away the suffrage from the blacks. By the amendment all the states, loyal as well as rebellious, were restricted in this respect to the same extent. But the wording of the restoring acts was wider in its scope than that of the amendment. The restored states were prohibited from narrowing the electorate on any ground ; the remaining states were prohibited only as to race, color or previous condition of servitude. If the conditions of restoration are valid, therefore, the ten reconstructed states still remain theoretically on a lower level of rights than the other states. Practically this distinction has disappeared. Mississippi in 1890 and South Carolina in 1895 amended their constitutions by establishing severe intelligence and property qualifications for the suffrage. The two states openly defied the acts of Congress restoring them to their rights after rebellion, and the defiance was based on the claim to equal rights with any of the other states of the Union.

In the restoration of Virginia, Texas and Mississippi, two further fundamental conditions were imposed. First, these states were forbidden to make the race, color or previous servitude of any citizen of the United States a disqualification for holding office, or to discriminate in qualifications for office between classes of citizens ; and second, their constitutions were never to be so amended as to deprive any United States citizens of the school rights and privileges secured therein.

The right to hold office is not expressly placed by the constitution under the guarantee of the United States.[1] The tendency of the Supreme Court's decisions does not indicate a probability that the right can be adjudged a privilege of United States citizenship, or be classed with those rights to which every state must give the equal protection of the laws. It is a historical fact that a determined effort was made, during the discussion of the Fifteenth Amendment in Congress, to include the right to hold office in the prohibition of that article. The proposition was passed at different times by both Senate and House, but finally disappeared in conference committee.[2] In view of this fact, the control of the whole subject seems to be still in the states, and the restriction placed upon Virginia, Mississippi and Texas deprives them of a right which is enjoyed by all the other members of the Union.

The guarantee of equal school privileges to all citizens of the United States within those three states was based on an assumption that educational

---

[1] Ultra-liberal construction might possibly regard it as incidental to a republican form of government, and thus justify its protection by Congress.

[2] Globe, 3d sess., 40th Cong., pp. 1040, 1428, 1481.

facilities were a right of United States citizenship. There is no ground in the constitution for this assumption. Education is a matter which was left wholly within state control. Whatever privileges in this direction are granted by a state to its citizens may, of course, be enjoyed by citizens of other states while within its boundaries. This enjoyment, however, is a privilege that results from state citizenship under the *ante-bellum* constitution. Citizens of the United States, as such, cannot claim it. The case is entirely analogous to that of the taxation of the land of non-residents. Unequal laws are unconstitutional so far as citizens of other states are concerned; citizens of the territories and of the District of Columbia are not thus protected. The act of Congress, therefore, which forbids any discrimination whatever in the three states limits their power to that extent within the bounds prescribed for the rest.[1]

IV

The review of the acts of Congress by which the powers of the various states have been restricted is now complete. It has been shown that

[1] The federal circuit court in Kentucky expressed its readiness to grant an injunction restraining the application of money raised by state taxes to schools open to white children exclusively. The ground was the Fourteenth Amendment. Claybrook *vs.* Owensboro, 23 Fed. Rep. 634.

a great majority of the compacts and fundamental conditions were such only in name, and were wholly without influence on the constitutional relations of the national and state governments. We have seen how several real and vital limitations imposed by law upon individual states were afterwards extended to all by amendment of the national constitution. The residuum of matters in which inequality may still be fairly held to exist is small and comparatively unimportant. In brief, it may be summed up thus: Ohio, Indiana, Illinois, Michigan, Wisconsin, Mississippi, Alabama, Louisiana, Arkansas, Minnesota, Iowa, Oregon, California, Kansas, Nevada, Nebraska, Colorado, Montana, the two Dakotas, Washington and Utah have not the right, enjoyed by the original states, of discriminating in land-taxation against citizens of the United States who are not citizens of any state; Ohio, Indiana, Illinois, Michigan, Wisconsin, Louisiana, Mississippi, Alabama, Nevada, Nebraska, Colorado, Montana, the two Dakotas, Washington and Utah are forbidden to establish any rule interfering with the freedom of worship or religious sentiment, while no such prohibition rests upon the other states; Montana, Washington, the two Dakotas and Utah are required to establish non-sectarian systems of public schools; Utah is forbidden to permit the existence of polygamy; Virginia, North Carolina, South Carolina, Georgia, Florida, Alabama, Mississippi, Arkansas, Louisiana and Texas are forbidden to amend the franchise clauses of their constitutions in certain respects as to which the rest of the states are free from restraint; and finally, Virginia, Mississippi and Texas are forbidden to make race, color or previous condition of servitude a disqualification for holding office, or to amend their constitutions so as to deprive any citizen of the United States of the school privileges secured therein.

The conclusion from all the historical facts seems to be that at no time since the formation of the present constitution have all the states of the Union been in the enjoyment of equal powers under the laws of Congress. A principle of constitutional law under our system can never be said to be fully established until it has received the positive sanction of all three co-ordinate departments of the government. Tested by this rule the theory of equal states falls to the ground. Neither by the judiciary nor by the executive has the doctrine been decisively affirmed; while the action of the legislature has been in many cases in positive contradiction of it. A century of legislation cannot but be regarded as making a pretty strong foundation for the interpretation of any part of the constitution. It is the legislature that must interpret the organic law in the first instance, and such interpretation must stand as sound until overruled by the Supreme Court. But in political questions the court has consistently

declined to take jurisdiction. In such matters
the action of the legislature is conclusive. There
seems to be good reason for considering the relation of the United States to the individual states
in respect to the terms of admission a political
question. If it is, the theory that all states have
equal powers must be regarded as finally defunct;
if it is not, the theory can only be galvanized into
life by a powerful act of judicial construction.

But while such is the technical position of the
doctrine in constitutional law, it enjoys a somewhat different rôle in general public opinion and in
practice. Whatever differences may exist in the
powers which the states *may* exercise over different subjects, the powers which they *do* exercise
are everywhere substantially the same. That the
maintenance of such a condition of things is at
present the wisest policy for the nation, will be
doubted by no one. Time, however, may change
all this. The differentiation of interests in the
vast region covered by the states may bring about
a situation in which the welfare of the whole will
be best subserved by an unequal distribution of
powers among the parts. When that time comes,
the theory of equal states will disappear as did
that of state-sovereignty, and possibly with as
tremendous a convulsion.

THE UNDOING OF RECONSTRUCTION

In July of 1870, when the law declaring Georgia entitled to representation in Congress was finally enacted, the process of reconstruction was, from the technical point of view, complete. Ten of the states which had seceded from the Union had been "made over" by a series of operations which involved, first, the creation in each of a new political people, in which the freedmen constituted an important element, and, second, the organization in each of a new government, in the working of which the participation of the blacks on equal terms with the whites was put under substantial guarantees. The leading motive of the reconstruction had been, at the inception of the process, to insure to the freedmen an effective protection of their civil rights, — of life, liberty and property. In the course of the process, the chief stress came to be laid on the endowment of the blacks with full political rights, — with the electoral franchise and eligibility to office. And by the time the process was complete, a very important, if not the most important, part had been played by the desire and the purpose to secure to the Republican Party the permanent control of several Southern states in which hitherto such a political organization had been unknown. This last motive had a plausible and widely accepted justification in the view that the rights of the negro and the "results of the war" in general would be secure only if the national government should remain indefinitely in Republican hands, and that therefore the strengthening of the party was a primary dictate of patriotism.

Through the operation of these various motives, successive and simultaneous, the completion of the reconstruction showed the following situation: (1) the negroes were in the enjoyment of equal political rights with the whites; (2) the Republican Party was in vigorous life in all the Southern states, and in firm control of many of them; and (3) the negroes exercised an influence in political affairs out of all relation to their intelligence or property, and, since so many of the whites were disfranchised, excessive even in proportion to their numbers. At the present day, in the same states, the negroes enjoy practically no political rights; the Republican Party is but the shadow of a name; and the influence of the negroes in political affairs is nil. This contrast suggests what has been involved in the undoing of reconstruction.

I

Before the last state was restored to the Union the process was well under way through which the resumption of control by the whites was to be effected. The tendency in this direction was greatly promoted by conditions within the Republican Party itself. Two years of supremacy in those states which had been restored in 1868 had revealed unmistakable evidences of moral and political weakness in the governments. The personnel of the party was declining in character through the return to the North of the more substantial of the carpet-baggers, who found Southern conditions, both social and industrial, far from what they had anticipated, and through the very frequent instances in which the " scalawags " ran to open disgrace. Along with this deterioration in the white element of the party, the negroes who rose to prominence and leadership were very frequently of a type which acquired and practiced the tricks and knavery rather than the useful arts of politics, and the vicious courses of these negroes strongly confirmed the prejudices of the whites. But at the same time that the incapacity of the party in power to administer any government was becoming demonstrable, the problems with which it was required to cope were made by its adversaries such as would have taxed the capacity of the most efficient statesmen the world could produce. Between 1868 and 1870, when the cessation of the national military authority left the new state governments to stand by their own strength, there developed that widespread series of disorders with which the name of the Ku Klux Klan is associated. While these were at their height the Republican Party was ousted from control in four of the old rebel states, namely, Tennessee, North Carolina, Georgia and Virginia. The inference was at once drawn that the whites of the South were pursuing a deliberate policy of overthrowing the negro party by violence. No attention was paid to the claim that the manifest inefficiency and viciousness of the Republican governments afforded a partial, if not a wholly adequate, explanation of their over-throw. Not even the relative quiet and order that followed the triumph of the whites in these states were recognized as justifying the new régime. The North was deeply moved by what it considered evidence of a new attack on its cherished ideals of liberty and equality, and when the Fifteenth Amendment had become part of the constitution, Congress passed the Enforcement Acts and the laws for the federal control of elections. To the forces making for the resumption of white government in the South was thus opposed that same apparently irresistible power which had originally overthrown it.

That the Ku Klux movement was to some extent the expression of a purpose not to submit to the political domination of the blacks, is doubtless true. But many other motives were at work in the dis-orders, and the purely political antithesis of the races was not so clear in the origin and develop-ment of the movement as in connection with the

efforts of the state governments to suppress it.
Thousands of respectable whites, who viewed the
Ku Klux outrages with horror, turned with equal
horror from the projects of the governments to
quell the disturbances by means of a negro militia.
Here was the crux of the race issue. Respectable
whites would not serve with the blacks in the
militia; the Republican state governments would
not — and indeed, from the very nature of the
case, could not — exclude the blacks from the
military service; the mere suggestion of employing the blacks alone in such service turned every
white into practically a sympathizer with the Ku
Klux: and thus the government was paralyzed at
the foundation of its authority. It was demonstrated again and again that the appearance of a
body of negroes under arms, whether authorized by
law or not, had for its most certain result an affray,
if not a pitched battle, with armed whites, in which
the negroes almost invariably got the worst of it.

On the assumption, then, that the white state
governments in the South were unwilling, and the
black governments were unable, to protect the
negro in his rights, Congress inaugurated the policy of the " Force Acts." The primary aim was
to protect the right to vote, but ultimately the
purely civil rights, and even the so-called " social
rights," were included in the legislation. By the
act of 1870,[1] a long series of minutely specified

---

[1] 16 Statutes at Large, 140.

offenses, involving violence, intimidation and fraud, with the effect or even the intention of denying equal rights to any citizens of the United States, were made crimes and misdemeanors, and were thus brought under the jurisdiction of the federal courts.   Great activity was at once displayed by the United States district attorneys throughout the South, and hundreds of indictments were brought in; but convictions were few.   The whites opposed to the process of the federal courts, supported by federal troops, no such undisguised resistance as had often been employed against state officers backed by a posse comitatus or a militia company of negroes.   But every advantage was taken of legal technicalities; in the regions where the Ku Klux were strong, juries and witnesses were almost invariably influenced by sympathy or terror to favor the accused; and the huge disproportion between the number of arrests and the number of convictions was skillfully employed to sustain the claim that the federal officers were using the law as the cover for a systematic intimidation and oppression of the whites.   As the effect of this first act seemed to be rather an increase than a decrease in the disorders of the South, Congress passed in the following year a more drastic law. This, known commonly as the Ku Klux Act,[1] healed many technical defects in the earlier law; **reformulated in most precise and far-reaching**

[1] 17 Statutes at Large, 13.

terms the conspiracy clause, which was especially designed to cover Ku Klux methods; and, finally, authorized the President, for a limited time, to suspend the writ of *habeas corpus* and employ military force in the suppression of violence and crime in any given district. In addition to the punitive system thus established, Congress at the same time instituted a rigorous preventive system through the Federal Elections Laws. By acts of 1871 and 1872,[1] every polling place, in any election for Congressmen, might be manned by officials appointed by the federal courts, with extensive powers for the detection of fraud, and with authority to employ the federal troops in the repression of violence.

Through the vigorous policy thus instituted by the national government the movement toward the resumption of control by the whites in the South met with a marked though temporary check. The number of convictions obtained under the Ku Klux Act was not large, and President Grant resorted in but a single instance — that of certain counties in South Carolina, in the autumn of 1871 — to the extraordinary powers conferred upon him. But the moral effect of what was done was very great, and the evidence that the whole power of the national government could and would be exerted on the side of the blacks produced a salutary change in method among the whites. The extreme and vio-

[1] U. S. Revised Statutes, § 2011 *et seq.*

lent element was reduced to quiescence, and haste was made more slowly. No additional state was redeemed by the whites until 1874. Meanwhile, the wholesale removal of political disabilities by Congress in 1872 brought many of the old and respected Southern politicians again into public life, with a corresponding improvement in the quality of Democratic leadership. More deference began to be paid to the Northern sentiment hostile to the Grant administration which had been revealed in the presidential campaign of 1872, and the policy of the Southern whites was directed especially so as to bring odium upon the use of the military forces in the states yet to be wrested from black control.

It was upon the support of the federal troops that the whole existence of the remaining black governments in the South came gradually to depend. Between 1872 and 1876 the Republican Party split in each of the states in which it still retained control, and the fusion of one faction with the Democrats gave rise to disputed elections, general disorder, and appeals by the radical Republicans to the President for aid in suppressing domestic violence. Alabama, Arkansas and Texas emerged from the turmoil in 1874 with the whites triumphant; and the federal troops, after performing useful service in keeping the factions from serious bloodshed, ceased to figure in politics. But in Louisiana and South Carolina the radical factions retained power exclusively through the presence of the troops, who were employed in the former state to reconstitute both the legislature and the executive at the bidding of one of the claimants of the gubernatorial office. The very extraordinary proceedings in New Orleans greatly emphasized the unfavorable feeling at the North toward "governments resting on bayonets"; and when, upon the approach of the state election of 1875 in Mississippi, the radical governor applied for troops to preserve order, President Grant rather tartly refused to furnish them. The result was the overthrow of black government in that state. Though strenuously denied at the time, it was no deep secret that the great negro majority in the state was overcome in this campaign by a quiet but general exertion of every possible form of pressure to keep the blacks from the polls. The extravagance and corruption of the state administration had become so intolerable to the whites that questionable means of terminating it were admitted by even the most honorable without question. There was relatively little "Ku-Kluxing" or open violence, but in countless ways the negroes were impressed with the idea that there would be peril for them in voting. "Intimidation" was the word that had vogue at the time, in describing such methods, and intimidation was illegal. But if a party of white men, with ropes conspicuous on their saddlebows, rode up to a polling place and announced that hanging would begin in fifteen minutes, though without any more definite reference to anybody, and a group of blacks who had assembled to vote heard the remark and promptly disappeared, votes were lost, but a conviction on a charge of intimidation was difficult. Or if an untraceable rumor that trouble was impending over the blacks was followed by the mysterious appearance of bodies of horsemen on the roads at midnight, firing guns and yelling at nobody in particular, votes again were lost, but no crime or misdemeanor could be brought home to any one. Devices like these were familiar in the South, but on this occasion they were accompanied by many other evidences of a purpose on the part of the whites to carry their point at all hazards. The negroes, though numerically much in excess of the whites, were very definitely demoralized by the aggressiveness and unanimity of the latter, and in the ultimate test of race strength the weaker gave way.

The "Mississippi plan" was enthusiastically applied in the remaining three states, Louisiana, South Carolina and Florida, in the elections of 1876. Here, however, the presence of the federal troops and of all the paraphernalia of the Federal Elections Laws materially stiffened the courage of the negroes, and the result of the state elections became closely involved in the controversy over the presidential count. The Southern Democratic

leaders fully appreciated the opportunity of their
position in this controversy, and, through one of
those bargains without words which are common
in great crises, the inauguration of President
Hayes was followed by the withdrawal of the
troops from the support of the last radical governments, and the peaceful lapse of the whole South
into the control of the whites.

II

With these events of 1877 the first period in the
undoing of reconstruction came to an end. The
second period, lasting till 1890, presented conditions so different from the first as entirely to
transform the methods by which the process was
continued. Two, indeed, of the three elements
which have been mentioned as summing up reconstruction still characterized the situation : the negroes were precisely equal in rights with the other
race, and the Republican Party was a powerful
organization in the South. As to the third element, the disproportionate political influence of
the blacks, a change had been effected, and their
power had been so reduced as to correspond much
more closely to their general social significance.
In the movement against the still enduring features of reconstruction the control of the state
governments by the whites was of course a new
condition of the utmost importance ; but not less

vital was the party complexion of the national government. From 1875 to 1889 neither of the great parties was at any one time in effective control of both the presidency and the two houses of Congress. As a consequence, no partisan legislation could be enacted. Though the state of affairs in the South was for years a party issue of the first magnitude, the legislative deadlock had for its general result a policy of non-interference by the national government, and the whites were left to work out in their own way the ends they had in view. Some time was necessary, however, to overcome the influence of the two bodies of legislation already on the national statute book, — the Force Acts and the Federal Elections Laws.

During the Hayes administration the latter laws were the subject of a prolonged and violent contest between the Democratic houses and the Republican President. The Democrats put great stress on the terror and intimidation of the whites and the violation of freemen's rights due to the presence of federal officials at the polls, and of federal troops near them. The Republicans insisted that these officials and troops were essential to enable the negroes to vote and to have their votes counted. As a matter of fact, neither of these contentions was of the highest significance so far as the South was concerned. The whites, once in control of the state electoral machinery, readily devised means of evading or neutralizing the influence of the federal officers. But the patronage in the hands of the administration party under these laws was enormous. The power to appoint supervisors and deputy marshals at election time was a tower of strength, from the standpoint both of direct votes and of indirect influence. Accordingly, the attack of the Democrats upon the laws was actuated mainly by the purpose of breaking down the Republican party organization in the South. The attack was successful in Mr. Hayes's time only to the extent that no appropriation was made for the payment of the supervisors and deputy marshals for their services in the elections of 1880. The system of federal supervision remained, but gradually lost all significance save as a biennial sign that the Republican Party still survived; and when Mr. Cleveland became President even this relation to its original character disappeared.

The Force Acts experienced a similar decline during the period we are considering. In 1875, just before the Republicans lost control of Congress, they passed, as a sort of memorial to Charles Sumner, who had long urged its adoption, a Supplementary Civil Rights Bill,[1] which made criminal, and put under the jurisdiction of the federal courts, any denial of equality to negroes in respect to accommodations in theatres, railway cars, hotels, and other such places. This was not

[1] 18 Statutes at Large, 335.

regarded by the most thoughtful Republicans as a very judicious piece of legislation ; but it was perceived that, with the Democrats about to control the House of Representatives, there was not likely to be a further opportunity for action in aid of the blacks, and so the act was permitted to go through and take its chances of good. Already, however, the courts had manifested a disposition to question the constitutionality of the most drastic provisions of the earlier Enforcement Acts. It has been said above that indictments under these acts had been many, but convictions few. Punishments were fewer still; for skillful counsel were ready to test the profound legal questions involved in the legislation, and numbers of cases crept slowly up on appeal to the Supreme Court. In 1875, this tribunal threw out an indictment under which a band of whites who had broken up a negro meeting in Louisiana had been convicted of conspiring to prevent negroes from assembling for lawful purposes and from carrying arms; for the right to assemble and the right to bear arms, the court declared, pertained to citizenship of a state, not of the United States, and therefore redress for interference with these rights must be sought in the courts of the state.[1] In the same year, in the case of United States *vs.* Reese,[2] two sections of the Enforcement Act of 1870 were declared unconstitutional, as involving the exercise by the United

[1] U. S. *vs.* Cruikshank, 92 U. S., 542.　　[2] 92 U. S., 214.

States of powers in excess of those granted by the
Fifteenth Amendment. It was not, however, till
1882 that the bottom was taken wholly out of the
Ku Klux Act. In the case of United States *vs*.
Harris[1] the conspiracy clause in its entirety was
declared unconstitutional. This was a case from
Tennessee, in which a band of whites had taken
a negro away from the officers of the law and mal-
treated him. The court held that, under the last
three amendments to the constitution, Congress
was authorized to guarantee equality in civil rights
against violation by a state through its officers or
agents, but not against violation by private individuals. Where assault or murder or other crime
was committed by a private individual, even if the
purpose was to deprive citizens of rights on the
ground of race, the jurisdiction, and the exclusive
jurisdiction, was in the state courts. And because
the conspiracy clause brought such offenses into
the jurisdiction of the United States it was unconstitutional and void. This decision finally disposed
of the theory that the failure of a state to protect
the negroes in their equal rights could be regarded
as a positive denial of such rights, and hence could
justify the United States in interfering. It left
the blacks practically at the mercy of white public
sentiment in the South. A year later, in 1883, the
court summarily disposed of the act of 1875 by
declaring that the rights which it endeavored to

[1] 106 U. S., 629.

guarantee were not strictly civil rights at all, but rather social rights, and that in either case the federal government had nothing to do with them. The act was therefore held unconstitutional.[1]

Thus passed the most characteristic features of the great system through which the Republicans had sought to prevent by normal action of the courts, independently of changes in public opinion and political majorities, the undoing of reconstruction. Side by side with the removal of the preventives, the Southern whites had made enormous positive advances in the suppression of the other race. In a very general way the process in this period, as contrasted with the earlier, may be said to have rested, in last resort, on legislation and fraud rather than on intimidation and force. The statute books of the states, especially of those in which negro rule had lasted the longest, abounded in provisions for partisan — that is, race — advantage. These were at once devoted as remorselessly to the extinction of black preponderance as they had been before devoted to the repression of the whites. Moreover, by revision of the constitutions and by sweeping modifications of the laws, many strongholds of the old régime were destroyed. Yet, with all that could be done in this way, the fact remained that in many localities the negroes so greatly outnumbered the whites as to render the political ascendency of the latter impossible,

[1] Civil Rights Cases, 109 U. S. 1.

except through some radical changes in the laws
touching the suffrage and the elections; and in
respect to these two points the sensitiveness of
Northern feeling rendered open and decided action
highly inexpedient. Before 1880 the anticipation,
and after that year the realization, of a "solid
South" played a prominent part in national politics. The permanence of white dominion in the
South seemed, in view of the past, to depend as
much on the exclusion of the Republicans from
power at Washington as on the maintenance of
white power at the state capitals. Under all the
circumstances, therefore, extra-legal devices had
still to be used in the "black belt."

The state legislation which contributed to con-
firm white control included many ingenious and
exaggerated applications of the gerrymander and
the prescription of various electoral regulations
that were designedly too intricate for the average
negro intelligence. In Mississippi appeared the
"shoestring district," three hundred miles long
and about twenty wide, including within its boundaries nearly all the densest black communities of
the state. In South Carolina, the requirement
that, with eight or more ballot boxes before him,
the voter must select the proper one for each
ballot, in order to insure its being counted, furnished an effective means of neutralizing the ignorant black vote; for though the negroes, unable
to read the lettering on the boxes, might acquire,

by proper coaching, the power to discriminate among them by their relative positions, a moment's work by the whites in transposing the boxes would render useless an hour's laborious instruction. For the efficient working of this method of suppression, it was indispensable, however, that the officers of election should be whites. This suggests at once the enormous advantage gained by securing control of the state government. In the hot days of negro supremacy the electoral machinery had been ruthlessly used for partisan purposes, and when conditions were reversed the practice was by no means abandoned. It was, indeed, through their exclusive and carefully maintained control of the voting and the count that the whites found the best opportunities for illegal methods.

Because of these opportunities the resort to bull-dozing and other violence steadily decreased. It penetrated gradually to the consciousness of the most brutal white politicians that the whipping or murder of a negro, no matter for what cause, was likely to become at once the occasion of a great outcry at the North, while by an unobtrusive manipulation of the balloting or the count very encouraging results could be obtained with little or no commotion. Hence that long series of practices, in the regions where the blacks were numerous, that give so grotesque a character to the testimony in the contested-election cases in Congress, and to the reminiscences of candid Southerners. Polling

places were established at points so remote from
the densest black communities that a journey of
from twenty to forty miles was necessary in order
to vote; and where the roads were interrupted by
ferries, the resolute negroes who attempted to
make the journey were very likely to find the
boats laid up for repairs. The number of polling
places was kept so small as to make rapid voting
indispensable to a full vote; and then the whites,
by challenges and carefully premeditated quarrels
among themselves, would amuse the blacks and
consume time, till only enough remained for the
casting of their own votes. The situation of the
polls was changed without notice to the negroes,
or, conversely, the report of a change was indus-
triously circulated when none had been made.
Open bribery on a large scale was too common to
excite comment. One rather ingenious scheme is
recorded which presents a variation on the old
theme. In several of the states a poll-tax receipt
was required as a qualification for voting. In an
important local election, one faction had assured
itself of the negro vote by a generous outlay in
the payment of the tax for a large number of the
blacks. The other faction, alarmed at the prospect
of almost certain defeat, availed itself of the opportunity presented by the providential advent of a
circus in the neighborhood, and the posters announced that poll-tax receipts would be accepted
for admission. As a result, the audience at the

circus was notable in respect to numbers, but the negro vote at the election was insignificant.

But exploitation of the poverty, ignorance, credulity, and general childishness of the blacks was supplemented, on occasion, by deliberate and high-handed fraud. Stuffing of the boxes with illegal ballots, and manipulation of the figures in making the count, were developed into serious arts. At the acme of the development undoubtedly stood the tissue ballot. There was in those days no prescription of uniformity in size and general character of the ballots. Hence miniature ballots of tissue paper were secretly prepared and distributed to trusted voters, who, folding as many, sometimes, as fifteen of the small tickets within one of the ordinary large tickets, passed the whole, without detection, into the box. Not till the box was opened were the tissue tickets discovered. Then, because the number of ballots exceeded the number of voters as indicated by the polling list, it became necessary, under the law, for the excess to be drawn out by a blindfolded man before the count began. So some one's eyes were solemnly bandaged, and he was set to drawing out ballots, on the theory that he could not distinguish those of one party from those of the other. The result is not hard to guess. In one case given by the Senate committee [1] through whose investigation of

---

[1] The report of this committee is in Sen. Rep. 3d sess., 45th Cong., vol. iv.

the elections of 1878, in South Carolina, the theory and practice of the tissue ballot were revealed to an astonished world, the figures were as follows: —

Number of ballots in box	1163
Names on polling list	620
Excess drawn out	543
Tissue ballots left to be counted	464

Not the least interesting feature of this episode was the explanation, given with entire gravity by the white committee, of the existence of the great mass of tissue ballots. They were prepared, it was said, in order to enable the blacks who wished to vote the Democratic ticket to do so secretly, and thus to escape the ostracism and other social penalties which would be meted out to them by the majority of their race.

Under the pressure applied by all these various methods upon the negroes, the black vote slowly disappeared. And with it the Republican Party faded into insignificance. In the presidential election of 1884 the total vote in South Carolina was, in round numbers, 91,000, as compared with 182,000 in 1876. In Mississippi the corresponding decrease was from 164,000 to 120,000; in Louisiana, from 160,000 to 108,000. The Republican party organization was maintained almost exclusively through the holders of federal offices in the postal and revenue service. When, in 1885, a Democratic administration assumed power, this basis for continued existence was very seriously weakened, and the decline of the party was much accelerated. Save for a few judicial positions held over from early appointments, the national offices, like those of the states, were hopelessly removed from the reach of any Republican's ambition. A comparison of the Congressional delegation from the states of the defunct Confederacy in the Forty-first Congress (1869–71) with that in the Fifty-first (1889–91) is eloquent of the transformation that the two decades had wrought: in the former, twenty out of the twenty-two Senators were Republican, and forty-four out of fifty-eight Representatives; in the latter, there were no Republican Senators and but three Representatives.

Summarily, then, it may be said that the second period in the undoing of reconstruction ends with the political equality of the negroes still recognized in law, though not in fact, and with the Republican Party, for all practical purposes, extinct in the South. The third period has had for its task the termination of equal rights in law as well as in fact.

III

The decline of negro suffrage and of the Republican Party in the South was the topic of much discussion in national politics and figured in the party platforms throughout the period from 1876 to 1888; but owing to the deadlock in the party control of the national legislature the discussion remained academic in character, and the issue was supplanted in public interest by the questions of tariff, currency and monopoly. By the elections of 1888, however, the Republicans secured not only the presidency, but also a majority in each house of Congress. The deadlock of thirteen years was broken, and at once an effort was made to resume the policy of the Enforcement Acts. A bill was brought in that was designed to make real the federal control of elections. The old acts for this purpose were, indeed, still on the statute book, but their operation was farcical; the new project, while maintaining the general lines of the old, would have imposed serious restraints on the influences that repressed the negro vote, and would have infused some vitality into the moribund Republican Party in the South. It was quickly demonstrated, however, that the time for this procedure had gone by. The bill received perfunctory support in the House of Representatives, where it passed by the regular party majority, but in the Senate it was rather contemptuously set aside by Republican votes. Public sentiment in the North, outside of Congress, manifested considerable hostility to the project, and its adoption as a party measure probably played a rôle in the tremendous reaction which swept the Republicans out of power in the House in 1890, and gave to the Democrats in 1892 the control of both houses of Congress and the presidency as well. The response of the Democrats to the futile project of their adversaries was prompt and decisive. In February, 1894, an act became law which repealed all existing statutes that provided for federal supervision of elections. Thus the last vestige disappeared of the system through which the political equality of the blacks had received direct support from the national government.

In the meantime, a process had been instituted in the Southern states that has given the most distinctive character to the last period in the undoing of reconstruction. The generation-long discussions of the political conditions in the South have evoked a variety of explanations by the whites of the disappearance of the black vote. These different explanations have of course all been current at all times since reconstruction was completed, and have embodied different degrees of plausibility and truth in different places. But it may fairly be said that in each of the three periods into which the undoing of reconstruction falls one particular view has been dominant and characteristic. In the first period, that of the Ku Klux and the Mississippi plan, it was generally maintained by the whites that the black vote was not suppressed, and that there was no political motive behind the disturbances that occurred. The victims of murder, bulldozing and other violence were represented as bad and socially dangerous men, and their treatment as merely incident to their own illegal and violent acts, and expressive of the tendency to self-help instead of judicial procedure, which had always been manifest in Southern life, and had been aggravated by the demoralization of war time. After 1877, when the falling off in the Republican vote became so conspicuous, the phenomenon was explained by the assertion that the negroes had seen the light, and had become Democrats. Mr. Lamar gravely maintained, in a famous controversy with Mr. Blaine,[1] that the original Republican theory as to the educative influence of the ballot had been proved correct by the fact that the enfranchised race had come to recognize that their true interests lay with the Democratic Party; the Republicans were estopped, he contended, by their own doctrine from finding fault with the result. A corollary of this idea that the negroes were Democrats was generally adopted later in the period, to the effect that, since there was practically no opposition to the Democracy, the negroes had lost interest in politics. They had got on the road to economic prosperity, it was said, and were too busy with their farms and their growing bank accounts to care for other things.

Whatever of soundness there may have been in any of these explanations, all have been superseded, during the last decade, by another, which, starting with the candid avowal that the whites are

---

[1] *North American Review*, vol. 128 (1879), p. 225.

determined to rule, concedes that the elimination of the blacks from politics has been effected by intimidation, fraud, or any other means, legal or illegal, that would promote the desired end. This admission has been accompanied by expressions of sincere regret that illegal means were necessary, and by a general movement toward clothing with the forms of law the disfranchisement which has been made a fact without them. In 1890, just when the Republicans in Congress were pushing their project for renewing the federal control of elections, Mississippi made the first step in the new direction. Her constitution was so revised as to provide that, to be a qualified elector, a citizen must produce evidence of having paid his taxes (including a poll tax) for the past two years, and must, in addition, "be able to read any section in the constitution of this state, or . . . be able to understand the same when read to him, or give a reasonable interpretation thereof." Much might be said in favor of such an alternative intelligence qualification in the abstract: the mere ability to read is far from conclusive of intellectual capacity. But the peculiar form of this particular provision was confessedly adopted, not from any consideration of its abstract excellence, but in order to vest in the election officers the power to disfranchise illiterate blacks without disfranchising illiterate whites. In practice, the white must be stupid indeed who cannot satisfy the official demand for a "reasonable interpretation," while the negro who can satisfy it must be a miracle of brilliancy.

Mississippi's bold and undisguised attack on negro suffrage excited much attention. In the South it met with practically unanimous approval among thoughtful and conscientious men, who had been distressed by the false position in which they had long been placed. And at the North, public opinion, accepting with a certain satirical complacency the confession of the Southerners that their earlier explanations of conditions had been false, acknowledged in turn that its views as to the political capacity of the blacks had been irrational, and manifested no disposition for a new crusade in favor of negro equality. The action of Mississippi raised certain questions of constitutional law which had to be tested before her solution of the race problem could be regarded as final. Like all the other seceded states, save Tennessee, she had been readmitted to representation in Congress, after reconstruction, on the express condition that her constitution should never be so amended as to disfranchise any who were entitled to vote under the existing provisions. The new amendment was a most explicit violation of this condition. Further, so far as the new clause could be shown to be directed against the negroes as a race, it was in contravention of the Fifteenth Amendment. These legal points had been elaborately discussed in the state convention, and the opinion had been adopted that, since neither race, color nor previous condition of servitude was made the basis of discrimination in the suffrage, the Fifteenth Amendment had no application, and that the prohibition to modify the constitution was entirely beyond the powers of Congress, and was therefore void. When the Supreme Court of the United States was required to consider the new clause of Mississippi's constitution, it sustained the validity of the enactment,[1] at least so long as injustice in its administration was shown to be possible only and not actual. There was still one contingency that the whites had to face in carrying out the new policy. By the Fourteenth Amendment it is provided that if a state restricts the franchise her representation in Congress shall be proportionately reduced. There was a strong sentiment in Mississippi, as there is throughout the South, that a reduction of representation would not be an intolerable price to pay for the legitimate extinction of negro suffrage. But loss of Congressmen was by no means longed for, and the possibility of such a thing was very carefully considered. The phrasing of the franchise clause may not have been actually determined with reference to this matter; but it is obvious that the application of the Fourteenth Amendment is, to say the least, not facilitated by the form used.

[1] Williams *vs.* Miss., 170 U. S., 213.

The action of Mississippi in 1890 throws a rather interesting light on the value of political prophecy, even when ventured upon by the most experienced and able politicians. Eleven years earlier, Mr. Blaine, writing of the possibility of disfranchisement by educational and property tests, declared: "But no Southern state will do this, and for two reasons: first, they will in no event consent to a reduction of representative strength; and, second, they could not make any disfranchisement of the negro that would not at the same time disfranchise an immense number of whites." How sadly Mr. Blaine misconceived the spirit and underrated the ingenuity of the Southerners Mississippi made clear to everybody. Five years later South Carolina dealt no less unkindly with Mr. Lamar, who at the same time with Mr. Blaine had dipped a little into prophecy on the other side. "Whenever," he said, — "and the time is not far distant, — political issues arise which divide the white men of the South, the negro will divide, too. . . . The white race, divided politically, will want him to divide." Incidentally to the conditions which produced the Populist Party, the whites of South Carolina, in the years succeeding 1890, became divided into two intensely hostile factions. The weaker manifested a purpose to draw on the negroes for support, and began to expose some of the devices by which the blacks had been prevented from voting.

The situation had arisen which Mr. Lamar had foreseen, but the result was as far as possible from fulfilling his prediction. Instead of competing with its rival for the black vote, the stronger faction, headed by Mr. Tillman, promptly took the ground that South Carolina must have a "white man's government," and put into effect the new Mississippi plan. A constitutional amendment was adopted in 1895 which applied the "under-standing clause" for two years, and after that required of every elector either the ability to read and write or the ownership of property to the amount of $300. In the convention which framed this amendment, the sentiment of the whites revealed very clearly, not only through its content, but especially through the frank and emphatic form in which it was expressed, that the aspirations of the negro to equality in political rights would never again receive the faintest recognition.

Since the action of South Carolina, four other states, Louisiana in 1898, North Carolina in 1900, Alabama (1901) and Virginia (1902), have excluded the blacks from the suffrage by analogous constitutional amendments. By Louisiana, however, a new method was devised for exempting the whites from the effect of the property and intelligence tests. The hereditary principle was introduced into the franchise by the provision that the right to vote should belong, regardless of education or property, to every one whose father or grandfather possessed the right on January 1, 1867. This "grandfather clause" was adopted by North Carolina, also, and, in a modified form, by Alabama and Virginia. The basis for the hereditary right in the latter states has been found, not in the possession of the franchise by the ancestor, but in the fact of his having served as a soldier of either the United States or the Confederacy. As compared with the Mississippi device for evading the Fifteenth Amendment, the "grandfather clause" has the merit of incorporating the discrimination in favor of the whites in the written law rather than referring it to the discretion of the election officers. Whether the Supreme Court of the United States will regard it as equally successful in screening its real purpose from judicial cognizance remains to be seen.

With the enactment of these constitutional amendments by the various states, the political equality of the negro is becoming as extinct in law as it has long been in fact, and the undoing of reconstruction is nearing completion. The many morals that may be drawn from the three decades of the process it is not my purpose to suggest. A single reflection seems pertinent, however, in view of the problems which have assumed such prominence in American politics since the war with Spain. During the two generations of debate and bloodshed over slavery in the United

States, certain of our statesmen consistently held that the mere chattel relationship of man to man was not the whole of the question at issue. Jefferson, Clay and Lincoln all saw more serious facts in the background. But in the frenzy of the war time public opinion fell into the train of the emotionalists, and accepted the teachings of Garrison and Sumner and Phillips and Chase, that abolition and negro suffrage would remove the last drag on our national progress. Slavery was abolished, and reconstruction gave the freedmen the franchise.

But with all the guarantees that the source of every evil was removed, it became obvious enough that the results were not what had been expected. Gradually there emerged again the idea of Jefferson and Clay and Lincoln, which had been hooted and hissed into obscurity during the prevalence of the abolitionist fever. This was that the ultimate root of the trouble in the South had been, not the institution of slavery, but the coexistence in one society of two races so distinct in characteristics as to render coalescence impossible; that slavery had been a *modus vivendi* through which social life was possible; and that, after its disappearance, its place must be taken by some set of conditions which, if more humane and beneficent in accidents, must in essence express the same fact of racial inequality. The progress in the acceptance of this idea in the North has measured the progress in the South of the undoing of reconstruction. In view of the questions which have been raised by our lately established relations with other races, it seems most improbable that the historian will soon, or ever, have to record a reversal of the conditions which this process has established.

INDEX

Admission of states: Vermont, Kentucky, Tennessee, 311; Ohio, 312; Louisiana, 313; Maine, Indiana, Illinois, Alabama, Mississippi, Missouri, 314; Arkansas, Michigan, Iowa, 316; Nevada, Nebraska, 317; Colorado, the Dakotas, Montana, Washington, Idaho, Wyoming, Utah, 318.

Alabama, part of third military district, 144; registration in, 188; disfranchisement in, 196; election on ratification of constitution, 204; bill to admit representatives of, to Congress, 210; restored to full rights, 215; organization of legislature in, 217; original admission to Union, 314; not equal with original states, 350; end of negro government in, 360; disfranchisement of negroes in, 382.

Amendment of the Constitution of the United States: proposed by Buchanan, 6; submitted by Congress in 1861, 7; the Fourth, 39; the Fifth, 40; the Thirteenth, 56, 70, 82, 93, 338; the Fourteenth, 116, 118, 120, 122, 222, 225, 336, 339; the Fifteenth, 227, 232, 243, 252; the first, 341.

Ames, General, appointed governor of Mississippi, 156.

Amnesty, offered by Lincoln, 66; by Johnson, 78; not to give right to vote in reconstruction, 183.

Arkansas, military situation in, 64; government organized in, 69; part

of fourth military district, 144; registration in, 188; disfranchisement in, 196; ratification of constitution of, 205; act admitting to representation, 212; organization of legislature in, 217; original admission to Union, 316; not equal with original states, 350; end of negro government in, 360.

Ashley, Representative, moves impeachment resolution, 255.

Bates, Attorney-General, opinion on suspension of *habeas corpus*, 20.

Black, Attorney-General, opinion on suppressing rebellion, 3.

Blaine, J. G., views on negro disfranchisement, 381.

Boutwell, Representative, leads in impeachment proceedings, 271.

Buchanan, President, message of December, 1860, 2, 6; attitude toward forts and property in the seceded states, 9, 10.

Bullock, governor of Georgia, 223; refuses to call special session of legislature, 242; attitude of, on final restoration, 246.

Butler, General B. F., treats slaves as contraband, 49; introduces bill for dealing with Georgia, 239; disappointed as to impeachment, 257; leads in impeachment proceedings, 271; secures adoption of article concerning Johnson's speeches, 274; on character of

387

Revised June, 1965

hαrper ⚜ τorch books

HUMANITIES AND SOCIAL SCIENCES

American Studies: General

THOMAS C. COCHRAN: The Inner Revolution: *Essays on the Social Sciences in History*   TB/1140

EDWARD S. CORWIN: American Constitutional History. *Essays edited by Alpheus T. Mason and Gerald Garvey*   TB/1136

A. HUNTER DUPREE: Science in the Federal Government: *A History of Policies and Activities to 1940*   TB/573

OSCAR HANDLIN, Ed.: This Was America: *As Recorded by European Travelers in the Eighteenth, Nineteenth and Twentieth Centuries. Illus.*   TB/1119

MARCUS LEE HANSEN· The Atlantic Migration: 1607-1860. *Edited by Arthur M. Schlesinger; Introduction by Osrar Handlin*   TB/1052

MARCUS LEE HANSEN: The Immigrant in American History. *Edited with a Foreword by Arthur M. Schlesinger*   TB/1120

JOHN HIGHAM, Ed.: The Reconstruction of American History   TB/1068

ROBERT H. JACKSON: The Supreme Court in the American System of Government   TB/1106

JOHN F. KENNEDY: A Nation of Immigrants. *Illus. Revised and Enlarged. Introduction by Robert F. Kennedy*   TB/1118

RALPH BARTON PERRY: Puritanism and Democracy   TB/1138

ARNOLD ROSE: The Negro in America: *The Condensed Version of Gunnar Myrdal's An American Dilemma*   TB/3048

MAURICE R. STEIN: The Eclipse of Community: *An Interpretation of American Studies*   TB/1128

W. LLOYD WARNER and Associates: Democracy in Jonesville: *A Study in Quality and Inequality* || TB/1129

W. LLOYD WARNER: Social Class in America: *The Evaluation of Status*   TB/1013

American Studies: Colonial

BERNARD BAILYN: The New England Merchants in the Seventeenth Century   TB/1149

JOSEPH CHARLES: The Origins of the American Party System   TB/1049

LAWRENCE HENRY GIPSON: The Coming of the Revolution: 1763-1775. † *Illus.*   TB/3007

LEONARD W. LEVY: Freedom of Speech and Press in Early American History: *Legacy of Suppression*   TB/1109

PERRY MILLER: Errand Into the Wilderness   TB/1139

PERRY MILLER & T. H. JOHNSON, Eds.: The Puritans: *A Sourcebook of Their Writings*
Vol. I TB/1093; Vol. II TB/1094

KENNETH B. MURDOCK: Literature and Theology in Colonial New England   TB/99

WALLACE NOTESTEIN: The English People on the Eve of Colonization: 1603-1630. † *Illus.*   TB/3006

LOUIS B. WRIGHT: The Cultural Life of the American Colonies: 1607-1763. † *Illus.*   TB/3005

American Studies: From the Revolution to the Civil War

JOHN R. ALDEN: The American Revolution: 1775-1783. † *Illus.*   TB/3011

RAY A. BILLINGTON: The Far Western Frontier: 1830-1860. † *Illus.*   TB/3012

GEORGE DANGERFIELD: The Awakening of American Nationalism: 1815-1828. † *Illus.*   TB/3061

CLEMENT EATON: The Freedom-of-Thought Struggle in the Old South. *Revised and Enlarged. Illus.*   TB/1150

CLEMENT EATON: The Growth of Southern Civilization: 1790-1860. † *Illus.*   TB/3040

LOUIS FILLER: The Crusade Against Slavery: 1830-1860. † *Illus*   TB/3029

DIXON RYAN FOX: The Decline of Aristocracy in the Politics of New York: 1801-1840. ‡ *Edited by Robert V. Remini*   TB/3064

FRANCIS J. GRUND: Aristocracy in America: *Social Class in the Formative Years of the New Nation* ‡   TB/1001

ALEXANDER HAMILTON: The Reports of Alexander Hamilton. ‡ *Edited by Jacob E. Cooke*   TB/3060

DANIEL R. HUNDLEY: Social Relations in Our Southern States. ‡ *Edited by William R. Taylor*   TB/3058

THOMAS JEFFERSON: Notes on the State of Virginia. ‡ *Edited by Thomas P. Abernethy*   TB/3052

BERNARD MAYO: Myths and Men: *Patrick Henry, George Washington, Thomas Jefferson*   TB/1108

JOHN C. MILLER: Alexander Hamilton and the Growth of the New Nation   TB/3057

RICHARD B. MORRIS, Ed.: The Era of the American Revolution   TB/1180

R. B. NYE: The Cultural Life of the New Nation: 1776-1801. † *Illus.*   TB/3026

GEORGE E. PROBST, Ed.: The Happy Republic: *A Reader in Tocqueville's America*   TB/1060

† The New American Nation Series, edited by Henry Steele Commager and Richard B. Morris.
‡ American Perspectives series, edited by Bernard Wishy and William E. Leuchtenburg.
* The Rise of Modern Europe series, edited by William L. Langer.
|| Researches in the Social, Cultural, and Behavioral Sciences, edited by Benjamin Nelson.
§ The Library of Religion and Culture, edited by Benjamin Nelson.
Σ Harper Modern Science Series, edited by James R. Newman.
° Not for sale in Canada.

FRANK THISTLETHWAITE: America and the Atlantic Community: *Anglo-American Aspects, 1790-1850* TB/1107

A. F. TYLER: Freedom's Ferment: *Phases of American Social History from the Revolution to the Outbreak of the Civil War. 31 illus.* TB/1074

GLYNDON G. VAN DEUSEN: The Jacksonian Era: 1828-1848. † *Illus.* TB/3028

LOUIS B. WRIGHT: Culture on the Moving Frontier TB/1053

American Studies: Since the Civil War

RAY STANNARD BAKER: Following the Color Line: *American Negro Citizenship in Progressive Era.* ‡ *Illus. Edited by Dewey W. Grantham, Jr.* TB/3053

RANDOLPH S. BOURNE: War and the Intellectuals: *Collected Essays, 1915-1919.* ‡ *Edited by Carl Resek* TB/3043

A. RUSSELL BUCHANAN: The United States and World War II. † *Illus.* Vol. I TB/3044; Vol. II TB/3045

ABRAHAM CAHAN: The Rise of David Levinsky: *a documentary novel of social mobility in early twentieth century America. Intro. by John Higham* TB/1028

THOMAS C. COCHRAN: The American Business System: *A Historical Perspective, 1900-1955* TB/1080

THOMAS C. COCHRAN & WILLIAM MILLER: The Age of Enterprise: *A Social History of Industrial America* TB/1054

FOSTER RHEA DULLES: America's Rise to World Power: 1898-1954. † *Illus.* TB/3021

W. A. DUNNING: Essays on the Civil War and Reconstruction. *Introduction by David Donald* TB/1181

W. A. DUNNING: Reconstruction, Political and Economic: 1865-1877 TB/1073

HAROLD U. FAULKNER: Politics, Reform and Expansion: 1890-1900. † *Illus.* TB/3020

JOHN D. HICKS: Republican Ascendancy: 1921-1933. † *Illus.* TB/3041

ROBERT HUNTER: Poverty: *Social Conscience in the Progressive Era.* ‡ *Edited by Robert d'A. Jones* TB/3065

HELEN HUNT JACKSON: A Century of Dishonor: *The Early Crusade for Indian Reform.* ‡ *Edited by Andrew F. Rolle* TB/3063

ALBERT D. KIRWAN: Revolt of the Rednecks: *Mississippi Politics, 1876-1925* TB/1199

WILLIAM L. LANGER & S. EVERETT GLEASON: The Challenge to Isolation: *The World Crisis of 1937-1940 and American Foreign Policy*
Vol. I TB/3054; Vol. II TB/3055

WILLIAM E. LEUCHTENBURG: Franklin D. Roosevelt and the New Deal: 1932-1940. † *Illus.* TB/3025

ARTHUR S. LINK: Woodrow Wilson and the Progressive Era: 1910-1917. † *Illus.* TB/3023

ROBERT GREEN MC CLOSKEY: American Conservatism in the Age of Enterprise: 1865-1910 TB/1137

GEORGE E. MOWRY: The Era of Theodore Roosevelt and the Birth of Modern America: 1900-1912. † *Illus.* TB/3022

WALTER RAUSCHENBUSCH: Christianity and the Social Crisis. ‡ *Edited by Robert D. Cross* TB/3059

CHARLES H. SHINN: Mining Camps: *A Study in American Frontier Government.* ‡ *Edited by Rodman W. Paul* TB/3062

TWELVE SOUTHERNERS: I'll Take My Stand: *The South and the Agrarian Tradition. Intro. by Louis D. Rubin, Jr.; Biographical Essays by Virginia Rock* TB/1072

WALTER E. WEYL: The New Democracy: *An Essay on Certain Political Tendencies in the United States.* ‡ *Edited by Charles B. Forcey* TB/3042

VERNON LANE WHARTON: The Negro in Mississippi: 1865-1890 TB/1178

Anthropology

JACQUES BARZUN: Race: *A Study in Superstition. Revised Edition* TB/1172

JOSEPH B. CASAGRANDE, Ed.: In the Company of Man: *Twenty Portraits of Anthropological Informants. Illus.* TB/3047

W. E. LE GROS CLARK: The Antecedents of Man: *An Introduction to the Evolution of the Primates.* ° *Illus.* TB/559

CORA DU BOIS: The People of Alor. *New Preface by the author. Illus.* Vol. I TB/1042; Vol. II TB/1043

RAYMOND FIRTH, Ed.: Man and Culture: *An Evaluation of the Work of Bronislaw Malinowski* || ° TB/1133

L. S. B. LEAKEY: Adam's Ancestors: *The Evolution of Man and His Culture. Illus.* TB/1019

ROBERT H. LOWIE: Primitive Society. *Introduction by Fred Eggan* TB/1056

SIR EDWARD TYLOR: The Origins of Culture. *Part I of "Primitive Culture."* § *Introduction by Paul Radin* TB/33

SIR EDWARD TYLOR: Religion in Primitive Culture. *Part II of "Primitive Culture."* § *Introduction by Paul Radin* TB/34

W. LLOYD WARNER: A Black Civilization: *A Study of an Australian Tribe.* || *Illus.* TB/3056

Art and Art History

WALTER LOWRIE: Art in the Early Church. *152 illus. Revised Edition* TB/124

EMILE MÂLE: The Gothic Image: *Religious Art in France of the Thirteenth Century.* § *190 illus.* TB/44

MILLARD MEISS: Painting in Florence and Siena after the Black Death: *The Arts, Religion and Society in the Mid-Fourteenth Century. 169 illus.* TB/1148

ERICH NEUMANN: The Archetypal World of Henry Moore. *107 illus.* TB/2020

DORA & ERWIN PANOFSKY: Pandora's Box: *The Changing Aspects of a Mythical Symbol. Revised Edition. Illus.* TB/2021

ERWIN PANOFSKY: Studies in Iconology: *Humanistic Themes in the Art of the Renaissance. 180 illustrations* TB/1077

ALEXANDRE PIANKOFF: The Shrines of Tut-Ankh-Amon. *Edited by N. Rambova. 117 illus.* TB/2011

JEAN SEZNEC: The Survival of the Pagan Gods: *The Mythological Tradition and Its Place in Renaissance Humanism and Art. 108 illustrations* TB/2004

OTTO VON SIMSON: The Gothic Cathedral: *Origins of Gothic Architecture and the Medieval Concept of Order. 58 illus.* TB/2018

HEINRICH ZIMMER: Myth and Symbols in Indian Art and Civilization. *70 illustrations* TB/2005

Business, Economics & Economic History

REINHARD BENDIX: Work and Authority in Industry: *Ideologies of Management in the Course of Industrialization* TB/3035

GILBERT BURCK & EDITORS OF FORTUNE: The Computer Age TB/1179

THOMAS C. COCHRAN: The American Business System: *A Historical Perspective, 1900-1955* TB/1080

THOMAS C. COCHRAN: The Inner Revolution: *Essays on the Social Sciences in History* TB/1140

THOMAS C. COCHRAN & WILLIAM MILLER: The Age of Enterprise: *A Social History of Industrial America* TB/1054

3

NICCOLÒ MACHIAVELLI: History of Florence and of the Affairs of Italy: *from the earliest times to the death of Lorenzo the Magnificent. Introduction by Felix Gilbert*　　　　　　　　　　　　TB/1027

ALFRED VON MARTIN: Sociology of the Renaissance. *Introduction by Wallace K. Ferguson*　　TB/1099

GARRETT MATTINGLY et al.: Renaissance Profiles. *Edited by J. H. Plumb*　　　　　　　　　TB/1162

MILLARD MEISS: Painting in Florence and Siena after the Black Death: *The Arts, Religion and Society in the Mid-Fourteenth Century. 169 illus.*　　TB/1148

J. E. NEALE: The Age of Catherine de Medici °　TB/1085

ERWIN PANOFSKY: Studies in Iconology: *Humanistic Themes in the Art of the Renaissance. 180 illustrations*　　　　　　　　　　　　TB/1077

J. H. PARRY: The Establishment of the European Hegemony: 1415-1715: *Trade and Exploration in the Age of the Renaissance*　　　　　TB/1045

J. H. PLUMB: The Italian Renaissance: *A Concise Survey of Its History and Culture*　　　TB/1161

GORDON RUPP: Luther's Progress to the Diet of Worms °　　　　　　　　　　　　　TB/120

FERDINAND SCHEVILL: The Medici. *Illus.*　TB/1010

FERDINAND SCHEVILL: Medieval and Renaissance Florence. *Illus.*　Volume I: *Medieval Florence* TB/1090 Volume II: *The Coming of Humanism and the Age of the Medici*　　　　　　　　　TB/1091

G. M. TREVELYAN: England in the Age of Wycliffe, 1368-1520 °　　　　　　　　　　TB/1112

VESPASIANO: Renaissance Princes, Popes, and Prelates: *The Vespasiano Memoirs: Lives of Illustrious Men of the XVth Century. Introduction by Myron P. Gilmore*　　　　　　　　　　　　TB/1111

History: Modern European

FREDERICK B. ARTZ: Reaction and Revolution, 1815-1832. * *Illus.*　　　　　　　　　TB/3034

MAX BELOFF: The Age of Absolutism, 1660-1815　　　　　　　　　　　　TB/1062

ROBERT C. BINKLEY: Realism and Nationalism, 1852-1871. * *Illus.*　　　　　　　　　TB/3038

CRANE BRINTON: A Decade of Revolution, 1789-1799. * *Illus.*　　　　　　　　　TB/3018

J. BRONOWSKI & BRUCE MAZLISH: The Western Intellectual Tradition: *From Leonardo to Hegel*　TB/3001

GEOFFREY BRUUN: Europe and the French Imperium, 1799-1814. * *Illus.*　　　　　　TB/3033

ALAN BULLOCK: Hitler, A Study in Tyranny. ° *Illus.*　　　　　　　　　　　　TB/1123

E. H. CARR: The Twenty Years' Crisis, 1919-1939: *An Introduction to the Study of International Relations* °　　　　　　　　　　　TB/1122

GORDON A. CRAIG: From Bismarck to Adenauer: *Aspects of German Statecraft. Revised Edition*　TB/1171

WALTER L. DORN: Competition for Empire, 1740-1763. * *Illus.*　　　　　　　　TB/3032

CARL J. FRIEDRICH: The Age of the Baroque, 1610-1660. * *Illus.*　　　　　　　　TB/3004

RENÉ FUELOEP-MILLER: The Mind and Face of Bolshevism: *An Examination of Cultural Life in Soviet Russia. New Epilogue by the Author*　TB/1188

M. DOROTHY GEORGE: London Life in the Eighteenth Century　　　　　　　　　TB/1182

LEO GERSHOY: From Despotism to Revolution, 1763-1789. * *Illus.*　　　　　　　TB/3017

C. C. GILLISPIE: Genesis and Geology: *The Decades before Darwin* §　　　　　　　TB/51

ALBERT GOODWIN: The French Revolution　TB/1064

ALBERT GUERARD: France in the Classical Age: *The Life and Death of an Ideal*　　　　TB/1183

CARLTON J. H. HAYES: A Generation of Materialism, 1871-1900. * *Illus.*　　　　　　　TB/3039

J. H. HEXTER: Reappraisals in History: *New Views on History and Society in Early Modern Europe*　　　　　　　　　　　　TB/1100

A. R. HUMPHREYS: The Augustan World: *Society, Thought, and Letters in Eighteenth Century England*　　　　　　　　　　　TB/1105

ALDOUS HUXLEY: The Devils of Loudun: *A Study in the Psychology of Power Politics and Mystical Religion in the France of Cardinal Richelieu* § °　TB/60

DAN N. JACOBS, Ed.: The New Communist Manifesto *and Related Documents. Third edition, revised*　　　　　　　　　　　　TB/1078

HANS KOHN, Ed.: The Mind of Modern Russia: *Historical and Political Thought of Russia's Great Age* TB/1065

KINGSLEY MARTIN: French Liberal Thought in the Eighteenth Century: *A Study of Political Ideas from Bayle to Condorcet*　　　　TB/1114

SIR LEWIS NAMIER: Personalities and Powers: *Selected Essays*　　　　　　　　　TB/1186

SIR LEWIS NAMIER: Vanished Supremacies: *Essays on European History, 1812-1918* °　TB/1088

JOHN U. NEF: Western Civilization Since the Renaissance: *Peace, War, Industry, and the Arts*　TB/1113

FREDERICK L. NUSSBAUM: The Triumph of Science and Reason, 1660-1685. * *Illus.*　　TB/3009

JOHN PLAMENATZ: German Marxism and Russian Communism. ° *New Preface by the Author*　TB/1189

RAYMOND W. POSTGATE, Ed.: Revolution from 1789 to 1906: *Selected Documents*　　TB/1063

PENFIELD ROBERTS: The Quest for Security, 1715-1740. * *Illus.*　　　　　　　　TB/3016

PRISCILLA ROBERTSON: Revolutions of 1848: *A Social History*　　　　　　　　TB/1025

ALBERT SOREL: Europe Under the Old Regime. *Translated by Francis H. Herrick*　　TB/1121

N. N. SUKHANOV: The Russian Revolution, 1917: *Eyewitness Account. Edited by Joel Carmichael*　Vol. I　TB/1066;　Vol. II　TB/1067

A. J. P. TAYLOR: The Habsburg Monarch, 1809-1918: *A History of the Austrian Empire and Austria-Hungary* °　　　　　　　　　TB/1187

JOHN B. WOLF: The Emergence of the Great Powers, 1685-1715. * *Illus.*　　　　　TB/3010

JOHN B. WOLF: France: 1814-1919: *The Rise of a Liberal-Democratic Society*　　　TB/3019

Intellectual History

HERSCHEL BAKER: The Image of Man: *A Study of the Idea of Human Dignity in Classical Antiquity, the Middle Ages, and the Renaissance*　TB/1047

R. R. BOLGAR: The Classical Heritage and Its Beneficiaries: *From the Carolingian Age to the End of the Renaissance*　　　　　　　TB/1125

J. BRONOWSKI & BRUCE MAZLISH: The Western Intellectual Tradition: *From Leonardo to Hegel*　TB/3001

ERNST CASSIRER: The Individual and the Cosmos in Renaissance Philosophy. *Translated with an Introduction by Mario Domandi*　　TB/1097

NORMAN COHN: The Pursuit of the Millennium: *Revolutionary Messianism in medieval and Reformation Europe and its bearing on modern Leftist and Rightist totalitarian movements*　　　TB/1037

4

5

RELIGION

Ancient & Classical

Biblical Thought & Literature

The Judaic Tradition

Christianity: Origins & Early Development

8

9

A. WOLF: A History of Science, Technology and Philosophy in the 16th and 17th Centuries. ° *Illus.*
Vol. I TB/508; Vol. II TB/509

A. WOLF: A History of Science, Technology, and Philosophy in the Eighteenth Century. ° *Illus.*
Vol. I TB/539; Vol. II TB/540

Mathematics

H. DAVENPORT: The Higher Arithmetic: *An Introduction to the Theory of Numbers* TB/526

H. G. FORDER: Geometry: *An Introduction* TB/548

GOTTLOB FREGE: The Foundations of Arithmetic: *A Logico-Mathematical Enquiry* TB/534

S. KÖRNER: The Philosophy of Mathematics: *An Introduction* TB/547

D. E. LITTLEWOOD: Skeleton Key of Mathematics: *A Simple Account of Complex Algebraic Problems* TB/525

GEORGE E. OWEN: Fundamentals of Scientific Mathematics TB/569

WILLARD VAN ORMAN QUINE: Mathematical Logic TB/558

O. G. SUTTON: Mathematics in Action. ° *Foreword by James R. Newman. Illus.* TB/518

FREDERICK WAISMANN: Introduction to Mathematical Thinking. *Foreword by Karl Menger* TB/511

Philosophy of Science

R. B. BRAITHWAITE: Scientific Explanation TB/515

J. BRONOWSKI: Science and Human Values. *Revised and Enlarged Edition* TB/505

ALBERT EINSTEIN et al.: Albert Einstein: Philosopher-Scientist. *Edited by Paul A. Schilpp* Vol. I TB/502
Vol. II TB/503

WERNER HEISENBERG: Physics and Philosophy: *The Revolution in Modern Science* TB/549

JOHN MAYNARD KEYNES: A Treatise on Probability. ° *Introduction by N. R. Hanson* TB/557

KARL R. POPPER: The Logic of Scientific Discovery TB/576

STEPHEN TOULMIN: Foresight and Understanding: *An Enquiry into the Aims of Science. Foreword by Jacques Barzun* TB/564

STEPHEN TOULMIN: The Philosophy of Science: *An Introduction* TB/513

G. J. WHITROW: The Natural Philosophy of Time ° TB/563

Physics and Cosmology

DAVID BOHM: Causality and Chance in Modern Physics. *Foreword by Louis de Broglie* TB/536

P. W. BRIDGMAN: The Nature of Thermodynamics TB/537

P. W. BRIDGMAN: A Sophisticate's Primer of Relativity TB/575

A. C. CROMBIE, Ed.: Turning Point in Physics TB/535

C. V. DURELL: Readable Relativity. *Foreword by Freeman J. Dyson* TB/530

ARTHUR EDDINGTON: Space, Time and Gravitation: *An outline of the General Relativity Theory* TB/510

GEORGE GAMOW: Biography of Physics Σ TB/567

MAX JAMMER: Concepts of Force: *A Study in the Foundation of Dynamics* TB/550

MAX JAMMER: Concepts of Mass *in Classical and Modern Physics* TB/571

MAX JAMMER: Concepts of Space: *The History of Theories of Space in Physics. Foreword by Albert Einstein* TB/533

EDMUND WHITTAKER: History of the Theories of Aether and Electricity
Volume I: *The Classical Theories* TB/531
Volume II: *The Modern Theories* TB/532

G. J. WHITROW: The Structure and Evolution of the Universe: *An Introduction to Cosmology. Illus.* TB/504

Code to Torchbook Libraries:

TB/1+	: The Cloister Library
TB/301+	: The Cathedral Library
TB/501+	: The Science Library
TB/1001+	: The Academy Library
TB/2001+	: The Bollingen Library
TB/3001+	: The University Library

A LETTER TO THE READER

Overseas, there is considerable belief
that we are a country of extreme conservatism and
that we cannot accommodate to social change.

Books about America in the hands of
readers abroad can help change those ideas.

The U. S. Information Agency cannot,
by itself, meet the vast need for books about
the United States.

You can help.

Harper Torchbooks provides three packets
of books on American history, economics,
sociology, literature and politics to
help meet the need.

To send a packet of Torchbooks [*] overseas,
all you need do is send your check for $7 (which
includes cost of shipping) to Harper & Row.
The U. S. Information Agency will distrib-
ute the books to libraries, schools, and other
centers all over the world.

I ask every American to support this
program, part of a worldwide BOOKS USA campaign.

I ask you to share in the opportunity to
help tell others about America.

EDWARD R. MURROW
Director,
U. S. Information Agency

[*retailing at $10.85 to $12.00]

PACKET I: *Twentieth Century America*

Dulles/America's Rise to World Power, 1898-1954
Cochran/The American Business System, 1900-1955
Zabel, Editor/Literary Opinion in America (two volumes)
Drucker/The New Society: *The Anatomy of Industrial Order*
Fortune Editors/America in the Sixties: *The Economy and the Society*

PACKET II: *American History*

Billington/The Far Western Frontier, 1830-1860
Mowry/The Era of Theodore Roosevelt and the
   Birth of Modern America, 1900-1912
Faulkner/Politics, Reform, and Expansion, 1890-1900
Cochran & Miller/The Age of Enterprise: *A Social History of
   Industrial America*
Tyler/Freedom's Ferment: *American Social History from the
   Revolution to the Civil War*

PACKET III: *American History*

Hansen/The Atlantic Migration, 1607-1860
Degler/Out of Our Past: *The Forces that Shaped Modern America*
Probst, Editor/The Happy Republic: *A Reader in Tocqueville's America*
Alden/The American Revolution, 1775-1783
Wright/The Cultural Life of the American Colonies, 1607-1763

*Your gift will be acknowledged directly to you by the overseas recipient.
Simply fill out the coupon, detach and mail with your check or money order.*

HARPER & ROW, PUBLISHERS · BOOKS USA DEPT.
49 East 33rd Street, New York 16, N. Y.

Packet I ☐   Packet II ☐   Packet III ☐

Please send the BOOKS USA library packet(s) indicated above, in my
name, to the area checked below. Enclosed is my remittance in the
amount of _____ for _____ packet(s) at $7.00 each.

_____ Africa   _____ Latin America

_____ Far East   _____ Near East

Name_____

Address_____

_____

NOTE: This offer expires December 31, 1966.

*A reference-list of Harper Torchbooks, classified
by subjects, is printed at the end of this volume.*

[handwritten marginal note:] Then accept your Social Darwinism and see Rap & Stkels in Hos light.

NATURAL SCIENCES AND MATHEMATICS